Magickal Almanac

Copyright © 1991 Llewellyn Publications
All rights reserved.

Printed in the United States of America
Typography property of Llewellyn Worldwide, Ltd.

ISBN: 0-87542-471-6

Edited and Designed by Raymond Buckland
Cover Painting by Randy Asplund-Faith

Contributing Writers: Raymond Buckland, Tara Buckland, Chic and Tabatha Cicero, Brian and Esther Crowley, Scott Cunningham, Norman Frankland, Migene González-Wippler, Hans Holzer, Gordon T. G. Hudson, Amber K, Susan Levitt, DeTraci Regula, Janina Renee, Gerald and Betty Schueler, Kisma K. Stepanich, Jenine E. Trayer

Illustration Credits: Esther Crowley—4, 9, 66, 69, 260, 263, 300, 320; Joann Colbert Beecher—19, 34; Jenine E. Trayer—20, 264, 324; Sandra Tabatha Cicero—114, 284; Robin Wood—304; Sallie Ann Glassman—353

Published by
LLEWELLYN PUBLICATIONS
P.O. Box 64383-471
St. Paul, MN 55164-0383

1991

JANUARY
S	M	T	W	T	F	S
		1	2	3	4	5
6	7	8	9	10	11	12
13	14	15	16	17	18	19
20	21	22	23	24	25	26
27	28	29	30	31		

FEBRUARY
S	M	T	W	T	F	S
					1	2
3	4	5	6	7	8	9
10	11	12	13	14	15	16
17	18	19	20	21	22	23
24	25	26	27	28		

MARCH
S	M	T	W	T	F	S
					1	2
3	4	5	6	7	8	9
10	11	12	13	14	15	16
17	18	19	20	21	22	23
24	25	26	27	28	29	30
31						

APRIL
S	M	T	W	T	F	S
	1	2	3	4	5	6
7	8	9	10	11	12	13
14	15	16	17	18	19	20
21	22	23	24	25	26	27
28	29	30				

MAY
S	M	T	W	T	F	S
			1	2	3	4
5	6	7	8	9	10	11
12	13	14	15	16	17	18
19	20	21	22	23	24	25
26	27	28	29	30	31	

JUNE
S	M	T	W	T	F	S
						1
2	3	4	5	6	7	8
9	10	11	12	13	14	15
16	17	18	19	20	21	22
23	24	25	26	27	28	29
30						

JULY
S	M	T	W	T	F	S
	1	2	3	4	5	6
7	8	9	10	11	12	13
14	15	16	17	18	19	20
21	22	23	24	25	26	27
28	29	30	31			

AUGUST
S	M	T	W	T	F	S
				1	2	3
4	5	6	7	8	9	10
11	12	13	14	15	16	17
18	19	20	21	22	23	24
25	26	27	28	29	30	31

SEPTEMBER
S	M	T	W	T	F	S
1	2	3	4	5	6	7
8	9	10	11	12	13	14
15	16	17	18	19	20	21
22	23	24	25	26	27	28
29	30					

OCTOBER
S	M	T	W	T	F	S
		1	2	3	4	5
6	7	8	9	10	11	12
13	14	15	16	17	18	19
20	21	22	23	24	25	26
27	28	29	30	31		

NOVEMBER
S	M	T	W	T	F	S
					1	2
3	4	5	6	7	8	9
10	11	12	13	14	15	16
17	18	19	20	21	22	23
24	25	26	27	28	29	30

DECEMBER
S	M	T	W	T	F	S
1	2	3	4	5	6	7
8	9	10	11	12	13	14
15	16	17	18	19	20	21
22	23	24	25	26	27	28
29	30	31				

1992

JANUARY
S	M	T	W	T	F	S
			1	2	3	4
5	6	7	8	9	10	11
12	13	14	15	16	17	18
19	20	21	22	23	24	25
26	27	28	29	30	31	

FEBRUARY
S	M	T	W	T	F	S
						1
2	3	4	5	6	7	8
9	10	11	12	13	14	15
16	17	18	19	20	21	22
23	24	25	26	27	28	29

MARCH
S	M	T	W	T	F	S
1	2	3	4	5	6	7
8	9	10	11	12	13	14
15	16	17	18	19	20	21
22	23	24	25	26	27	28
29	30	31				

APRIL
S	M	T	W	T	F	S
			1	2	3	4
5	6	7	8	9	10	11
12	13	14	15	16	17	18
19	20	21	22	23	24	25
26	27	28	29	30		

MAY
S	M	T	W	T	F	S
					1	2
3	4	5	6	7	8	9
10	11	12	13	14	15	16
17	18	19	20	21	22	23
24	25	26	27	28	29	30
31						

JUNE
S	M	T	W	T	F	S
	1	2	3	4	5	6
7	8	9	10	11	12	13
14	15	16	17	18	19	20
21	22	23	24	25	26	27
28	29	30				

JULY
S	M	T	W	T	F	S
			1	2	3	4
5	6	7	8	9	10	11
12	13	14	15	16	17	18
19	20	21	22	23	24	25
26	27	28	29	30	31	

AUGUST
S	M	T	W	T	F	S
						1
2	3	4	5	6	7	8
9	10	11	12	13	14	15
16	17	18	19	20	21	22
23	24	25	26	27	28	29
30	31					

SEPTEMBER
S	M	T	W	T	F	S
		1	2	3	4	5
6	7	8	9	10	11	12
13	14	15	16	17	18	19
20	21	22	23	24	25	26
27	28	29	30			

OCTOBER
S	M	T	W	T	F	S
				1	2	3
4	5	6	7	8	9	10
11	12	13	14	15	16	17
18	19	20	21	22	23	24
25	26	27	28	29	30	31

NOVEMBER
S	M	T	W	T	F	S
1	2	3	4	5	6	7
8	9	10	11	12	13	14
15	16	17	18	19	20	21
22	23	24	25	26	27	28
29	30					

DECEMBER
S	M	T	W	T	F	S
		1	2	3	4	5
6	7	8	9	10	11	12
13	14	15	16	17	18	19
20	21	22	23	24	25	26
27	28	29	30	31		

1993

JANUARY
S	M	T	W	T	F	S
					1	2
3	4	5	6	7	8	9
10	11	12	13	14	15	16
17	18	19	20	21	22	23
24	25	26	27	28	29	30
31						

FEBRUARY
S	M	T	W	T	F	S
	1	2	3	4	5	6
7	8	9	10	11	12	13
14	15	16	17	18	19	20
21	22	23	24	25	26	27
28						

MARCH
S	M	T	W	T	F	S
	1	2	3	4	5	6
7	8	9	10	11	12	13
14	15	16	17	18	19	20
21	22	23	24	25	26	27
28	29	30	31			

APRIL
S	M	T	W	T	F	S
				1	2	3
4	5	6	7	8	9	10
11	12	13	14	15	16	17
18	19	20	21	22	23	24
25	26	27	28	29	30	

MAY
S	M	T	W	T	F	S
						1
2	3	4	5	6	7	8
9	10	11	12	13	14	15
16	17	18	19	20	21	22
23	24	25	26	27	28	29
30	31					

JUNE
S	M	T	W	T	F	S
		1	2	3	4	5
6	7	8	9	10	11	12
13	14	15	16	17	18	19
20	21	22	23	24	25	26
27	28	29	30			

JULY
S	M	T	W	T	F	S
				1	2	3
4	5	6	7	8	9	10
11	12	13	14	15	16	17
18	19	20	21	22	23	24
25	26	27	28	29	30	31

AUGUST
S	M	T	W	T	F	S
1	2	3	4	5	6	7
8	9	10	11	12	13	14
15	16	17	18	19	20	21
22	23	24	25	26	27	28
29	30	31				

SEPTEMBER
S	M	T	W	T	F	S
			1	2	3	4
5	6	7	8	9	10	11
12	13	14	15	16	17	18
19	20	21	22	23	24	25
26	27	28	29	30		

OCTOBER
S	M	T	W	T	F	S
					1	2
3	4	5	6	7	8	9
10	11	12	13	14	15	16
17	18	19	20	21	22	23
24	25	26	27	28	29	30
31						

NOVEMBER
S	M	T	W	T	F	S
	1	2	3	4	5	6
7	8	9	10	11	12	13
14	15	16	17	18	19	20
21	22	23	24	25	26	27
28	29	30				

DECEMBER
S	M	T	W	T	F	S
			1	2	3	4
5	6	7	8	9	10	11
12	13	14	15	16	17	18
19	20	21	22	23	24	25
26	27	28	29	30	31	

Table of Contents

Evocation

Llewellyn's *Magickal Almanac* has now become entrenched as a firm favorite among the many students and practitioners of magick in its various forms, both in this country and abroad. Shamans, Ceremonialists, Wiccans, Voodooists, Enochians, and a broad range of others have found the articles and almanac information to be great resource material. The articles, we are told, are entertaining and informative.

Speaking of last year's edition, *Voices From Spirit* magazine referred to the almanac as "a superb collection of articles, poetry, spells, information on ancient deities, from magickal beliefs and practices around the world by an assortment of authors expert on their subjects." *New Moon Rising* magazine said, "This is not an almanac that you will discard at the end of the year . . . there is enough variety and quantity that most readers will find plenty of interest." And *Sisterspirit* said, "this [is] a fun and enlightening addition to your bookshelf."

We like to get feedback. We like to know what you like, and don't like and what you would like to see that we have not yet covered. The field of magick is vast, and many different forms are practiced by people around the globe. Gerald Gardner would be delighted to find that his form of Witchcraft—*Wicca*—has become a world religion within 30 years of his death. Dr. John Dee would probably be amazed to find that his system of Enochian magick is popular 400 years after his death. Ramses II might well be unable to comprehend that Egyptian magick is riding high in popularity 3,300 years after his death. Yet these three forms, and many others, have been found to be "just right" for thousands of individual seekers around the world.

Our job is to make this arcane knowledge available so that seekers *can* satisfy their souls. The almanac serves as a sampler, a collection of bite-size pieces of many different regimens. Here you may taste and see which "tickles your palate." Here you may get an idea of what is involved in practices and beliefs that normally you may have heard of only in passing. If something catches your fancy, follow up on it. The authors of the articles herein are all experts in their fields and many have books published by Llewellyn Publications. If you enjoy an article here, seek out the books by that author and read more. Let the *Magickal Almanac* be the appetizer for your feast of knowledge.

This year we have a number of old favorites returning and being joined by several new writers. Welcome, please:

RAYMOND BUCKLAND—"The man who introduced Wicca to the U.S.," author of such best-selling books as *Buckland's Complete Book of Witchcraft, Practical Candleburning Rituals, Practical Color Magick, Secrets of Gypsy Fortunetelling, Love Magick, Dream Reading,* etc.

TARA BUCKLAND—Teacher, musician and author of *How To Make an Easy Charm to Bring Love into Your Life* and *Beauty Secrets of the Ancient Egyptians.*

CHIC and TABATHA CICERO—Chic has been a practicing ceremonial magician for 25 years; Tabatha painted *The New Golden Dawn Ritual Tarot.* Together they have co- authored *The New Golden Dawn Ritual Tarot Book.*

BRIAN and ESTHER CROWLEY—Authors and co-authors of many books including *The Face On Mars, Hotting Up* (Brian), *Joga in die Buitelug, The Living Waters of Yoga and Meditation* (Esther); and *Words Of Power: Sacred Sounds of East and West* (together).

SCOTT CUNNINGHAM—Popular author of *Cunningham's Encyclopedia of Magical Herbs, Earth Power, Magical Herbalism, The Magical Household, The Magic in Food* and many others.

NORMAN FRANKLAND—Poet and student of Native American lore.

MIGENE GONZÁLEZ-WIPPLER—Author of many books, including *The Complete Book of Spells, Ceremonies and Magic* and *A Kabbalah for the Modern World*.

HANS HOLZER—Professor of Parapsychology, noted ghosthunter, writer/producer of television and feature films, author of nearly 90 books.

GORDON T. G. HUDSON—Egyptologist, founder and preceptor of the University of Egyptian Arts, author of *History and Mystery of Ancient Egypt*.

AMBER K—Wiccan Priestess, teacher, experienced practitioner of magick, author of *True Magick, Picture Book of Goddesses, Lithomancy* and others.

SUSAN LEVITT—Metaphysical counselor and ritual facilitator, author of an upcoming book *Tarot: Mysteries of the Ancients*.

DETRACI REGULA—Priestess of Isis and author of an upcoming book on that Goddess.

JANINA RENEE—Scholar of folklore, mythology, Jungian psychology, magic and religion; author of *Tarot Spells*.

GERALD and BETTY SCHUELER—Authors of the series of books on Enochian magick, including *An Advanced Guide to Enochian Magic, Enochian Physics, Enochian Yoga* and *The Enochian Tarot* and *Enochian Tarot Deck*.

KISMA K. STEPANICH—Longtime student of Gaia, of Faeries, and Gypsy mysticism; author of *The Gaia Tradition*.

JENINE E. TRAYER—An artist, solitary Wiccan, editor of *WPPA Trade Magazine*, involves her large family in as much magick as possible.

    To new readers of the almanac, I say, "Welcome." To old readers, I say, "Welcome back." I think you will find something here to interest you. If not, let us know. We aim to make this an annual you will all want to come back to.

Raymond Buckland

Did Moses use Sanskrit words of power to part the Red Sea?

Using the Name of Power

Brian Crowley

IN THE JEWISH TRADITION THE NAME OF GOD
HAS NOT BEEN UTTERED FOR CENTURIES. BUT
WAS IT USED BY MOSES, JESUS AND OTHERS
FOR MAGICAL PURPOSES?

There has been much speculation down the ages regarding
the nature of the "miracles" performed by various famous biblical personages, such as Moses and Jesus. Were these indeed miraculous supernatural events beyond the capabilities of the ordinary mortal, or were they a demonstration of magick as we
know it today? And, more importantly, did Moses and the others use the sacred name of God in their rituals?

Before and after its official ban in spoken or sung Jewish
Temple worship, following the destruction of the First Temple
at Jerusalem in 507 B.C.E., the four-lettered Holy Name of God
enjoyed widespread secret use as a magical symbol or word of
power. This is confirmed in the *Sefer ha-Razim* ("The Book of Secrets"), a Jewish magical work of the late Roman era, and in
Origen's *Contra Celsum*, which describes the magical power of
certain Jewish formulae for use in spells and exorcisms, including the power invested in the Name of God and also the name of
Jesus, particularly when used in the realm of the spirits.

Saint Stephen tells us that "Moses was learned in all the
wisdom of the Egyptians, and was mighty in words and in
deeds" (*Acts 7:22*). The future Hebrew leader was in fact raised
as an Egyptian prince, and it is almost certain that his court tui-
tion would have included some lessons in Egyptian magic and

5

in particular in the use of *hekau* or *words of power*. Later, Moses would have been initiated into the Hebrew religio/mystical tradition known as *Kabbalah* and learned the intricacies of incantantion for specified purposes in the Hebrew language.

It may be considered relevant to note here that in the Hebrew tradition there is a distinct difference made between magic and miracle. Jewish lore states that magic is a mere metaphysical operation that involves a mastery of the so-called "World of Formation" and can be attained by anyone who is prepared to work hard upon the higher centers of the psyche. Miracles, on the other hand, occur through the operation of spiritual energies emanating from the upper World of Creation, via the agency of someone whose psyche has developed more naturally through emphasis on more spiritual refinement and sensitization. Kabalists consider these spiritual energies as "gifts" from subtler worlds that are not to be used for any occult or magical manipulation on the earth plane.

In the Talmud it is clearly stated: "He who practices magic will not enter Heaven"—meaning that anyone who concentrates solely on operating in the World of Formation (i.e., our physical world and what is known as the astral level) for their own gain may become trapped there and find it difficult to progress into the World of the Spirit. Persons who, however, perform miracles are acting only as conduits for higher forces, without any thought of self gain.

This rather rigid interpretation of the operation and control of super-physical forces is, of course, open to debate.

The miracles of Moses ranged from turning his staff into a snake and calling up sundry plagues to irritate the Egyptians to parting the waters of the Red Sea so that the Hebrews might pass on dry land and the finding of drinking water from solid rock in the arid Sinai desert.

However, ancient references inform us that the Egyptian magicians could also convert sticks into snakes, and back again, or part the waters of a lake or river; the Bible tells us very clearly that the Pharaoh's sorcerers were easily able to duplicate some, although not all, of the miracles performed by Moses. But as an indication of the apparently superior magical power at Moses's command the snake created from his staff easily devoured those called into life by his Egyptian rivals.

It has been claimed that to part the Red Sea Moses actually used a magical Sanskrit-based mantra consisting of a mystical sound formula normally used for protection at a critical time. This phrase runs as follows: Ut-*Re-Ma-Fa-Sol-La-Ne*; with "ut" as in put, and the remainder of the invocation sounding much like part of the familiar musical scale.

Legend also tells us that the staff Moses always carried bore an inscription of the magical four-lettered Holy Name of God or "Tetragrammaton." According to Rabbi Dr. Philip Berg, former head of the Kabbalah Institute, Jerusalem, and a notable writer on Hebrew mysticism, the ancient *Zohar*, original handbook of the kabbalists, states clearly that in the Exodus story Moses killed an Egyptian overseer through the energy transmitted by utterance of a Holy Name—"There can be no doubt that Moses was on that elevated metaphysical plane and was thoroughly knowledgable of all the Names of the Almighty."[1]

In his intriguing book *Jesus the Magician*, Morton Smith, professor of history at Columbia University, postulates that Jesus "did his miracles and even raised himself from the dead by magical use of the divine Name, the greatest of all spells."[2]

By all accounts, Jesus the Nazarene was a miracle worker unsurpassed by any other. He healed the sick and lame, cast out devils and exorcized unclean spirits, walked on water, stilled a terrible storm at sea, once fed 5,000 people with five loaves of bread and a few fishes, turned water into wine, and even raised people from the dead—including himself, in his final great miracle.

Apocryphal Gnostic texts list many more of Jesus's miracles, with a number of the healings and exorcisms described including the use of special words of power to accomplish specific effects. It is possible that the method used by Jesus to exorcise unclean spirits might have involved spells actually screamed out by him, plus a certain amount of gesticulation which matched the mad in their fury—this being normal practice for magicians of the time. In *Mark 3:21* Jesus is described as being "beside himself" and is immediately accused of being possessed by the demon Beelzebub, the "prince of devils."

Jesus also appears as a miracle worker in the Islamic holy book, the *Qur'an*. When still a child, he is described as breathing life into the clay figurine of a bird. According to this reference, he made several figures of sparrows and other birds for his playmates. They flew about or stood on his hands as he ordered them, and also ate and drank at his command.

There are several references in the Bible relating to words actually used by Jesus to perform miracles of healing, such as, for instance, in the stories of the Roman Centurion in the *Matthew* gospel, the deaf and dumb man in *Mark*, and the young daughter of Jairus, also in *Mark*, when he used the expression *Talitha Koumi*, which literally translated means simply "Young girl, arise!"

The Gnostic *Pistis Sophia*, a Coptic codex of the 5th and 6th centuries taken from a Greek original, details the supposed secret metaphysical teachings of Jesus and even records the words he allegedly used in his own resurrection process: *Zama Zama Ozza Rachama Ozai!* Is it not also likely that he would have used the Ineffable Name itself, as the most powerful of all Hebrew expressions?

Moses and Jesus are not the only prominent Jewish miracle workers to use sacred sound for specified effect. There are several such references in the *Zohar* itself. Of more recent equal standing is the 17th century Eastern European Israel ben Eliezer, known to posterity as the *Baal ShemTov* or "Master of the Good Name," a title which probably indicates his mastery over the use of the Tetragrammaton for magical/mystical purposes.

The Baal Shem was founder of the charismatic Jewish Hassidic sect and bringer to the persecuted Jewish people of a new ecstatic religious expression in which members danced and chanted in glorification of the Lord. He was, like Jesus, also apparently able to walk on water, exorcise evil spirits, and heal the sick by his touch. Moreover, in a magical/miracle sense it is said that by using the Holy Name of God he could physically bring back to life a person who was at death's door.

"New Age" Hassidic writer Reb Zalman Schachter encapsulates the method and basic philosophy of the Baal Shem Tov:

"He was capable of using the Divine Name for purposes of *changing things as they were to what they ought to be*, because there is always such a discrepancy between how things are and how they ought to be." (*our italics.*)[3]

What is this famous Divine Name of Power used by Moses, Jesus, the Baal Shem Tov and others to perform their miracles—and how is it pronounced?

The answer to the first question is simple, and taken from scripture. When Moses first asked God by what name the Israelltes should call Him, the reply was *Ehyeh Asher Ehyeh*—"I Am That I Am" (Exodus 3:13-14). Other appellations for God are also used elsewhere in the Hebrew biblical texts (*El Shaddai, Elohim, Eli*, etc.), but the actual Holy Name is written in Hebrew *yod, hey, vau, hey*, which is generally translated into English as YHWH. This has been in the past badly mistranslated as *Jehovah*. It appears exactly 6,832 times in the Old Testament and is held to possess unbounded power sufficient, it is said, to shake the very foundations of Heaven and Earth and to inspire even the angels with astonishment and terror!

The Ineffable Name of God in Hebrew characters

Whenever anyone reads aloud from the Jewish Bible, the *Torah*, or other scriptural source, a substitute name is applied, usually *Adonai* ("my Lord") or simply *Ha Shem* ("The Name"). Of course, any person who does not feel constrained by the Jewish traditions imposed in the first century may be inclined to verbalize the Name of God without offending any personal inhibitions. The only problem is that no one is completely certain how it should be pronounced!

The clumsy "Jehovah" is certainly incorrect; the term *Yahweh is* probably closer to the original sounding. In the Phoenecian and early Hebrew alphabets, all vowels except *aleph*, the first letter, were not written down. As a result, there is really no knowing the original pronunciation of many ancient Hebrew words. In his *Wars of the Jews* (5:5:7), the Roman/Jewish historian Josephus states that the sacred name consisted of four vowels. The Egyptian word for the source of all being is, incidentally, written in hieroglyphs as for vowel sounds and might be vocalized something like *IAAW*. However, in his writings in the *Zohar*, the 11th century kabbalist, Solomon Ben Yehuda Ibn Gebirol (known also as Avicebron, the undisputed master Jewish sage of his time), claims seven vowels. Distinguished poet and mythologist Robert Graves also argues seven vowels, pointing to a distinct link between Egyptian priestly hymns (which consisted of uttering seven vowels in succession), the secret name of the transcendental god of the mythical Greek Hyperboreans, some Celtic and other connections, and the Ineffable Name—which he suggests could be sounded *IAOOUA*, with accents on the second *O* and final *A*.[4]

Whatever the precise sounding of the Name of God, it remains that traditionally it is held to carry more power of a universal, all-embracing nature than any other word or name, in any or all of Earth's numerous tongues, past and present.

Mention has been made of the strict Jewish prohibition involving the use of the Holy Name. This injunction has to a large extent been based on the Exodus 20 text, which reads: "Thou shalt not take the name of the Lord thy God in vain ..." and represents a clear warning that (if it is to be used at all) the Ineffable Name should never be vocalized irreverently, either in oath or especially in magical practice related to personal acquisition in any form.

Notes:

1. Berg, Dr. Philip. *The Kabbalah Connection*. Jerusalem: Research Center of Kabbalah, 1983. p.82.

2. Smith, Horton. *Jesus the Magician*.London: Victor Gollancz, 1978. p. 49.

3. Schachter, Reb Zalman. *Fragments of a Future Scroll*. Germantown PA; Leaves of Grass Press, 1975. p. 10.

4. Graves, Robert. *The White Goddess*. London: Faber and Faber, 1962. pp. 285-287.

Main reference:

Crowley, Brian & Esther. *Words of Power: Sacred Sounds of East and West*. St Paul: Llewellyn, 1991.

Other references:

Budge, E. A. Wallis. *Egyptian Magic*. New York: Dover, 1971.

James, Montague Rhodes. *The Apocryphal New Testament*. London: Oxford University Press, 1924.

Mandal, Dr. Sant Ramah. *Aum and Other Words of Power*. San Francisco CA: The Universal Brotherhood Temple, undated.

First Footing

Raymond Buckland

The ritual of "First Footing" used to be found in many parts of Britain but today is only alive in the north of England and in Scotland.

It was believed that the first person to cross the threshold of a house at the start of the new year represented what was to come throughout the rest of the year. If it was someone who was old, poor and decrepit, then your year was going to be a most unfortunate one. However, if it was a strong, rich, handsome young man, then your year was going to be most prosperous.

To help direct the Fates, as it were, it was usually arranged that the very first person to set foot across your threshold should be the best. Many times the most handsome, strongest man in the village was given the task of visiting each and every house, to be invited in, or two or three men would cover the territory if it was large. Tradition dictated that he be dark (definitely not red-haired, except in parts of Yorkshire) and that he bear gifts. These might be salt or a green branch (fertility), bread (food), wine (sustenance), money (riches), and/or coal (warmth). No householder would allow anyone to enter the house after midnight New Year's Eve until the First Footer had been in to assure luck for the coming year.

Fortunetelling With Cats

Janina Renee

There are many superstitions surrounding the behavior of cats, including omens and portents. Since folk belief has it that cats' behavior can give clues to what luck is in store, cats can participate in fortunetelling practices on Halloween, May Eve, New Year's Eve, or any of the other times when peeking into the future is traditional.

To find out what future portents your own cat has to reveal, simply allow Kitty into the room when your family or friends are assembled and just observe how it reacts to the various guests:

• If the cat sits down quietly next to a person, peace and prosperity is foretold.

• If the cat rubs itself against a person, that person is in for a run of good luck.

• An extremely good run of luck is portended if the cat jumps into a person's lap.

• If the cat yawns while sitting near a person, an opportunity is about to arise which that person must be careful not to miss.

• If the cat runs away from a person, he or she is hiding a secret which will, however, come to light in the near future.

When you try this method, be sure to be very quiet and don't coax or cajole the cat. Otherwise, ironically, the recipients of the best predictions of luck are likely to be the cat haters! Why? Cat experts have determined that the reason cats always go to people who hate them or are allergic to them is because those are the persons least likely to intrude on the cat's personal space.

The Oneness of Gaia

Kisma K. Stepanich

With each step we take we are stepping on the Mother of all life—our supreme life-support system, planet Earth, alias Gaia! Deep within the center of Earth (the heart space of Gaia) vibrates a rich and powerful energy. This energy vibration rises in the same rhythm as a beating of the heart; it rises up through the deepest and densest physicality of life. When it reaches the surface of the planet it radiates out this physical reality of life ecology.

The heartbeat of Gaia continually vibrates. We receive it into the soles of our feet. The energy also rises up and enters our bodies through the solar plexus as if through an umbilical cord stretching from our belly buttons into the very core of Mother Earth, in much the same way a baby is connected to the mother's placenta at birth. But the invisible umbilical cord that stretches between our bodies and Mother Earth is never cut away, for this connection—this vibrating cord of energy—is the essential lifeline that fills our bodies with the animated "soul-stuff" of nature.

Detecting Gaia's heartbeat is very easy to achieve. If we kick off our shoes and walk on the grass, or lay our hands down on the earth, or press our ear against the side of a smooth granite cliff, the heartbeat of Mother Earth is felt and/or heard as a *buzzing* in very much the same way as the electrical synapse as it flashes along a telephone wire. It is not the fuzzy or static electrical sound heard over the airwaves, such as on the radio or television, but is the very pure *buzzing* of life, the beating heart rhythm that vibrates at such an undetectably high rate as it moves through every physical aspect of physical reality. This buzzing, if slowed down tremendously, would be the very sound of "dum-dum dum-dum," the opening and shutting sounds of the heart valves as monitored through a stethoscope.

The undetected or sleeping power of Gaia's heartbeat resides inside of us until through our own consciousness-raising efforts we strike a chord within that awakens part of the cell memory of our DNA. This awakening allows us to shift our energy vibration, allowing the internal energy to begin vibrating at a higher rate. When this higher energy vibration is achieved we move into a new level of awareness, a sensitive level of awareness where we begin to faintly feel this other heartbeat that is not our own. This awakening in our deep-seeded ecology takes us to the very core of consciousness—in essence back to our origin—for it awakens a primordial part of our being that sparks an ancient fire or burst of existence equivalent to the Big Bang.

As we are roused from slumber and Gaia's heartbeat resounds fully inside, we become aware that all living creatures are animated by Gaia's heartbeat. Through this "heartbeat connection" it becomes clear that all life, all physicality, is of the Earth, comes from the Earth, is formed from the Earth and that, therefore, it is one and the same thing. One. In the most abstract essence, there *is only one life*—Gaia.

In this oneness, this deep ecological connection, through the soul animation of Gaia's heartbeat, after the conscious awakening to this reality, a revelation is given—a breakthrough of all seven veils of human ignorance—which is: *in our oneness of life we are an extension of Gaia*.

From the substance of her body, our forms are created. Her body is composed of the four elements: water, fire, air, and earth, just as our bodies are comprised of the same four elements. Through the pulsing of her heartbeat—the soul-stuff of life—we become animated creatures filled with our own beating heart rhythm grounded deep into the soul of nature.

Be me and I will speak through you.
Feel me and I will feel through you.
See me and I will show you the way.
Honor me and I honor you.

Dance my dance and I dance through you.
Hold me and I hold you.
Know me and know life,
And keep the wheel turning.

There are many ways, but one Gaia.
Bring all ways to me, to one Gaia.
Connect all ways to my energy (to one Gaia).
And peace will prevail, to one Gaia.
Then life will be on its way to transcending

To one Gaia.
To one Gaia.
To one Gaia.
*To one Gaia.**

As extensions of Gaia who have conscious awareness, it is important for us not to forget our origins. It has become apparent that now is the time to move beyond the comfort zone which we have been living in and pass through the threshold into the next level of attunement. We are working hard at uncovering our inner spirits, the inner spirit which embraces both the light side and shadow side of our "self." Through this effort, we become aware of the need to defend our Mother Earth from destruction and the importance of healing our planet.

We have been dwelling in an age of "anthropocentrism" (human chauvinism), the age where humans believe themselves superior over all creation. This consciousness has been deeply etched in our culture. Because of this, it has become important for us as a whole people to embark upon a journey that will bring us closer to nature.

---

* "To One Gaia" chant, Stepanich, Kisma K., *The Gaia Tradition: Celebrating the Earth in Her Seasons*, Llewellyn Publications, 1991.

Now is the time to move further into our awareness. Further into the beginning of our origin, deeper into the core of our connection to Gaia and all life. Celebrating Gaia is part of the ancient tradition of life. The tradition which goes beyond organized religions and heritage and political involvements to the very basic, underlying principle of existence.

In the last few years, the popularity of Earth Day has helped initiate the mass consciousness into shifting their awareness and taking the first steps toward making the awakening realization toward caretaking Gaia. For those of us who have been working with this awareness for years, we must begin guiding our communities in this awakening awareness deeper into the connection of life-oneness.

> *The Earth is our mother*
> *we must take care of her,*
> *the earth is our mother*
> *we must take care of her.*
>
> *Hey nawa, ho nawa, hey na na.*
> *Hey nawa, ho nawa, hey na na.*
>
> *Her sacred ground we walk upon*
> *with every step we take.*
> *Her sacred ground we walk upon*
> *with every step we take.*

Being connected and very much aware of Gaia's seasonal cycle is vitally important for living in a harmonious way. Today we experience never-ending trauma to the senses because we are inundated with pollutions and congestion and lack of open land (especially those of us who subject ourselves to city living). We recognize that we live in a society of modern conveniences that are not compatible with natural living. As each age passes we develop our lifestyles further and further away from the earth and her cycles and closer to an environment that is confined to fluorecent lights and white concrete walls. To escape from this setup will become increasingly impossible. The end

Priestess of the Moon

result will be a death of the natural cycles, and the survival of our species will rely on a totally man-made world. How unfortunate, for we too shall die from lack of contact to our home, the soil upon which we now so carelessly tread.

The disparity of living in the world today (a time when each moment could be our last due to the threat of nuclear warfare) makes it increasingly difficult to function in a natural way. It is so very important and relatively easy to connect with Mother Earth and her cycles. The first step is simply becoming more aware of the seasons, those four counterparts that equate to one year: Spring, Summer, Autumn and Winter. By witnessing the seasons first, then celebrating them on a regular annum, a chain reaction of awareness will develop. As we become more in tune with the naural energy shifts, we gain living skills that provide us with the ability to create a more balanced and harmonious environment in which to live.

When we work with the seasons we merge with the natural order of this great planet and flow with her energy rather than against it, and in time the celebration of the seasons and Mother Earth will be brought back into the interior of our communities, providing the necessary cohesive ingredient for us to bond together and create a unity that, in our deepest sense of ecology, we recognize as missing today.

As our attunement to Gaia begins to form, and as our connection to the life force becomes embedded within our consciousness, the layers of anthropocentrism will shed away and a beautiful spirit will begin to reveal itself, a spirit as fresh and as free as the very essence of sacredness. Our hearts will beat in time with the pulse of the mystical life vibration emanating from the center of all living organisms around us. Our minds will begin to merge with a greatness beyond any conceivable imagining, and many wonderful secrets and supposed "mysteries" will be revealed. As we become stronger in our deep-seeded ecology and oneness, our very personal dance of life will suddenly flow and we will join with the purpose of creativity.

Magical Personalities of Egypt: Hatshepsut

Gordon T. G. Hudson

It must be remembered that regnant queens were never popular in Egypt, but because the line of succession went through the distaff side, one custom for anyone aspiring to the Lotus Throne was to legitimize his claim by marrying the sister-wife of the late Pharaoh, and only by marriage could a man legally secure the throne for himself.

A ruler was bound to take as his Great Wife a princess of the royal blood. In the normal course of events the king was succeeded by the oldest son of his Great Wife. If she bore only daughters, the oldest of them and the husband selected for her (preferably the king's son by a secondary wife or concubine) inherited the throne. Since women could not rule, an heiress princess needed a husband; a properly legitimate crown-prince, though, could rule in his own right.

This would account for the custom of brother-sister marriages, even in Greco-Roman times. In Egypt only members of

When considering the time period Egypt's ancient history comprised, it is profitable to go, very briefly, into the question of times and comparisons.

(a) The period covered by the 18th and 19th dynasties comprised 370 years: 250 years for the 18th and 120 years for the 19th, much longer in duration than the time from George Washington to the present day!

(b) Alexander the Great (356-323 B.C.), whose sarcophagus was a national shrine and the wonder of the Ptolemaic Era, lived closer to our time than he did to the building of the pyramids of Giza.

G.T.G.H.

royal families indulged in this practice, the purpose being to keep inheritance within the family and prevent interlopers gaining power or property by marrying an heiress.

Hatshepsut was soft and feminine looking and was brought up in Thebes, a garrison town which must have been an exciting place to live in. Its streets echoed to the tramp of soldiers; its pillared halls often thronged with the young officers of chariotry, freshly returned from campaigns with fascinating stories of foreign lands. The following is one story of the birth of Hatshepsut.

In the land of the Gods, Amen-Ra held court to see how best Egypt could be served. On his right sat Osiris, Isis, Nephthys, Hathor, Horus and Anubis, and on his left sat Mentu, Geb, Nut, Atmu, Shu and Tefnut. To the assembled gods he spoke these words:

"I will make a great queen who shall rule over Egypt and Syria, Nubia and Punt, so that all lands may be united under her sway. Worthy must the maiden be of her great dominions, for she shall rule the whole world."

As he spoke the god Thoth entered, he who has the form of an ibis so that he may fly more swiftly than the swiftest arrow. In silence he listened to the words of Amen-Ra, the mightiest of gods, the maker of men.

Then he said,

"Behold, Amen-Ra, there is in the land of Egypt a maiden of much beauty. The sun shines not on anything fairer than she. Surely it is fitting that she be the mother of the great queen of whom thou speakest."

"Thou sayest well," Amen-Ra replied, "Where shall we find this fairest of mortals, and what is her name?"

"Her name is Aahmes, and she is wife to the king and dwelleth in his palace. I shall take you to her."

"It is well." said Amen-Ra.

Then Thoth in the shape of an ibis flew to the land of Egypt and with him went Amen-Ra in the form of Pharaoh of Egypt, and Neith and Selket, all of whom carried ankhs which are the sign of life.

Silently the gods and goddesses entered the sleeping pal-

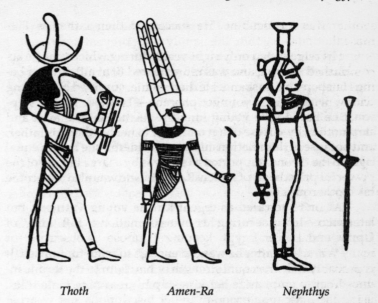

Thoth	Amen-Ra	Nephthys

ace and were conducted by Thoth to the bedchamber of Queen Aahmes, and as they gazed upon her they saw that she was indeed the fairest mortal alive. As they watched, she awoke and looked with astonishment on her supernatural visitors, magnificently attired in their heavenly raiment. She looked toward Amen-Ra, the best dressed of the gods, and saw her husband and was glad in her heart that he was there. Amen-Ra placed in her hand the sign of life and the emblem of power.

At length the gods returned to the land of Punt, and Amen-Ra called for Khnum, the potter, creator and fashioner of bodies.

"Fashion for me the body of my daughter and the body also of her ka," he instructed Khnum. "A great queen shall I make of her, and honor and power shall be hers."

So it was done, Khnum fashioning the body and ka of Hatshepsut in obedience to Amen-Ra. Aahmes became pregnant and in time Hatshepsut was born.

Her father, Tutmose I, informed the court that she was to be his successor. At 15 she married her half-brother, whose

mother was a concubine. He succeeded their father as Tutmose II.

His reign lasted only eight years, during which time he accomplished nothing and was remembered (if at all) only for being Hatshepsut's husband. He died young, survived by a young
widow with a much younger pharaoh—Tutmose III, her step-
son. She bore to the young king the relationship of aunt and
stepmother, by virture of her marriage to her brother, his father,
and because of this relationship she considered she had an equal
right to the throne, supported as she was by a large faction of the
powerful priesthood of Amen-Ra. Later she was also to become
his mother-in-law.

At first she ruled as regent for the young Tutmose, but
later succeeded in securing her own coronation as full "king" of
Upper and Lower Egypt, keeping Tutmose in obscurity for
many years, long after he was old enough to reign for himself. It
is probably that the equal strength of his claim to the throne induced her to emphasize her kingship by assuming male titles,
using the masculine pronoun in her inscriptions and wearing
male costume, at least on her statues and monuments.

Having become Pharaoh in her own right by downright
chicanery (which today would be called a technicality!), peace-
loving Hatshepsut attempted to heal the wounds of foreign rule
and long wars. To that end she found no necessity for military
action in Nubia, the favorite hunting grounds of the Pharaohs,
for the south remained at peace during her tenure of the Lotus
Throne, although she personally led one military expedition to
Nubia while she was queen. The country enjoyed a period of
peace and prosperity when great architectural projects flourished, as well as trade and the arts. Her vessels were laden with
myrrh trees, ivory, perfumes and the like, rather than the ac-
coutrements of war.

The queen's favorite minister and advisor, Sennemut, who
was also tutor of the royal children, wielded great power. He
was at the head of most of her great undertakings, notably as the
architect of her magnificent temple at Deir el Bahri, on the west
bank of the Nile at Thebes, on the walls of which are carved
(with the highest technical mastery) detailed scenes of outstand-

ing events of her reign. This temple is a masterpiece, designed with an inspired regard for its setting in a natural bay of the towering cliffs of the western desert, and even in its present ruined state is one of the most impressive sights in Egypt. The chief exploits of the queen's reign were depicted in carvings along the porticos.

The sed festival is the jubilee of the ruler held at the end of the first 30 years of a pharaoh's reign and repeated at shorter intervals thereafter, though most kings celebrated it earlier. It was an occasion for renewal of royal vitality and confirmation of the king's god-given right to the Two Lands. It was during this festival that the uniting of the Two Lands and the founding of the first palace were re-enacted and the king's title to the succession reaffirmed. Traditionally it was held in Memphis, the seat of the first kings of united Egypt, but in Hatshepsut's case, it was held at Deir el Bahri. In her Jubilee year, known as the "Myriad of Years," a feast celebrated the arrival of four obelisks at Deir el Bahri. Sennemut was supervising close by.

Hatshepsut's life held much triumph. This was one of her proudest days. The new structure at Deir el Bahri lacked nothing, it seems, as Sennemut had thought of everything to make his queen and his love a happy woman.

A palace or any great house had its own performers. She would have maintained her own orchestra and dancing troupe, the musicians playing oboes, lutes, lyres and drums. One cookbook of the New Kingdom era contains recipes for 40 cakes. The favorite in Hatshepsut's time was the shat cake, made of date flour and honey, then fried.

Despite their triumph, queen and commoner were not destined to enjoy *la belle vie* for much longer because the family feud was at length resolved, either by her deposition or death, when Tutmose III came at last into his heritage, becoming one of the most spectacular of Egypt's warrior kings. He is sometimes referred to as the Napoleon of the ancient world.

Upon his succession, Tutmose obliterated all traces of Hatshepsut by the erasure of her cartouches wherever they could be found. It can be imagined how the queen and her followers were abhorred by Tutmose and became the subject of his vindictiveness (amounting, at times, to pettiness), which is amply borne out by the systematic erasure of Hatshepsut's name and the usurpation of her monuments. One, though, remains. Tutmose couldn't destroy it, so he built a wall around it to hide it, but in time the wall itself disappeared and Hatshepsut's obelisk still stands proudly, almost 100 feet tall, defiantly and (it seems) impervious to the vicissitudes of Mother Nature, the deletorious effects of Father Time or the capriciousness of mankind.

She was the daughter of Tutmose I, the sister-wife of Tutmose II and the setpmother-aunt of Tutmose III, all bellicose individuals. She had two daughters, Neferure, who died young, and Meryetre (known as the younger Hatshepsut), who was married to Tutmose III. She was the only female ruler whose reign wasn't calamitous, for Nitokris ended the Old Kingdom, Sebekneferure ended the Middle Kingdom, Twosre ended the 19th dynasty and Cleopatra ended everything!

She elevated the Chief Priests of An-u, Memphis, Abydos, Thebes, Esna, Edfu and Syene to the rank of High Priest, their title being First Prophet (see article in Llewellyn's *1991 Magical Almanac*).

A Fanciful Herb Garden

Amber K

(with tongue firmly in cheek)

Herbs are wonderful creations with a thousand uses, but alas, the common varieties cannot do everything. Here are some wild plants we wish were growing in our garden.

LESSER DOGNAP—Sort of the antithesis to catnip; sprinkle a little of the ground leaves in the Chihuahua Chow of your small, yappy, hyperactive dog (or your neighbor's), and he will mellow right out.

BOODLE-COME-HITHER—Hang the berries over your front door, and people who owe you money will have an overpowering desire to share their wealth with you.

GREATER PESTBANE—Worn as an amulet around the neck, it keeps away borrowers, religious fanatics and other pesky people.

FALSE WORRYWORT—When the roots are powdered and burned as incense, the vapors suddenly make it clear to you that all the stuff you worry about is really going to turn out all right.

MONTESSORI DOMESTICUS—Drunk as a tea, gives children the irresistible urge to pick up their toys and place them neatly in color-coded bins.

MORNINGLOW FLOWER—When soaked in your scrub water, makes floors totally impervious forever to dirt and food by eliminating friction: food scraps and dust particles just sort of slide right out the door. When added to bath water, does the same for children.

QUENCHA TWIG—One cup of the tea at dinner means that little ones will never yell for a drink of water at 11 p.m., yet it has no effect on tiny bladders. Also strengthens their retinal cells so they don't require half the house lights blazing at bedtime, plus the aroma drives monsters from under beds and out of the closet, to a galaxy far far away.

FOGHORN SUMAC—Chewing one of the leaves will raise the volume of your voice by several decibels; ideal for athletic coaches, youth group leaders, and organizers of political rallies.

MUGWARN—Carry the roots in your purse or pocket. If threatened by a pursesnatcher, pinch them and the high-pitched squealing sound will drive away the would-be thief.

JOCK-IN-THE-PULPIT—Used at an inhalant, the powdered flowers are said to enhance the spiritual awareness of athletes.

Of course these and other herbs should be used only under the guidance of an experienced herbalist. Perhaps you'll find them growing in your neighborhood—good luck!

A Primer in Natural Magic and Spells and Rituals

Scott Cunningham

A Primer in Natural Magic

Natural magic is the branch of these occult (hidden) arts that was once public knowledge. It's a beautiful, loving use of natural energies to create positive change. Though it's been cloaked in secrecy for centuries, it's just as effective today as it was in a distant past. If you've never practiced natural magic before, here are the basics:

- Magic is the movement of natural energies to cause needed change.
- Magic isn't dangerous or evil.
- Magic is a genuine (but little understood) practice.
- Magic utilizes natural energies: those within your body, as well as those within plants, stones, symbols and colors
- You can feel this energy within yourself while exercising, walking up stairs, or performing other physical activities.
- You can stir up this energy, at will, by tightening your muscles.
- This energy is given purpose and direction by the nature of the spell, which may involve creating pictures or images in your mind.
- This energy is then released through relaxation of the muscles and by pushing it out toward its goal, which may be a candle, a stone, an herb, a tub of water or even the atmosphere.
- Magic is used for positive reasons.
- Magic is never used to cause harm.

- Magic isn't used for others without their permission.
- Magic can always be used to help yourself (indeed, this is the best reason for using it).

Does this seem simple? It is. Does this seem complex? It is. Why are these two statements seemingly contradictory? Find the answer in the practice of natural magic.

Natural magic is a precious legacy that earlier generations have given to us.

Spells and Rituals

The following spells can be performed by anyone, anywhere, as long as a need exists. These spells address common needs: money, love and protection. They're non-religious, require little specialized equipment, and can be surprisingly effective. For maximum results, perform one spell at a time. If you have many needs, decide which is the most important and concentrate on that.

Perform these rites with the proper attitude: *expect results*. Realize that most magical rituals must be repeated several times. Know that magic isn't supernatural, and its effects don't materialize before your astonished eyes in a supernatural way. The more you practice natural magic, the more aware you'll become of its possible positive applications in your life. Natural magic is a powerful tool of positive change.

The Cornucopia Spell
(to attract needed money)

Items Needed: a wooden, ceramic or glass bowl; 3 tablespoons ground cinnamon; 3 tablespoons ground cloves; a smaller, non-metallic bowl or cup.

Wash the bowl well. Dry. Place it somewhere in the house where it can remain for at least three weeks.

Measure the ground spices and pour them into the smaller bowl. Mix well with your fingers, while saying in a low voice, with great intent, as you tighten the muscles in your fingers, arms and shoulders:

> *Spices fragrant;*
> *Spices enfold;*
> *Bring me money,*
> *Silver and gold.*

Say this chant at least five times while mixing the ground cinnamon and cloves. *Feel* the energy that vibrates within the spices.

Place the small bowl beside the larger bowl. Fish out a few coins from your pocket or purse. Place them into the larger bowl. Then take a pinch of the powdered spices and sprinkle this on top of the coins while repeating the "Spices fragrant" chant. See a stream of money attracting energy beaming out from the bowl. At least once a day, or more often if you wish, add a few coins to the money cornucopia, sprinkle on a pinch of the spices, and say the chant. Continue this until the spices are gone. Money will come to you.

(Note: Don't remove any of the coins that you've placed in the bowl. Allow them to rest there, adding their own money energies to those of the spices. When you've used up the spices, remove the coins and spend them in whatever way you wish. If desired, recharge the spices with the above chant, wash the dish, and restart the spell.)

The Love Stone
(to attract love)

For this ritual you'll need nothing but yourself and your deep need for a loving relationship.

Go to a spring, visit the beach, or walk beside a river or a lake. A dry river bed (in desert regions) is also fine. Let a stone find you (don't look for one). One stone, and only one stone, will be suitable: it will be small enough to fit into your hands and will probably be smooth.

Once you have the stone, hold it loosely between your palms. See yourself enjoying a loving relationship, not with "Joe Smith," "Jessica Thompson" or a specific person, but with someone who, perhaps, you haven't yet met.

Build up an image in your mind. See the two of you having a quiet dinner, listening to music, and enjoying mutual interests. Make this picture real in you mind.

Now press your palms tightly together against the stone. Pour this energy into the stone. Force it from your palms. The rock is a sponge, a solid yet permeable sponge, sopping up your need for a loving relationship.

When you've forced out as much energy as you can, transfer the stone to your talented hand (your writing hand) and throw it into the spring, the ocean, the river, lake or dry lake bed. Fling it from you, knowing that your energy goes with it.

As it contacts the water (or the sand), it releases the energy that you've lent it. Forces will be set into motion. Be active. Someone, eventually, will find you.

The Flaming Key
(a house protection rite)

Items needed: a duplicate key to your house (that you won't need to use at any time); a red candle; a book of matches.

At dawn, or as near to sunrise as possible, take the key, the candle and the matches to the inside of your front door. Realize that the key can open or shut off entrance to your home. Realize that it can stop both physical as well as non-physical intruders.

Set down the key and the matches. Hold the candle between the palms of your hands. See your home as a safe, guarded, protected place, a place of sanctuary and security. See it as a fortress against unwanted persons or energies.

Say these or similar words:

> *Guard this house*
> *To the core.*
> *Guard it now*
> *From roof to floor.*

Pour this protective energy into the candle. Feel it rushing from your hands into the taper. Do this until you feel that you'll burst.

Transfer the candle to your left hand, if you're right-handed. (If left-handed, to the right). Still holding the candle, pick up the book of matches with your free hand and strike one of the matches. Light the candle's wick.

Set down the book of matches. As the candle's flame rises, say:

> *Guard this house,*
> *Guard it well.*
> *Guard ths house*
> *By this spell.*

Hold the candle before the door for at least a minute. Sense its energies stirring and rising through the flame as the wax melts.

Now pick up the key, the magical instrument which will protect your place of residence. Holding it in your left hand (if right-handed), smash the key down onto the candle's flame, quenching it and, simultaneously, transferring all the candle's power into the key.

Set aside the candle. Touch the key to the front door's lock and say:

> *Guard well this house,*
> *O Flaming Key.*
> *This is my will,*
> *So Mote It Be!*

Place the key somewhere inside the house near the front door (perhaps under the rug or carpeting). It will guard your home so long as it's never used to open the front door.

Quando io sono partito, da questo mondo,
Qualunque cosa che avrete bisogna,
Una volta al mese quando la luna
E piena... Dovrete venire in
luogo diserto, in una selva tutte insieme, E adorane lo spirito
potente di mia madre Diana. E chi vorra
imparare la stregoneria, Che non la sopra, mia
madre le insegnera, tutte cose... Sarete liberi dalla
schiaviti! E così divennete tutti liberi!...
—Aradia

Aradia

The Gypsy Fay

Kisma K. Stepanich

The dancing magick of moonlight shimmers down upon the glen. There in the forming moonbeam circle spark dozens of tiny lights. Tinkling chimes whisper through the night veil like butterfly gossamer wings fluttering by. The gentle music calls forth into the misty night, awakening the inner spirit of the Sprite.

> *From the hill and from the glen*
> *come the Faerie widdershin.*
> *Calling from the depths of life*
> *dancing under full moon light.*
>
> *Come unto us—*
> *come unto us—*
> *come dance,*
> *come sing,*
> *come unto us.*
>
> *From the moon-ring shimmering bright*
> *comes forth the magick of goddess life.*
> *We are the Fays, gentle and gay,*
> *we are the Angels fallen from grace.*

Lured to the enchanting mysterious world, the *gajo** does creep. Down to the glen he slithers like a snake, mystified, mesmerized, unable to wake from the stirring that the Faerie blast in his face.

---

* Non-Gypsy Male.

At the edge of their magickal circle he does lay; their swirling and dancing bodies lift him away into a world, quite different from his, superimposed, distant, gray.

> This night is upon you,
> a shimmering veil of mystical light.
> Into our circle, into our hands,
> you now commend your life.
>
> Come unto us—
> come unto us—
> come dance,
> come sing,
> come unto us.
>
> Forever now, as you walk through the day
> your mind and heart will forever stray—
> Into the realm revealed by the moon
> into the world of dancing Fays.

As the *gajo* lay helpless deep in trance, the dancing Faerie swiftly did part. There in the center of their moonlit grove stood a Lady covered with blue shimmering veils.

> Aradia, Aradia—
> Queen of Faerie
> comes to you.
>
> Lucky you, lucky you.
> Blessed with the presence
> of her mighty dew.
>
> Aradia, Aradia—
> Queen of Faerie
> speaks to you.
>
> Listen you, listen you.
> With open ears
> and heart so true.

As the Lady stepped forward, the ruffling of her gown resounded as if a symphony of thousands of tiny, delicate bells had been rung. The Faeries at the sound breathed deeply in, clutched their hands to heart and issued forth one big sigh.

The *Romni** knelt next to the *gajo* and gently laid her hand on his face. So sweet his eyes and the dimples of his cheek. She swooned over his beauty, bent and kissed his lips, touched the place of his heart, then disappeared in a mist.

The *gajo* sat up and blinked, looking around. No sight of the Fay or the magickal moon-ring was found.

"Yo, ho, Kirel, where be ya lad?" a voice did call.

Kirel stood slowly, shaking his head. "Over here, good brother; I got lost in the mists." Kirel told his brother of the Faerie and the beautiful Lady. "I must find her," Kirel said heart-forlorn.

"Let her go, man," the brother did say. "She's not of this world—she's a Fay! She's only a Gypsy who's tried to steal your heart. Give her up, man. Forget her this day!"

Kirel touched his face where her hand once lay and issued forth a sigh. "She stole my heart with her gentle."

The brother patted Kirel on the shoulder and guided him away from the glen, now empty, no magick therein.

Days passed, weeks tugged by. The season changed one into the next. And all the while Kirel's heart and mind drifted ever back to the world of Faerie.

One day, as the land dressed in blossoms of every hue, Kirel ventured back to the glen and found himself sitting at the same spot where the moon-ring had been. He sighed and he cried; he looked to the sky and wondered why his Gypsy Fay had gone away. Then out of the corner of his eye, a shimmering form jumped up and down. Yet, each time he looked directly at the movement, nothing was there.

"Look straight ahead," a whispering bell tinkled on the warm summer breeze. "Here is the secret to win her heart into your keep forever and a day.

"Find yourself a holey stone, and three slender branches of the flowering alder. The scent of roses attracts the White Lady, so make thee some rose-scented water by taking 21 measures of

---

* Gypsy wife.

rose petals and steeping them in a copper kettle under lid. Leave them to soak for the space of Full Moon to Full Moon. Next market day purchase ye a veil of crimson color embroidered richly with Moon thread, and a small silver bell.

"At the dark of the Moon next, anoint your hair and body with the rose water and get ye to this spot as the Sun begins to set.

"With the three flowering alder branches sweep a moonring widdershins, then sprinkle with the rose water. Place the crimson veil in the center with the holey stone. As the night black covers the land, with silver bell in hand, stand within the circle and face ye the east and whisper to the breeze:

> I call to thee Elemental Faeries.
> I call out to ye.
> Come unto me, come unto me.
> Come dance, come sing,
> Come unto me.

"Say this to each direction, south, west, then north. Then turn ye into the center, kneel at the crimson veil, and look down into the hole of the stone and say:

> In innocent purity, I shall see thee,
> I call unto thee, Mareynae,
> By thy Faerie name.
> I call ye so true, for I need you.
> Serve me well as I do you.

> I call unto thee, Mareynae,
> Bind thee unto me, comest to me.
> My virtues to thee, I hast shown.
> Thus, I may see thee in this stone.

"Then stand back and ring the silver bell three tones. Close your eyes and hold your breath, for into the stone your true love shall go."

The blackness hung heavy like a clock and the silver bell rang out three times in the night. Kirel stepped back, closed his eyes and held his breath.

A thunderclap hit the sky; a screaming wind rushed by. A light rain began to fall and a symphony of thousands of tiny, delicate bells began to ring.

The gentle touch of a hand on Kirel's face made him start. As he opened his eyes, there before him stood the beautiful White Lady wrapped in a crimson veil. A smile she gave him so warm and intimate.

"I am the Gypsy Fay come to you this day. At your bidding I now must stay. This warning I give: *never turn your back on me*— for if you do, escape I shall and with me your heart will be under my spell, which will cause you to mourn until the end of your days! Forsake me not!"

In the distance, a chorus spilled out into the night:

> *Aradia, Aradia—*
> *Queen of Faerie*
> *comes to you.*
>
> *Lucky you, lucky you.*
> *Blessed with the presence*
> *of her mighty dew.*
>
> *Aradia, Aradia—*
> *Queen of Faerie*
> *comes to you.*
>
> *Listen you, listen you.*
> *now you must*
> *serve her and forever be true.*

Erotic Magic

Hans Holzer

Ever since men desired women, and vice versa, ever since people had unfullfilled needs in their everyday lives, some of us have been looking for a better way to get what we really want.

In this computer-dominated word that way naturally involves increased knowledge, learning, training, the right contacts and the right approach once we have found those important individuals who can make our dreams come true. All this is strictly logical and rational, and the success of our drives depends on factors we can easily estimate, if not the actual end result itself.

But a small sector of humanity has always known there is an *alternate road to getting yours:* the way of magick. What is magick? Not stage manipulation, tricks that make your maiden aunt Sarah take her skirt off onstage or allow the magician to extract his handkerchief from your ear. Nothing so obviously contrived. *That* is "magic," not "magick" with a k. The magick I'm talking about is the ancient art of understanding and manipulating the forces of nature, in such a way that they serve you better than the one who is unaware of their laws and his own powers. Nothing supernatural about it, either: no laws of science are violated, no miracles performed. What *is* being done, however, may indeed *look* like a suspension of ordinary laws of science to the average person. But it really isn't. What it is is simply a way of harnessing energies within to powers outside and focusing them in the desired direction. Naturally, you have to abandon the old materialistic concept that man is simply flesh and blood and death is the end, and we're just a living machine of sorts, because that simply isn't true.

What makes the concept of magick work is the realization that man is a living power center, with ray guns called eyes, with antennas called nervous system, with computers called brains and with television cameras in miniature called visualization centers. If you look at it that way perhaps you will understand the power of magick a lot better.

Thoughts are not just imaginary nothings drifting through an otherwise empty mind, but are formulated telepathic messages, programmed broadcasts at times, with substance, direction and impact. The trick is to know how, when and to whom to apply these "broadcasts," of course, and it is a trick that can be learned once you understand the guiding principles of magick.

Now the word *erotic* has really very little to do with that sweet little angelic Greek boy-god Eros, at least not the way we and the majority of humanity understand the term today. Actually Eros was the god of life and, together with his dark twin Thanatos, symbolized the flow of man's life energies from birth to death, from day to night. In our concept of Erotic Magick, however, we deal with the love and love-making aspects of the term. As such we must address ourselves to Sexual Magick, as it appears to be the area of greatest impact in our lives next to the survival instinct itself. The sexual drive then is both a blessing and a curse: a blessing in that it causes the harnessing of the energies within us and a curse when the drive is frustrated or aborted.

Since time immemorial the power of sex has been the greatest power of them all. Men and women possessed with unusual physical attributes, or perhaps only those whose attributes were ordinary (such as Cleopatra) but who knew how to make them count, have been in commanding positions in more ways than one, as far back as the age of the caveman. But it was also that same primitive progenitor of the human race who recognized a second, equally powerful force in his world: the power of the occult, of the gods and demons, of the forces of nature he could not yet understand and even less control. Just as the choice specimens among men and women were worshipped (and sought after) for their sexual proclivities, so the purveyors of the occult, the priests, magicians, sorcerers, were much in demand . . . for as long as they could deliver (just as their sexual colleagues).

To this day the twin powers of sex and religion are among the world's most controversial attributes, even when they are taken only at their conventional level. But when sex becomes "sex all the way," and religion becomes "The Occult," the controversial aspects become explosive causes. It would be much too easy to say that sex deals with the body and the occult with the spirit; both expressions involve a far more sophisticated system of interlocking stimuli and they cannot be categorized in such a cut and dried manner at all. Sex does involve certain emotional/spiritual processes, and the occult, in some of its aspects, is *deeply sexual*.

Power is derived from a knowing combination of these forces in the hands of the user. This is the more difficult as few if any sources exist where one can find direct, factual information, the kind that could lead to actual experimentation.

What sex is and why it brings fullfillment need scarcely be discussed. But the powers derived from occult utilization of the sex drive are of two kinds: the power to attract, possibly dominate, others and the power to enjoy on levels vastly superior to those ordinarily reached without its application.

"Sexual congress" is of course possible only if two people actually meet; therefore, the *power to attract* another person is of considerable importance here. The important thing to remember is that eye contact is the hook to achieve desired results. Visualization of the thought of desire, followed by rapid "broadcasting" of a glance at the opposite person establishes a link. This is followed by a combination of thought patterns and bodily movements.

Example: George went to a party. Only one girl interested him, but she was with another man. George visualized *himself* in his place, held that picture for a while and sought to step into the direct line of view of the girl. As soon as she looked at him, George shot the visualization "at her." She blinked, but ten minutes later *she* sought *him* out and the rest was not difficult.

Example: Marie had been living with Fred for nearly a

year. Theirs was a harmonious relationship until he ran into another woman, Bea. His interest shifted to Bea. Marie's interest remained with Fred. But she recalled her esoteric training, the year she spent among a coven of white witches in Vermont. Little by little, every day, she projected a "holding pattern" on Fred, stripped down to a few essential thought ideas. At the same time she visualized herself making love to him; then she visualized the other woman in her stead, and followed this by blotting her out and replacing her with her own visualization. What Marie was doing was, of course, retracing her own situation, but with a new end result! She did this especially at times when Fred was about to fall asleep or wake up; i.e., when the bonds between his conscious and unconscious minds were weakest and thus most susceptible to outside impressions. Within two weeks he broke off with Bea and returned to Marie, puzzled as to why he had ever tried to leave her in the first place!

Here we have the occult utilization of *mind power* to obtain desired results. *Body power*, on the other hand, is derived from a different center. The same glandular system which supplies sexual fluids also manufactures psychic energy. This energy is normally invisible, but occasionally becomes visible in red light as the so-called *ectoplasm* of the séance room: it is an albumen-rich substance drawn from the "solar plexus" centers at the top of the head and in back of the stomach, and usually exteriorized through mouth, nose and sexual organs. It *must* be returned into the body eventually or serious weakness will result. It is also sensitive to white light and must not be exposed to it. However, when the psychic energy is invisible and has not reached the stage of visible density, it can be extremely useful in the so-called *Psycho-Ecstasy* process. By carefully arousing the power centers during the preparatory stages of sexual relations, the rising psychic power can add great depths and additional dimensions to the sensory experience itself. In India this is referred to as *kundalini*, the "dormant serpent" which is aroused to create the fire of passion in lovers. In the West, we have still lots to learn about our hidden powers.

Example: John and Sue were very much in love, but their sexual atunement had been less than perfect. John was considerably more nervous in her presence than desirable, and the results were poor, threatening a dissolution of their relationship. At that point Sue read of Psycho-Ecstasy and decided to test it. Following the basic instructions, she prepared a harmonious background for the experiment: the kind of colors, music, and scent both liked. Then they abstained from sex for a week, although that had not been required in their instructions. On the appointed night, both stretched out side by side in comfort and began by gently commanding their life forces to enter the two solar plexus areas, from the peripheral nerve centers where they normally are. Shortly after both felt intense heat in the stomach and head areas, but they knew this was to be expected so it did not cause them to worry. Next, they verbally commanded this "force" to rise into their conscious selves, at the same time silently visualizing the "opening up" of each to the other person. As they did so, their skin began to tingle as if they had plugged themselves into an electric circuit, which, in a way, they had ... their own, unused potential!

As the tingling became intoxicating, they *finally touched:* the experience lasted for nearly an hour and was a far cry from the relations they had been having until then. What John and Sue had discovered was nothing more mysterious than a way to harness and control the electric tension within us in such a way that it hypersensitized their nerve impulses, thus leading to extremely high sensory pleasures.

The powers of occult sex are, after all, not so strange. What is strange is how few people know about them, and how many regard them as imaginary. Imaginary, indeed! Ask John and Sue....

MYSTICAL CRYPTIC CROSSWORD PUZZLE

Raymond Buckland

Across

1. A tarot suit that runs over. (3)
3. Initially a travel organization when headed by an American. (2)
5. 3 Across on reflection. (2)
7. Fairy Queen. (3)
9. It contains the Autumnal Equinox. (9)
12. Exclamation of relief starts ahead. (2)
14. Untrue recumbant posture? (3)
15. H. Rider Haggard knew of her. (3)
16. Half a semi is directional. (2)
17. To pass a rope through a hole in a block. (5)

20. Alternative to land. (2, 3)
22. Protective barriers for magicians who get around. (6,7)
25. The start of South Dakota Magick. (3)
26. Babylonian god of the waters is short for each. (2)
27. Briefly a Doctor of Scientology. (2)
28. The opposite of Pacific Standard Time is three-quarters best. (3)
29. No sitting around when this sign goes up. (3)
31. Russian river flows backwards for a brief second. (2)
33. The start of the Rosicrucian Society. (2)
35. These usually go with more than one of 12 Across. (3)
37. The ineffable name loses a printer's measure. (13)
41. Rush as fast as you can to hide the Hindu Goddess of Dawn. (5)
42. "U" can't win! (1,4)
43. Just an afterthought. (2)
44. Female saint briefly begins stealing. (3)
46. A rumpled bed is the start of the East Delaware Buddhists. (3)
47. Brief British thank-you. (2)
48. Roman Catholic goddess? (3,6)
50. A pair. (3)
51. Briefly with regard to the symbol for rhenium. (2)
52. Tapuyan Indian starts gesticulating. (2)
53. You can do this if you can afford to. (3)

Down
 1. Amulets that fascinate. (6)
 2. The beginning of psychiatry is added on. (2)
 3. Not the whole thing. (1, 5)
 4. Consumed three-quarters of date. (3)
 5. Short Americans. (3)
 6. They say that Nature does it to a vacuum. (6)
 7. Brief gentleman. (2)
 8. Where Diana had many, it usually comes in pairs. (6)
10. Mr. Presley loses his end, mixed-up live. (4)
11. Backward Canadian Indian (4)
13. Egyptian ones were freqiently elaborate. (9)
16. Those segs get confused to view an apparition. (4,5)
18. Mixed up diamond starts the Egyptian Gnostic Magi. (3)
19. Stands for a leader of ritual or politician. (2)

21. Half sleeps. (3)
23. Known as the Egyptian second self. (2)
24. Psychoanalytically the short identity of Idaho? (2)
29. If you can work magick you can't be this. (6)
30. The middle of brother is also a large part of both. (3)
31. Young man has achieved success. (6)
32. Go backwards. (2)
33. Sun god is half rare. (2)
34. Do it with sage and make a mark. (6)
35. Coming or going it's still Crowley's order of doing things. (3)
36. Yes ank becomes furtive. (6)
38. Hasty, spotted magician is this? (4)
39. With 33 Down could be encouraging. (2)
40. Two thirds of ancient Britain. (4)
45. Palindromic first lady. (3)
46. Harvest rune turns into energy. (3)
48. Where you're going is in the middle of castoffs. (2)
49. Mark well what the Latin scholar says. (2)

Solution on page 354.

Getting Started in Magick

Amber K

This is a pop quiz. Check one of the following:
"Real magick is...

a) ...miraculous deeds performed by ancient wizards with incredible natural talents and decades of training by other ancient wizards."

b) ...supernatural exploits performed by misguided people under the influence of the devil."

c) ...amazing feats performed by the heroes of fantasy-adventure tales, having no basis in reality."

d) ...tricks and sleight-of-hard illusions performed by skillful performers for public entertainment."

e) ...wonderful accomplishment performed by ordinary people who work hard to learn and practice the art of changing consciousness at will."

Yes, the answer is *e*. Fortunately, since few of us are fantasy heroes, ancient wizards, devil-worshippers, or entertainers.

Magick is a skill that can be learned. As with scuba diving or quilting, some people learn faster than others either because they have some natural talent or the motivation to work hard. It is initially an internal process, "changing consciousness"—which, however, can have effects in the external world: protection, healing, prosperity etc. What magick does best is to change the magickian. You can grow spiritually, achieve new insights into yourself and the world, release bad habits, deepen your good qualities and more.

That's all very positive: what about curses and hexes, harming enemies or making people love you? Be aware that there is a boomerang effect to magick: whatever you send out returns to you amplified. If you harm or force another, you will be hurt worse. It's guaranteed. So focus your magick on making you, and your life, better.

How do you get started in magick? By finding an ethical and experienced teacher. By reading good books, like those recommended at the end of this article. And by having a good purpose, knowing your heart's desire.

It helps immensely if you are healthy and emotionally stable, free of addictions. You must be able to center yourself, and to develop faith in yourself, a vivid imagination, a strong will, and the ability to enter the silent space at the core of your being. Then you need to learn new skills: primarily raising, channeling and grounding psychic energy.

You can raise power by drumming, dancing, chanting, singing and breathing, to name a few common methods. You will know you have energy building; your whole body will feel tingly and vibrating. Channelling energy is a matter of focus or concentration. Visualize your goal, target or recipient as vividly as possible; then release the energy toward that goal. But you won't release all the energy immediately. You will still feel tingly and "hyperactive," so you must get the excess energy out of your nervous system before it leads to insomnia, raised blood pressure or other problems. Do this by "grounding" or "earthing" the energy. Usually you can stand or sit on the ground and consciously send it into the earth through your hands or the end of your spine. Do this until you feel relaxed and cleansed rather than tense.

Working with the power is the core of any ritual, but there are other important elements. First, you must be very clear in your purpose, and it must be an ethical one. Second, you must choose the place and the timing. Third, you must design the order and nature of your ritual. And fourth, you need to prepare your attire and tools.

Many Pagans prefer an outdoor setting whenever possible: a peaceful grove, a secluded beach, a mountain meadow or the like. A mossy log or flat stone can be your altar, and all the energies of Nature are present to aid you in the worthy work you will do. However, you may also perform magickal rites in a special temple in your home, or a living room adapted for the purpose. The room must be clean and neat, and arranged and decorated for the work you have in mind.

Timing can be important. Work during the waxing Moon for growth and new projects; at the Full Moon for healing and empowerment; during the waning Moon to banish, release or cleanse; and in the dark of the Moon for divination. The day and hour of the working also have an influence, but beginners can do well enough by paying attention to lunar phases.

Next, outline your ritual. It is well to include these steps:

1. Be sure the temple or ritual area is prepared and all tools and materials are at hand.

2. Do a small rite of cleansing and purification for yourself.

3. Ground and center yourself.

4. Asperge (cleanse) the ritual space, perhaps by sprinkling consecrated saltwater or by smudging with incense.

5. Cast the circle, creating sacred space. The circle keeps out distracting energies and focuses the power raised inside it. One method is to begin at the altar and move deosil with your athame, sword, wand or staff, pointing at the ground and imaging a boundary of intense blue light being formed at its tip. Speak aloud the words, "I conjure thee, O circle of power, that thou beest a boundary between the world of humanity and the realms of the Mighty Ones, a guardian and a protection, to preserve and contain the power we shall raise within. Wherefore do I bless and consecrate thee."

6. Call the quarters: that is, invite the spirits of Earth, Air, Fire and Water to lend their energies to your magick. These correspond to body, mind, energy and emotions (among other things), and calling them is also a way of involving your total self in the ritual.

7. Invoke the God and the Goddess, the masculine and feminine personifications of the Divine, by whatever names and attributes seem appropriate to you.

8. State your purpose aloud.

9. Raise power, by one of the methods suggested earlier. Channel it toward your goal, and earth the excess energy.

10. Partake of "cakes and wine" or other light refreshment to help ground yourself.

11. Thank all the Powers who helped you, and say farewell.

12. Open the circle by walking *widdershins* (counterclockwise), and drawing the energy back into your athame, sword or wand.

Once you have the steps of your ritual firmly in mind, prepare your tools and attire. Some Witches work "skyclad," that is without clothing, so that they can feel the flow of psychic energy more easily. Others wear long, hooded robes of various colors, bound at the waist by a cord or "cingulum." If you work with an established coven, it will have traditions to guide you.

The four basic, traditional tools of the Wiccan magickian are the athame (ah-THAY-mee), wand, cup or chalice and the pentacle. You can create such tools yourself, commission artisans to make them to your designs or purchase them readymade from craftspeople or occult shops. They must sometimes be cleansed, and always consecrated.

Other tools used by magickians include the staff, bells, herbs, candles, runestones, Tarot cards, the cauldron and many others. Space does not permit an exploration of their design and uses here, but good magickal texts can help you.

When all is prepared, you perform the magick. Then, afterwards, you "act in accord"; that is, you begin the practical, mundane work which allows the magick to manifest either in you or on the physical plane. If you are doing magick to lose weight, go throw out the candy bars and chips and plan some slimming vegetarian meals. If your magick is for a new job, read the want ads, apply, and hustle around as though you had never heard of magick.

Magick will not miraculously drop riches, spiritual enlightenment or a new personality in your lap. It works by seeming coincidence, by serendipity, by sudden insights and by unexpected opportunities. But you still have to live and work toward your goals on the material plane. And if you do, magick can give you a powerful boost toward accomplishing your dreams.

The rules of chess can be learned in a few minutes, but it takes years of practice to become a Grand Master. So it is with magick. I have outlined the basics here in few pages, yet you can study for a lifetime and still be learning. Good books help. Among others, you may wish to read *Positive Magick* by Marion Weinstein, *True Maglck: A Beginner's Guide* by myself, *The Ritual Book Of Maglck* by Clifford Bias and works by William Gray, Israel Regardie or William Butler and many of the fine Llewellyn books. If you can find an experienced and ethical teacher or teaching coven, so much the better.

The study and practice of magick is not for everyone. If it is for you, may the Lady and the Lord of All Magicks guide you on the path.

Finding Magic in the New Year

Janina Renee

There's an old superstition that whatever you find yourself doing on New Year's Day—that's what you'll spend most of your time at during the rest of the year.

In past times and places where people took this belief seriously, they would try to make this self-fulfilling prophecy a good one. They would surround themselves with revelry and cheer on New Year's day—primarily with feasting and visiting friends. (Although we must assume that the compulsive workaholics among them would also try to fit in some productive accomplishments as well.)

Like so many old superstitions, this practice can be seen to have both magical and psycological benefits. If you hold to this belief, you consciously create enjoyable experiences. The intent is that these actions will manifest continuing positive circumstances throughout the year. This is an act of imitative magic. It also reminds you that in order to maintain emotional well-being, you have to make room in your life for merriment and playfulness.

If you want to adopt this custom of starting the New Year out auspiciously, make it special by incorporating a number of magical practices:

• Start the day with some simple rite to help you focus on your ideals. Exercises that combine visualization of goals with prana breathing, candle burning, crystal work, tarot meditation, etc. are widely available (Llewellyn's series especially have much to offer in this respect).

• Positive affirmations stating what a lucky prosperous,

rewarding, and fulfilling year you're going to have are likely to be more meaningful and effetive than New Year's resolutions.

• Try to arrange your day so that you can incorporate something to give pleasure to each of your five senses: sight, hearing, touch, smell, and taste.

• Recognize the need for balance between active and reflective states and expansive and contractive phases. Be aware of the balance of yin ard yang principles in your day. Seek a harmonious relationship between work and relaxation.

• Be sure to include a special salutation to your personal deities to ensure their inspiring presence throughout the year. One further thought: magically oriented people, being the eclectic types that they are, may have more than one New Year to celebrate. Spring Equinox marked the start of the year for the Persians, many Native American groups, and others who felt it the best time for new beginnings. Some ancient cultures celebrated New Year's Day twice annually, because they divided the year into halves. The Celts and some Teutonic groups reckoned Beltaine (the beginning of the warm season—May 1) and Samhain (the beginning of the cold season—Nov. 1) as the special dates dividing the year. Other Teutonic tribes and some ancient Grecian subgroups reckoned by the summer and winter solstices, and some Mesopotamian groups divided the year between Autumn and Spring. Among the many other dates, past and present, marking the beginning of a new year are *Rosh Hashanah*, commemorating the Creation, dedicated to self-improvement, and observed by Jews around mid-September; the flooding of the Nile River in ancient Egypt (around July 19); and the first New Moon in the Chinese lunar calendar, usually between Jan. 21 and Feb. 19. With so many potential new beginnings to observe, you can make a point of renewing yourself and your ideals throughout the year!

Seed and Wheel

Norman Frankland

Said the seed to the wheel

"You make a great deal
About spinning so fast
When the first shall be last."

Said the wheel to the seed

"You should understand my speed,
For it's not through greed
That I pay no heed,
For before I've stopped spinning
You'll be the one winning,
And me, I'll be drinkin' my mead."

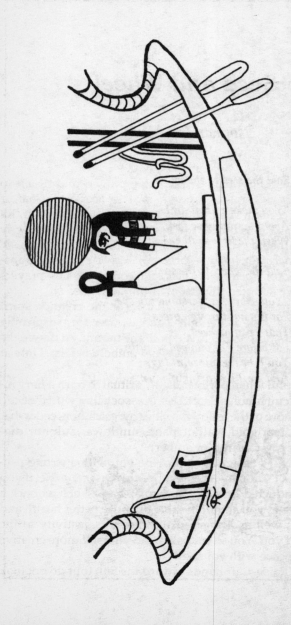

Ritual of the Sun God, Ra

The Ritual of the Sun God, Ra

Gerald and Betty Schueler

The ancient Egyptians wrote many prayers and rituals to the sun god, Ra. Several of the chapters of the *Book of the Dead*, or *Pert Em Hru*, contain such prayers and rituals. As a result, Ra (also known as Re) is one of the best known gods of the early Egyptian Pantheon.

The *Ritual of Ra*, included in the *Book of the Dead* and translated in our book, *Coming Into the Light*, contains many prayers to Ra. We have adapted this ritual for modern use.

The ritual text informs us that Ra is the creative spirit whose physical body is the Sun. The best time for performing this ritual is at noon on the first day of the month. At dawn, the sun is the body of Khepera. At dusk, it embodies Tem. Only at noon is it truly Ra.

It is helpful when performing this ritual to burn a fiery incense such as cinnamon. Also, to aid in associating with the Sun, place one or more of the following close by: carnation, cedar, hazel, lime, rice, marigold, walnut, palm, sunflower, sulphur, diamond, quartz crystal, and/or amber.

This ritual is designed to provide you with a strong psychic link to Ra. (You may use the more current name, Re, if you prefer.) If conducted on a fairly regular basis, such as once a month for a year, you should be able to notice better health and well-being as well as a marked increase in sensitivity to the world around you. You should also find yourself more creative and more at peace with yourself.

STEP 1. Raise your hands toward the Sun (but do not look

directly at it). Begin by saying the following:

Honor to you, O Sustainer of the Spirit, O Tem-Hor-Khuit, when you ascend over the horizon. May a prayer to you be on the mouth of every person. Your beauty is renewed every day in the form of the Solar Disk in those regions near your mother, Hathor.

Now you can make my heart expand throughout eternity when you pass through this house, wherein obeisance is given to you.

STEP 2. Say the following prayer:

A prayer for your radiant light in order for it to ascend over the horizon of the sky. You shoot turquoise rays into the world, O Ra, who is Hor-Khuit, O God of Renewed Existence, O Heir of Eternity, O Begetter who gave birth to himself, O King of this Earth and Ruler of the Tuat. O god of all life who desires life for every person. May your nature elevate you to a King of the Gods, a creation of the goddess Nuit. Your face embraces justice and is renewed at every season, and you are exalted thereby. May your path carry me above the Earth in order to return to you.

O Lord of Heaven and Lord of Earth, O King of Justice, O Lord of Eternity whose authority is forever, O Prince of all of the gods, O god who·made eternal life, who knows the heavens and establishes solidity in the subtle regions. The Company of the Gods give praise for your radiant light. The Earth is for those initiates who see your radiant light. You sail across heaven every day. You are strong. It is said that your mother, Nuit, repeats your journey across heaven.

STEP 3. Visualize the sun as the Boat of Ra in the form of the Sektet Boat. (Sektet is currently spelled Seqtet.) Visualize this boat made of shining green stone and containing colorful images of the Egyptian gods. Imagine a heaven above you of Star Gods and purifying waters. The boat should be a great structure, with as much detail as possible. Next, form a mental image of Ra facing north. Make him realistic, with colors and animation.

Visualize him sitting in the bow of his boat (as shown in the illustration facing the first page of this article). See yourself sitting in this boat next to Ra. Address Ra and say:

The Sektet Boat perfects consciousness and brings solidification in the South, North, West, and East. Your face is praised by the Two Companies of the Gods. The Earth manifests itself according to your thought. Isis and Nephthys ascend with you in that boat and they carry protective spells. You are a Master of the Universe.

You are embodied in the Sun. You have initiated justice and truth. You have divided up those gods who follow your boat which sails again to the Great Ancient Gods at your word. Your ways have influence. You have gathered together your body components. You turn your face toward the beautiful Amentet. You pass there, truly, every day.

STEP 4. Now, see yourself as a Great Ancient One and say:

May I have the strength of a Master of the Earth in the Magickal

Universe. May I rise up to see Ra and be strengthened every day without faltering.

I am truth-speaking. May beauty be seen with both eyes, and heard with both ears, with justice and truth. I am a Master of the Universe, a Master of the Universe. I am like a god.

STEP 5. Visualize the figure of a mighty hawk standing up with the White Crown of the South upon his head and the figures of Tem, Shu, Tefnut, Seb, Nuit, Osiris, Isis, and Nephthys. See them in full colors and have them face to the North, for realism. See them in your boat with you. Exhibit a great calmness of thought. Address the deities and say:

Honor to you who are in the Boat of Radiant Light, the Boat of Radiant Light. Sunlight, or even a ray of sunlight, is said to exalt a person for millions of years so that one's true Will will be turned toward the spiritual people who dwell in radiant light. The god Khepera is in his boat. He has overcome the serpent Apep. It is said that the Children of Seb will cast down my enemies, if I am truth-speaking, and will fortify me. May they fortify me in the Boat of Ra.

STEP 6. If this ritual is performed properly, you will now exist as a perfect spirit, in the Boat of Ra, and you will retain your memory while you are in the Magickal Universe. If you have performed this correctly, you will be able to exist like Thoth; you will be worthy of respect by the living; you will not be cast down at the time of the royal flame of the goddess Bast, and you will go about in strength as a mighty and beautiful prince. Say:

Honor to you, O Ra, in the form of radiant light. O Tem-Horus-Khuit, you are praised for your good qualities. Before my two eyes appears your shining spirit that is above flesh. You pass in strength and then you set in the Sektet Boat. Your heart expands with the breaths of truth in the Atet Boat. My heart is delighted by your cyclic pilgrimage across heaven, and by your setting with those who have cast down all of your enemies.

(Note: From sunrise to noon, Ra's boat is called the Atet Boat. From noon to sunset, his boat is called the Sektet boat.)

STEP 7. Address Ra as the spiritual being whose body is the Sun and say:

Honor to you, O Ra, who shines as the god Tem when you set. Beautiful is your radiant light. You shine upon your own mother. You rise up as the King of the Gods, and cause the Goddess of the Night Sky to show obeisance to your face. You are embraced by justice and you are renewed at dawn and dusk. Your cyclic pilgrimage across heaven expands your heart.

May you shine light upon my face. I praise you in the morning, and I rest with you in the evening. May my ba (soul) go forth with you over heaven.

May your peace be mine. I see your beautiful rays. I see Horus as a Guardian at the Helm of the Boat of Ra with Thoth and Maat at his sides. My way begins with the Sektet Boat and ends with the Atet Boat. I am allowed to view the solar disk and to look upon the Moon until all light is in the East. My soul (ba) can come forth and swiftly travel to any place it so desires at the invocation of my name.

Honor to you, O Ra, creator of immortal man, Tem-Hor-Khuit, the one god who lives in truth, creator of things that are, discerner of things that will be, ruler of the spirit body of men and women who came forth from his Eye, Lord of Heaven, Lord of Earth, creator of beings below man and above heaven.

Praise be unto you, O Creator of the Gods, O Tem who brought man into manifestation, Lord of Bliss and Mighty One of Desires. You are the shining light and the life of every face of man. I give praises to you in the evening. I rest when you set from the living. The Sektet Boat is with gladness. The Atet Boat is with joy.

STEP 8. Close by concentrating on Ra. See Ra in the Magickal Universe surrounded by all who are with him while saying:

> *You set in the horizon. You are beautiful in the form of Ra every day. You give existence to my ba. You initiate with shining light when you shine upon my body. I can see the solar disk and the dead who are perfected spirits in the Magickal Universe. May these creative ones assist me.*

Mantras for Everyday Use

Brian and Esther Crowley

There are literally thousands of mantras, chants and invocations in ancient languages, such as Arabic, Egyptian, Hebrew, Sanskrit and Tibetan, to be used for specified purposes. A small selection found to be of great personal benefit down the years is given below.

The ideal chant for opening and/or closing a meditation session is the well-known Sanskrit/Tibetan *Om*—generally pronounced (Aa...oo...mm). Sounding of the Om puts the user in touch with her/his higher self and with the source of all creation.

> *Lord of the Universe*
> *enrich our lives with Thy love.*
> *Guard the treasure*
> *of our innermost souls*
>
> *Aum*
> *(Ah...oo...mm)*
> (Repeat at least 3 times for best effect)

The Hebrew chant Qadosh, Qadosh, Qadosh Adonai Tzeba'oth (Holy, Holy, Holy is the Lord of Hosts) is found in Isaiah and Revelation in the Bible as the sound sung constantly at the feet of the Creator by His angelic choir. Used as a protective shield or helmet of light placed around the head of the chanter, it will ensure that only those influences emanating from the highest possible source will enter into the consciousness.

The Tibetan Buddha of Compassion, Avalokitesvara,
sounds the sacred OM.

Hearken to the inner voice:
tune in to the heartbeat of thy neighbor.
If all world listen thus,
we would live in a glorious world.

Qadosh Qadosh Qadosh
(Qa-*dosh*, Qa-*dosh*, Qa-*dosh*)
Adonai Tzeba'oth
(Ad-o-*noy* Tze-ba-*ot'h*)
(Repeat 12 or 24 times for best effect)

A wonderful Sanskrit mantra to be used for calming mind, body and soul is the chant *Om Namah Shivaya* (Om, reverence to the name of Shiva), especially when intoned in a long drawn-out fashion. Shiva is invoked as the dissipator of all negativity.

Justice is our karma.
We reap what we sow in life.
The law is immutable,
and is the key to all things.
The door closes;
we turn the key
it opens...

Om Namah Shivaya
(Aaaaauuuuu-mmmmm Na-*mah*-aah
Sseeva-ah-ah-ah-*yah*)

Repetition of the Arabic expression Ya-Rahman (God the Beneficent) not only tunes in the user with one of the many names of Allah, but brings immediate clarity to a tired mind and a more active clear-sightedness.

Our vision becomes clear,
nature will become alive for us;
We will become vital,
and the Spirit will shine
in our ears.

Ya-Rahman
(Yah Rah-maan)

Another good attention stimulator and energy provoker is the Egyptian chant Asar-djedu (Pillar of Osiris). Repeated use brings an effect on both the physical and paraphysical levels:

United, we are as one!
Unity is the strength of God,
for He is all thought.

Asair-djedu
(Os'r Dje-doo)

Several mantras (out of many hundreds of possibilities) can be specifically recommended for healing purposes, for those who are ill in body, mind, soul or spirit. The Hebrew *Shel Shem Geburah* calls upon the name of an Angel of Healing who works directly on the seven chakras or energy vortice of the body:

Center of the macrocosm,
direct Thy rays of power
to those who are part of Thee.

Shel Shem Geburah
(Shel Shem Ge-bu-*rah*)
(Repeat 12 times)

The Sun has long been a symbol of good health, and many ancient cultures developed so-called Sun chants as a source of bodily healing. One such is the Sanskrit *Om Suryaya Namah* (Om, salutations to the Supreme), which is best intoned facing the Sun at sunrise:

O nature, fill us with thy essence;
fill us with divine life,
so that we may radiate the life force.

Om Suryaya Namah
(Aum Sur-yai-ah Namah)

To bring peace to one's immediate surroundings, and into the world at large, chants in several different languages can be used. Below is a composite chant for use at all times:

Hold this world perfect in thy thought—
hold the thought of a world of love—
and, on the ethereal plane,
our thoughts of peace will manifest a thousandfold.

Shalom (Hebrew)
(Shalom)
Peace

Ya-Salaam (Arabic)
(Yah Sah-laam)
The Source of Peace

Om Santi, Santi, Santi (Sanskrit)
(Aum -SSan-tee, Ssan-tee, Ssan-tee)
Om. Peace! Peace! Peace!

SHALOM!—Peace!

Too Soon Old and Too Late Smart... Is the Art of Pow-Wow All (gone)?

Jenine E. Trayer

Ask 60-year-old residents of South Central Pennsylvania about Pow-Wow and five out of ten will tell you that they received a miraculous healing from one when they were a child. The other five will tell you that they had a friend or relative who was cured "way back."

Ask those in their 20s, from the same area about Pow-Wow. Nine out of ten will give you a totally empty stare. Some of them will ask you if you are inquiring on their knowledge of Indian Councils.

What is involved in this elusive art that has caused so much consternation among Pennsylvania families for almost 300 years? Why did good Christian daughters and sons burn stacks of books, bedding and other personal effects of their parents and grandparents the very day they passed away? What skeleton were they trying to frantically shove to the very bottom of the proverbial family closet, sincerely believing it would not have the nerve to pop back out again? What power did they so greatly fear that they felt the need to bind, suppress, discredit and destroy? What topic "makes no never mind"?

When William Penn (a charismatic Quaker born under the sign of Libra) acquired Pennsylvania in 1681, he dreamed of creating a haven of religious freedom for all faiths. He traveled all over Europe, asking persecuted families to consider joining him in America. He mapped out an acceptable form of government, sailed to Africa, and introduced himself to the native Africans.

The Delaware Indians accepted Penn, exchanging food,

71

ideas and customs. Penn learned that the word for the tribe's medicine man, priest and healer, was *Powaw*—meaning "he who dreams." These people believed that the Shaman of the tribe received a great percentage of his power and healing capabilities through dreams and vision question.

As a result of his preaching crusade in Europe 50 ships, bearing persecuted souls from England, Ireland, Wales and the Rhineland, anchored in the Delaware River. The first of many waves of emigrants.

These people, driven by threat of death (many had already been exterminated due to new dictates of the Roman Catholic Church) arrived with plain and colorful customs, varied religious beliefs and the magick of gypsy spells and charms. As with any group of perfect strangers suddenly lumped together in both common cause and environment, an exchange of religious and mundane practices occurred. This resulted in new concepts with twists and turns of old memories. The magick and practice of Pow-Wow was born.

By the early 1800s the Protestant beliefs of the various communities took a firm hold. Pow-Wow, like many magickal practices across the globe, was strongly affected by the religious system of the area. Pow-Wow artists made a great effort to veil the origins of their magick. Although they were practicing a fine mixture of Native American beliefs married to the charms and spells of the sloe-eyed Gypsies left behind in Europe, they refused to admit it. Leaving the practical applications intact, they revamped the chants and spells to the status of "prayers" that revolved around God and his son, Jesus Christ. Little or no reference was left to Mary or any other female deity.

In 1819, John Hohman of Berks County wrote the first (and just about only) book on the practice of Pow-Wow. Entitled *Long Lost Friends*, it was originally written in German and contained a mish-mash of charms, healings and spells for the country folk. Hohman and others of his kind appear to have campaigned long and hard to convince locals that they were not practicing Witchcraft and supported the myth that Witches worshipped Satan in order to guarantee the survival of Pow-Wow.

A great deal of the art focuses around the eradication of bodily affliction from humans and animals by the use of sympathetic magick. Although healing is the predominant magick, turning away mad dogs and snakes and eliminating slander were skills employed by the Pow-Wow as well.

Pow-Wows were (and are) predominately female. This was due more to their availability than to any particular skill. Farmers and their sons traveled from farm to farm in cooperative labor to ensure the stability of the community. The mothers and grandmothers remained near the main house, caring for livestock, gardens and, of course, the home and the small children therein. Extended family units were quite prevalent, with sons and daughters building on to the main house with each generation. Female Pow-Wows then served as midwives as well.

Because they served a community need—that of caring for the sick, injured and birthing babies (much needed for the continuance of farm life) they were permitted to practice with only a few difficulties from local clergy until the 1920s.

Like other magickal practitioners, Pow-Wows used wands cut the first night of Christmas. These tools were used to dowse for iron, water and other ores. They used herbs, byproducts of animals, and other natural substances.

Most of the charms and spells were of an ethical nature, though some might be considered borderline. For example, to win every hand in a card game, one would tie the heart of a bat to the right arm with red thread.

Talismans were also employed, and magickal writing was used often. A spell would be written on a slip of white paper and then be shoved between the slats of a barn to protect it from fire and theft. Pow-Wows also turned away evil with a great many practical actions. If someone was causing you physical discomfort, you would pinch a piece of your clothing between the door. This would rid you of the evil and send it back.

Campaigns waged by both the church and the medical profession heightened in 1928, when a fellow by the name of Rehmeyer was murdered by three men who swore that he had put a hex on them. Whether or not Rehmeyer really practiced Pow-Wow is now a moot point. The event provided plenty of ammunition for those who were against the practice.

The church systematically taught the children of the Pow-Wow that their parents or grandparents were entertaining evil. It was directly responsible for their own downfall, as it was their religion, and to argue against it would have been to discredit their own faith. The medical profession urged young mothers and fathers to partake of "expert" medical care rather than cower before local "superstition," as Pow-Wow came to be known.

There is little reference material to tell us the complete nature of the Pow-Wow. Even the translated material is subject to error, as those involved felt that some of the information was evil and either removed it totally from the texts or reworded it to fit their own religious background. Trying to find a practicing Pow-Wow is not an easy task. When making inquiries, one will usually hear, "Oh! I knew one. She was really GOOD! But... of course, she's dead this long time." Other responses range from snorts to upturned noses!

The concept and practice of Magick never dies. It may hibernate, move into closets or work under a cloaked environment. But... it NEVER dies. Rest assured then, that some Pow-Wow artists remain, though they are few and well protected by their clients.

As the Pennsylvania Dutch would say: "They aren't all... yet!"

The Qabalistic Cross of the Tarot

Chic Cicero and Sandra Tabatha Cicero

The Qabalistic Cross is one of the simplest yet most effective rituals for aligning the body, the mind and the Voice (or Will) to the single purpose of communion with the Divine. In this rite the lower self is consecrated through the vibration of Divine names so that the Higher Self may descend and give guidance and purity. It is also possible to use certain cards of the Tarot in conjunction with the Qabalistic Cross to form a sort of Divine circuitry through which Qabalistic energies can be explored and enhanced. The following rite employs four Tarot Trumps for this purpose.

1. Prepare the temple. From a consecrated pack of Tarot cards containing the traditional Qabalistic symbolism, remove the following: THE HIGH PRIESTESS, TEMPERANCE, THE UNIVERSE, and STRENGTH. Place the four trump cards upon the altar as indicated in the diagram.

2. Take a Ritual Bath.

3. Place the index finger of your right hand just above the crown of your head. Bring your hand down as if drawing the Divine Light into your body. Touch your forehead and intone the word, "ATAH" (Ah-tah). This means "I Am." Visualize a Bright light centered at the crown of your head.

4. Bring your finger down to the middle of your chest and vibrate the name, "MALKUTH" (Mahl-kooth) which means "The Kingdom." After touching your chest, draw the hand down to the level of the groin and point toward the floor. Imagine a shaft of white light extending from the top of your head down to your feet and ankles. Concentrate for a minute on this white pillar of light stretching from Kether to Malkuth.

5. Touch your right shoulder and intone the name, "VE-GEBURAH" (V'-geh-boo-rah) which means "And the Power." See another point of white light beginning at your shoulder.

6. Bring your index finger directly across your body to the left shoulder. Vibrate the name, "VE-GEDULAH" (V'-geh-doo-lah), which means, "And the Glory." See a brilliant white shaft of light perpendicular to the first one which connects both shoulders.

7. Put both hands out in front of you and clasp them together as if praying. Then bring the clasped hands close to your body and position them straight up, just in front of your heart. Intone "LE-OLAHM, AMEN" (lay-oh-lahm, Ah-men), which means "Forever, Unto the Ages." Visualize a complete cross of light formed within yourself, which consecrates the temple of the body through the power of the Divine Names.

Once you have established the Qabalistic Cross you may initiate the Cross of the Tarot. However the image of the Cross of Light must remain firmly fixed in your mind. With your index finger touch the four points on your body a second time, and repeat the names from ATAH through VE-GEDULAH, but add the following visualizations:

8. At the crown of your head, imagine a brilliant spiral shape contained within the point of light at KETHER. This is the symbol of the First Whirlings ⊙ .

9. At the bottom of the first shaft of light, visualize the symbol of the cross within a circle. See this sigil at your feet in black. This represents MALKUTH, the manifested kingdom ⊗ .

10. At your right shoulder, see the red symbol of Mars flaming within the white shaft of Light. This symbol alludes to

GEBURAH, the Sphere of Severity ♂

11. At your left shoulder, picture within the point of light, the blue sigil of Jupiter. This suggests CHESED, the Sephirah of Mercy ♃ .

12. Now return to the complete image of the Cross within your body. Vibrate the name of the Hebrew letter "GIMEL" (Gee-mahl). See the first shaft of it from Kether begin to change to the color blue. The blue light descends from your head to the area of your heart and stops there. Concentrate your thoughts on the image of THE HIGH PRIESTESS from the second Key of the Tarot. The High Priestess controls the flow of Divine Power from its eternal Source in Kether to the rest of the temple (you— as a reflection of the Tree of Life). Through her you experience all spiritual events. She controls and regulates all life, and she connects that which is above to that which is below. Contemplate her image for a few moments.

13. Intone the name of the Hebrew letter "SAMEKH" (Sahm-ehk). The shaft of light turns brilliant blue from your heart down to your groin area. Visualize the figure of TEMPERANCE from the 14th Key of the Tarot. The feminine, angelic form of TEMPERANCE blends the opposing elements of Fire and Water, Sun and Moon, Intellect and Emotion, Force and Form. She harmonizes these contradictory elements of your personality into a mixture of perfect balance, clearing the way for real spiritual growth to take place. Meditate upon this image for a short period of time.

14. Vibrate the name of the Hebrew letter "TAU" (Taw). The shaft of light leading from your groin to your feet turns indigo or violet-blue in color. Imagine the female figure from THE UNIVERSE, the 21st Key of the Tarot. The form of the Dancing Goddess gives final form to the Manifest Universe. She is the womb of Heaven, giving birth to the signs of the Zodiac, the Planets and the Elements. She is the completion of the Grand Design in the Mind of the Eternal. Take time to mediate upon this image.

15. Vibrate the name of the Hebrew letter "TETH" (Tayth). Envision the second shaft of white light which connects

the two shoulders begin to turn bright yellow, starting at Geburah. Imagine the woman from STRENGTH, the eighth Key of the Tarot. She holds the fierce and mighty lion under perfect control through the power of her Will. She has tamed the raw, fiery energy of the beast and transformed it by discipline. The strength generated from passion and intellect working together under will is tremendous. Feel the sense of inner strength given off by this image.

16. Repeat once more the words "LE-OLAHM, AMEN" while making the appropriate gestures. Visualize the complete Cross for the final time in glowing white light.

Thus ends the ritual.

The Yule Tree

Scott Cunningham

The Yule Tree, once a Pagan symbol of rebirth honored at the Winter Solstice, has now been firmly entrenched in the contemporary Christian religious holiday that takes place at about the same time. Even so, the curious custom of bringing a tree indoors, decorating it, and honoring it during the month of December has never lost its Pagan origins, and it never will.

There are many stories of how and why this custom originated. Suffice it to say that the Yule Tree is a survival of earlier times, in which Pagan peoples, suffering through the winter, revered a living pine or fir tree as a symbol of the continuing fertility of the Earth. In other words, the Yule Tree represents the hidden seeds that will soon, with the coming of spring, burst forth into profuse growth, destroying the specter of winter and ushering in yet another cycle of fertility.

In magic, pine (and fir) is used for its purifying energies. Bringing a pine tree into the house during the shuttered month of December is an excellent method of magically freshening your home.

While many Christian customs have been layered onto this tradition, the true essence of Yule Tree rites is far older, far more earthy and magical. Here are some of these rites.

The Tree Itself

If you choose a cut tree, realize that the tree has given its life for your celebration. If you've chosen a living tree, know that it shouldn't be kept indoors for more than two weeks (in warm weather areas) and should be placed near a window to receive a bit of sunlight.

The Dedication

After you've brought it into your home and set it into place, hold your hands palms outward toward the tree and commune. Feel its life-energies still pulsing within it. (If it's a cut tree, thank the tree for its sacrifice.)

Now say these or words of similar intent:

> O strong and noble, fragrant pine,
> That once shivered beneath the skies:
> Glimmer and shine now in my (our) home;
> Remind me (us) of the fertile loam
> That, far beneath the snow, still lies.

The Adorning

Yule tree decorations are available in wide variety each year. Originally, apples, pears, walnuts, and other fruits and nuts were hung from the boughs, in further honor of the occasion: the rebirth of the Sun God at the Winter Solstice.

The shiny glass globes are modern representations of these earlier vegetative ornaments, and they can be used; so can real fruit. Apples can be hung from their stems, and small tangerines and oranges can be propped among the boughs. Blownglass ornaments in the shapes of bunches of grapes, snow-frosted pine cones and other natural shapes are usually available, and are a fine substitute for the real fruit. Garlands of cranberries and popcorn can also, of course, be made and used.

Avoid the use of plastic ornaments on the tree.

Lights are the modern (and safer) equivalent of the candles that once perched on sturdy boughs. They represent the Sun's glow, and can certainly be used if desired.

Decorate the tree as best as you see fit. When it's finished, stand back and admire it for its symbolism and for its real energies.

The Yule Tree's Passing

By tradition, all Yule decorations are removed by February 1st. Usually, however, the tree is taken down long before this date. Even so, by the time the Winter Solstice has passed, a cut Yule Tree is usually dry, even if you've placed it in water. (See below for information regarding living trees.) The tree's life force is ebbing even as the Sun grows in strength and glory. Remove the decorations. Return the tree to its original, unadorned appearance.

Now take a small bowl. Gently collect some of the dried needles from the tree, placing them into the bowl. When you've gathered a few handfuls, hold the bowl before the tree in both hands. Say these or similar words:

> *I thank you for your presence.*
> *Continue to shine in my life.*

Hold the bowl up to the top of the tree, wait a second, then move the bowl, clockwise, around the tree's perimeter: from the top, down the right-hand side, to the trunk, up the left side, and back to the top once again.

As you move the bowl, feel the tree's fleeting energies streaming from every branch into the bowl. Transfer its powers into the needles that you've collected.

Place the gathered needles into an airtight jar. Once this has been done, take the tree to a recycling center (if one is available); use it for firewood (so that it can, once more, symbolize the Sun's energy); or mulch it (so that it can directly replenish the Earth's fertility).

Treasure the collected needles. During the winter, whenever the weather turns foul, or whenever you feel the need for refreshment, remove the top of the jar and inhale the needles' sweet, piney fragrance. Accept the energies of your Yule Tree until the waxing Sun melts the Earth's ice prison, spurring the rebirth of emerald fertility.

(If you've used a living tree, remove its decorations to return it to its original appearance. Keep inside, move to a porch, or place it ouside. Give it proper care and you should be able to use it again the following Yule.)

Plow Monday

Raymond Buckland

Traditionally, the first Monday after the Christmas season—that is after January 6th, the "twelfth day of Christmas"—is the day for everyone to return to work. It is the day to plow the fields so that the January frosts can break up the soil ready for the planting. However, in England it used to be "any excuse for a festival!" Plow Monday became a day to celebrate the going back to work and thereby not actually working!

The men of the village, dressed in gaily bedecked costumes, would haul a decorated plow about the village. The decorations on the men included horse-brasses, bells and ribbons and they were referred to as "Plow Witches" or "Plow Jacks." In many aspects of English country tradition there is a figure of a woman played by a man, and usually called the "Betsy" or "Bessy." She/he appears with Morris dancers and also appears with the plow. Indeed, the local Morris dancers often accompanied the plow on its rounds. The main reason for having the Betsy, however, was so that she/he could carry a collection box and obtain gifts (money, ale, food) from the villagers as the procession went by. If anyone refused to contribute, they might well find their front path plowed up!

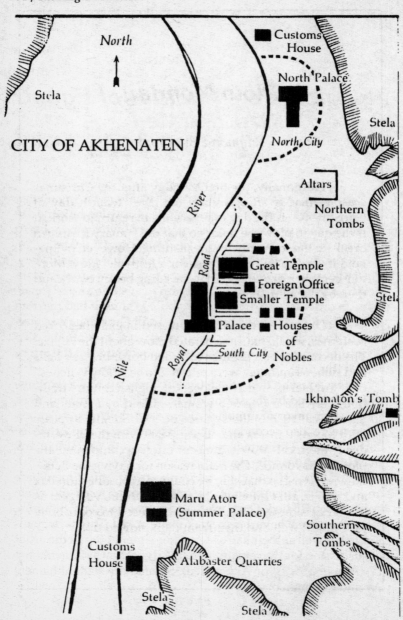

North

Stela

CITY OF AKHENATEN

River

Road

Royal

Nile

Royal

South City

Customs
House

Customs
House

North Palace

North City

Altars

Northern
Tombs

Great Temple

Foreign Office

Smaller Temple

Palace

Houses
of
Nobles

Stela

Stela

Stela

Ikhnaton's Tomb

Maru Aton
(Summer Palace)

Alabaster Quarries

Southern
Tombs

Stela

Stela

Magical Personalities of Egypt: Akhenaten

Gordon T. A. Hudson

In approximately 1392 B.C. a child was born to Amenhotep III and Queen Tiy, a son whose life was destined to be quite different from the lives of all preceding and following pharaohs. At the time of his birth, his father had reigned for 25 years.

The child's skull was malformed and he was a sickly boy. His father must have wondered if the boy would grow to manhood, and this may have decided him to arrange an early marriage in order to secure the succession. He himself had married Queen Tiy when he was about 12 years old. The prince was married to Tadukhipa, a princess of Mitanni, but it seems she died soon after her arrival in Egypt. It isn't known how old the prince was at this time.

The household in which the boy grew up was a feminine one, dominated by the strong queen (who, it is rumored, even then was in favor of opposing the powerful priests of Amon). There were also secondary queens, concubines and other assorted ladies. This atmosphere didn't help to encourage any masculine traits in the young prince.

Amenhotep III's other children were Nefertiti, Smenkhare and probably Tutankhamen, who was about 3 years old when Amenhotep III died. There was also another daughter, Sitamun, who may even have been Smenkhare's and Tutankhamen's mother as well as their half sister. After Amenhotep III the order of succession for the remainder of the dynasty was Amenhotep IV (Amenophis IV or Akhenaten), Smenkhare, Tutankhamen, Ay and Horemheb.

At age 11 Amenophis became Amenhotep IV and for a few years his mother, Queen Tiy, acted as regent. Shortly after occupying the Lotus Throne he married his sister Nefertiti. Six daughters were born of that marriage. We don't know much about the three youngest except that they appear every now and then in the family paintings, but of the others, the oldest, Meritaten, married her young half uncle Smenkhare; the next, Maketaten, died young; and Ankhsenpaaten married her even younger half uncle Tutankhamen.

It may be conjectured that in the early part of his reign Amenhotep worshipped both Amen and Aten, the former in his role of monarch and the latter from personal preference in his private sanctuary. When he was alive his father had established a small Aton chapel, and the prince spent much time worshipping there—a portent of things to come.

He was about 14 or 15 years of age at the time he began to change his religious views, and it is felt he was encouraged in this by the dowager queen Tiy. Realizing that the pantheon of gods was ineffective and that the priests were sometimes more powerful than Pharaoh, Amenophis IV tried to establish a new religion—monotheism. However, the flaw in this was his declaration that he was the living embodiment of Aten the Sun disc, thereby defeating his own object. Cautiously, even hesitantly at first, the new pharaoh wielded his power to overthrow Amon, symbolic god-ruler of Egypt's pantheon, and in Amon's place he elevated the Aten to the rank of primary deity.

From his original subordinate position as the abode of Ra, the material disc wherein the Sun god had his dwelling (Ra in his Aten), Aten came in time to signify both the god and the actual solar disc.

Early in his reign Amenophis built the great temple complex at Karnak. By the sixth year of his reign, he took a second dramatic step by changing his name to Akhenaten and, together with his family and friends, sailed northward from angry Thebes to inhabit a newly built city where the new religion might flourish unchecked. Akhenaten had declared that this city must be built on virgin soil, standing on ground never before dedicated to another god. A few years earlier (soon after his succession), he had discovered what he wanted 200 miles north of Thebes, which is where Luxor stands today. Tel el Amarna was the site which Akhenaten decided would be suitable for the proper worship of Aten the Sun disc and here, sheltered in the embrace of the cliffs and close to the life-giving river, the city of Akhetaten arose; fresh, glittering, dedicated, with quays and harbors, temples and palaces, gardens and groves.

In the late 19th century some clay tablets were discovered which, when they were finally brought to the museums in Berlin and London, were recognized as genuine documents written in cuneiform in the 18th dynasty. These letters led to the excavations at Tel el Amarna and the discovery of the ancient capital of Akhetaten. The tablets were the files of the Foreign Office of the time and thanks to their discovery we now know a great deal more about that period of history. They also tell of the religious revolution which shook Egypt for many years. Through the letters archaeologists were able to find the lost city, the bust of Nefertiti, tombs, stele, etc.

The Akhenaten Temple Project Team has located and photographed 35,000 decorated blocks, all part of Akhenaten's temple, which is estimated to have approached a mile in length. The new temples to the Aten, the Sun god, were open to the sunlight.

Akhenaten drove his own chariot through the wide new avenues and let himself be seen in affectionate scenes with his wife and children. He also insisted that statues and paintings of himself show him as he really was—by all accounts a man with peculiar physical characteristics: hatchet chin, slender neck, bulbous belly and thighs and spindly lower legs. A statue shows him to have an unusually large abdomen and hips, slanting eyes, a very long jaw and protruding lips. It is almost certain that he was an epileptic. Even Nefertiti was caught up in this new game of show and tell and was caricatured. In spite of his unprepossessing appearance, he was very strong intellectually and physically courageous.

As a matter of record, the relaxed "Amarna" spirit had been evolving in Egypt for several generations. For a while, Akhenaten was exhilarated in his new capital, enjoying his family and busying himself with affairs of the Empire. Intensifying his fight against Amen-Ra, he had the god's name hacked off all Egyptian monuments; but powerful forces were against him. In his conflict with the priesthood, there is strong circumstantial evidence that Queen Tiy, his mother, was sympathetic to the priests, although it was she who had started him on the path of Atonism.

Tiy was a commoner. Her father was Yuya, a priest, and her mother Tuya was a royal servant. They acted as advisors to Amenhotep III and had the respect of the court. Yuya's mummy is the best preserved of any discovered. Tiy was the recipient of many honors as temples, monuments and statues were erected in her name. Her husband wasn't interested in religion or politics, and slowly the queen took up the running of the government.

Amenhotep III was only 36 when he died, and even then there was a threat to the throne by the Hittites. They had invaded Mitanni and were advancing into Syria. What Egypt needed was another Tutmose III, but what she got was a mystic who believed in peace and gentleness, a sensitive man who didn't wish for conquest or bloodshed.

At the time Tiy decided to pay her son a state visit, there was discontent in Egypt. The bulk of the population felt a deep attachment to Amon-Ra, and the army was growing restive. Where there is no vision the people perish; Pharaoh had removed one of the main struts of the Egyptians' security. Many court members maintained homes in both Amarna and Thebes and were loth to commit themselves wholly to either Atonism or Amonism. There were nobles who were completely loyal to the king and his new religion, but many more preferred to straddle the fence and hedge their bets.

Soon after Tiy' s arrival Nefertiti was apparently banished to a separate part of the city and stripped of her royal titles.

Akhenaten took one of his daughters as his chief wife and made no further moves against Amon-Ra. He died five years later.

It is strongly suspected that Akhenaten and Nefertiti were both mystics in the modern sense of the word, and therefore military supremacy was subordinated to intellectual and spiritual endowments and accomplishments. But although Nefertiti remained a fanatic on the subject till her dying day, it looks very much as if Akhenaten, not long before he died, saw that things were getting so bad on the frontiers that if he was to survive as pharaoh at all he must give way a little and patch it up somehow with the priests at Thebes. So, having co-opted Smenkhare onto the throne, he sent him and Meritaten back to Thebes to hold out something like an olive branch. When Smenkhare went to Thebes, his departure *appeared* to cause a rift between Akhenaten and Nefertiti, and she retired from court life.

Nefertiti had always believed in and encouraged the new religion, and her marriage had apparently been a very happy one.

It has been put forward that it was she who suggested her removal from the king' s palace, taking Tutankhamen with her, partly to safeguard the boy when it appeared that Atonism would be overthrown, and she was trying to protect him. Smenkhare was co-regent and Tutankhamen was the heir apparent.

After Akhenaten's death nearly all inscribed objects had on them the name of Nefertiti and a fair proportion the names of Tutankhame and his wife Ankhsenpaaten, but hardly one with Akhenaten's name. However, before he died, Akhenaten had Nefertiti's name chipped away wherever it occurred and Meritaten's substituted, but somehow Nefertiti managed to take Tutankhamen into exile with her and, of course, all the supporters she could muster.

None of the defacements of Akhenaten's name could possibly have been done when he was alive. In exile, though, Nefertiti's name appears without that of Pharaoh, which indicates a rift in their marriage and their kingdom. It is a gray area which has troubled historians for years. She tried to keep her young pharaoh-brother true to the Aten cult. Smenkhare, still at Thebes, had died somewhere about this time, almost certainly of foul play. When Tutankhamen succeeded Smenkhare as phar- aoh through his marriage to a daughter of Akhenaten, he was only about ten years old and Nefertiti still had a firm hold on things. But it was nearly the end for, not long after, Nefertiti her- self perished.

It was the end, not only of the leading figures in the whole affair, but of Atenism itself—the priests had won! Within 15 years of his coronation, Akhenaten witnessed the virtual col- lapse of his empire. After his death the Egyptian court reverted back to its traditional polytheism, the royal headquarters moved back to Thebes and the Aten temple at Karnak was can- nibalized for new monuments.

Smenkhare reigned very briefly after Akhenaten, then (following the reigns of Tutankhamen and Ay) general Horem- heb, a commoner, became king. He sought by every means pos- sible to erase memories of the Aten and its royal sponsor. The wholesale violence against the late pharaoh and his heresy did- n't break out until several years later, not until Tutankhamen's death at Thebes when he was 18 years old. Only then did the tur- moil erupt, paralleling Tutmose III's anger against the memory of his stepmother. The priests couldn't very well do anything to dishonor those so close to the reigning pharaoh, but it wasn't long after Tutankhamen's death that they began wiping out every vestige or Atenism and of its author, Akhenaten. Then, everything went: his names and portraits, Nefertiti's as well, and the painted and carved symbols of Aten worship. No one knew where Nefertiti's remains were laid, or indeed if any honor was paid her in death. Everything then settled back safely into the old ways.

The severity of the shock felt at the changes wrought by Akhenaten in the state religion can scarcely be understood to- day, when there are so many different sects in this country, but Egypt had only one religion and the ruler was a god.

As an aside, Amenhotep III owned a barge which bore the name "Aton Gleams." Little could he have realized the irony of such a name and what it would mean to his family and country in later years.

Days of the Week

According to Hydn's Dictionary of Dates (1866), the names of the days of the week are derived from the Saxon names for the gods, which correspond to Roman deities:

DAY	SAXON	LATIN
Sunday	Sun's Day	*Dies Solis* (Day of the Sun)
Monday	Moon's Day	*Dies Lunae* (Day of the Moon)
Tuesday	Tiw's Day	*Dies Martis* (Day of Mars)
Wednesday	Woden's Day	*Dies Mercurii* (Day of Mercury)
Thursday	Thor's Day	*Dies Jovis* (Day of Jupiter)
Friday	Friga's Day	*Dies Veneris* (Day of Venus)
Saturday	Saterne's Day	*Dies Saturni* (Day of Saturn)

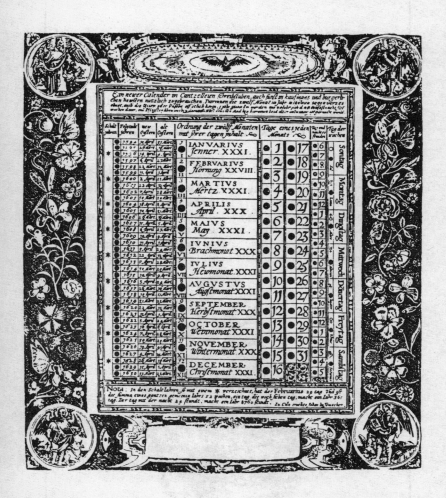

Divining with
the Coconut Shells

Migene González-Wippler

Maria kept her Warriors in a small cabinet in her room. Whenever she wanted to question any of these saints, she opened the door of the cabinet so they could hear her and proceeded with the divination ceremony. During one of these sessions she asked me to write down the ritual in detail. "So that you don't forget it later," she said with a smile. "But after a while, you learn it so well you never forget again."

When I was ready with pencil and paper she took a coconut from a shelf, broke the hard shell with a small hammer, and used the blade of a kitchen knife to dislodge the brown rind from the shell. Gathering the coconut's milk in a glass, she set it aside and cut five pieces of the rind into uneven squares about three by four inches in diameter.

"Coconut milk is good for many things," Maria told me. "Don't throw it away. You can use it for kidney trouble; to make hair grow strong. But best of all, you can use it to get rid of *fibu* (danger) and everything *burucu* (evil). It brings good luck, *orobo*. Bathe your forehead with it and it clears your mind. Then throw the rest on your doorstep and you'll be healthy and happy, *arani*."

She filled a small gourd with water and placed it in front of the cabinet where Eleggua and the Warriors were kept.

"Water is important," she explained, "because Obi—the coconut—must be refreshed all the time. Otherwise he gets heated and his answers are no good."

She opened the door to the cabinet and pulled out the clay vessel where the cement head representing Eleggua was reposing. The head had small cowrie shells for its eyes and mouth, and from the top of its skull protruded a tiny blade. Coins, stones, candies, a cigar and other attributes of Eleggua surrounded the orisha's head. Alongside Eleggua stood a small cauldron with all the metal implements of Oggun and Ochosi, who are known as "the Warriors."

Maria sprinkled water three times in front of Eleggua and started an invocation in Yoruba:

Omi tutu a Eleggua, omi tutu a mi ile, Oloddumare, modupues. Boquo iworo iyalocha babalocha babalawo oluo iku embelese ybae baye tonu . . . Boquo iworo ashe semilenu, cosi iku, cosi ano, cosi allo, cosi ofo, ariku Babagwa . . . .

I translated this prayer many years later—with much difficulty due to the increasingly corrupted spelling and pronunciation of the Yoruba language in the New World.

"I give you some water to refresh Eleggua, I give you some water to refresh my home and I thank you, O Great Lord of the Universe. I salute all the faithful santeras, santeros, bablawos, and great seers who have died and are at the feet of eternity. May they all rest in peace . . . I greet all the santeros and ask their blessing, so that I will be safe from death, from illness, from tragedy, from shame.

"Greetings, Holy Father."

This invocation, known as *moyubar* in Santeria, is sometimes much longer. Some santeros believe it is better to name individually all the dead elders to ensure their blessing. The blessings of the santero's madrina or padrina (godmother or godfather), who are his sponsors in the religion, are also requested *in absenita*.

After she finished the invocation, Maria picked four of the five pieces of coconut and washed them with water. The fifth piece is kept in reserve in case one of the other pieces breaks. Then she proceeded to tear with her nails three bits of coconut from each rind and sprinkle them over Eleggua's head.

"Remember, florecita," she told me, "You must always tear three pieces of each coconut and sprinkle them over Eleggua when you are consulting him. That is his sacred number. If you were speaking with one of the other orishas, you would tear as many bits of coconut as the number of the orisha. Six for Chango, five for Oshun, seven for Yemaya, and so on."

Holding the rinds in her left hand, she touched the floor and Eleggua's image three times with her right hand. "*Ilé mokué, Eleggua mokué*," she prayed three times, asking Eleggua to bless the home. "Now you say *Acuellé*, florecita," she added, "to get Eleggua's blessing."

"*Acuellé*," I said obediently, without the slightest idea of what I was saying.

"*Unlle Obi a Eleggua*," said Maria, and turned to me once more. "Say *Asoñá*, florecita. It means amen."

"*Asoñá*," I repeated, scribbling down all the strange words as fast as I could.

During this session of giving coconut to Eleggua, Maria wanted to ask him if I could receive the necklaces—*elekes*—of Santeria. I was not to attend high school for another two years, but to Maria's mind the "big school" was a sinister place full of dangers. Therefore she wanted me to have the necklaces—with the orishas' protection—as soon as possible.

She held the rinds against her chest and began to question the orisha.

"Eleggua, my father, please tell me if this little *obini* should receive the *elekes* for her protection."

As she finished speaking, Maria threw the coconut rinds on the floor in front of Eleggua's image. The white sides of all four rinds came up, in the pattern known as Alafia.

"*Alafia! Alafia omo, Alafia awo, Alafia osi Ariku Babagwa!*" cried Maria joyfully. "Kiss the floor, florecita. That means Alafia. Eleggua gives you his blessing!"

I kissed the floor in front of Eleggua.

"Does that mean I can have the necklaces?" I asked hopefully.

"Alafia is not a sure answer," said Maria. "It means the orisha gives you his blessing, but that's all. I must ask the same question again."

She repeated the question and again threw the coconut.

This time, three of the dark sides of the coconut came up and only one white, in the pattern known as Ocana Sode.

Maria's face was a study in consternation.

"Ocana Sode," she said, with dismay, "means no. And sometimes it means something bad is coming."

She refreshed the coconut rinds with water. "Eleggua, my father, please tell me, is there something wrong—some danger for the little obini?"

She threw the rinds down and watched anxiously as they rolled on the floor and finally settled in a pattern—Alafia again, but this time one of the rinds fell on top of another.

Maria's face relaxed. "Alafia with *Irè*!" she exclaimed with a sigh of relief. "It's all right. There's no danger. Eleggua just doesn't think you should have the *elekes*—at least not now."

As she spoke, she poured some water on top of the two rinds that had fallen together and offered them to me.

"Drink," she smiled. "That way you'll receive the *Irè*—the good luck—of Eleggua. And if you want, you can make a wish and he'll grant it."

I drank the water and looked at her dubiously.

"What I want are the necklaces, Maria. When can I have them?"

"I don't know, florecita. Maybe later on, when you grow up. There's no danger for you. Eleggua said so, and he knows. But let me ask him again to be sure."

She picked the rinds again, refreshed them, and faced the orisha once more. "Eleggua, my father," she asked respectfully. "Can the little *obini* receive the *elekes* when she grows up?"

This time the resulting pattern was made of two dark and two white sides.

Maria smiled. "That's Ellife, florecita, the strongest of the answers, and it means yes. Be patient, and someday you'll have your *elekes*."

The fourth pattern, Itagua, where three white sides and one dark side come up, is a dubious answer and means something is not clear. The orisha must be questioned again. When I remember that day I wonder what Maria's reaction would have been if the dreaded pattern, Oyekun, with four dark sides, had fallen during her consultation. For Oyekun means no, but also predicts death and destruction, and all sorts of protective measures have to be undertaken to dispel its evil influence.

The Shamanic Tools of the Gaia Tradition

Kisma K. Stepanich

The Gaia Tradition is based on the shamanic principle of continual self-analysis (looking at your life in connection with cycles around you) and, through the enlightenment attained through each season, to transform your spirit each year to a higher level of attunement with Mother Earth.

This principle is best put into practice in conjunction with the understanding of the Wheel of the Year. Each year we travel round an imaginary wheel consisting of eight energy shifts and four distinct seasons. The wheel begins and ends repeatedly throughout the years of our lives. It is a wheel based upon nature—the basic nature of Gaia and the heavens, not of humankind.

The eight energy shifts occur on the following dates annually.

- March 21-23   Vernal/Spring Equinox
  April 31-May 1   Beltaine
- June 21   Summer Solstice/Midsummer
  August 1   Lamas/First Harvest
- September 21-23 Autumnal Equinox
  October 31   Samhain/Hallows Eve
  December 21-23   Winter Solstice/Yule
  February 2   Imbolg/Candlemas

Connection with the energy shifts is elevating to our spirit vibration, for it allows the opportunity to become one with the

---

* Four Seasons

elements of nature and therefore gain a better understanding, in a basic sense, of the cycles of nature. We become grounded in Mother Earth and our "center" opens to channel the seasonal energy.

The season of Spring contains the following energy shifts:

Vernal Equinox (March 21-23)—One of the four seasonal shifts based first on the astronomical level of the Sun's ecliptic in relationship to the celestial equator of the Earth. There is complete balance on this day as both night and day are equal in length: 12 hours each. The energy surges forth, flowing with inspiration and creativity. The intellect is sparked; ideas are formulated. The Mental Body is most sensitive to and stimulated by this energy.

The Shamanic tools to be used during the season of Spring are seed-planting ceremonies, study of attitude, Tiger's Eye (self expression/identity) and mirror magick.

The Summer season contains two energy shifts, which are:

Beltain (April 31-May 1)—Theme of fertility. The Sun is entering the constellation of Taurus, which is the primary sign in the zodiacal celestial sphere that represents the Goddess, or Mother of Creation. The energy shift is transformed into a receptive mode. Creativity is nurtured and the foundations from the ideas inspired in the Mental Body during the Vernal Equinox are being laid down. This is the energy by which the Emotional Body is most stimulated and nurtured.

Summer Solstice (June 21-23)—The Sun has traveled its ecliptic to the maximum position north of the celestial equator, and the Northern Hemisphere of the earth is receiving the fullest force of the Sun's light and energy. The daylight is at its longest duration and dominates the night at this midsummer time. The receptivity of the Emotional Body has nurtured the energy of Beltain and shifted into swift action, sparking the Physical Body into full force. Spirit is given the flame of life and allowed to passionately take control. The Physical Body is most stimulated and activated at this time.

Shamanic tools to use at this time are healing ceremonies, fertility rituals, pyromancy/candle burning and affirmations/

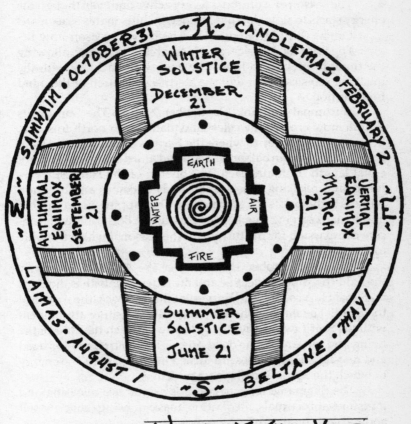

WHEEL OF THE YEAR

chanting.

The season of Autumn is a very active one even though the energy starts to slow down. The energy shifts in this season are:

Lamas (July 31-August 1)—The harvest season now begins. Together the Physical and Mental Bodies merge, allowing the thought process to flow. The energy is crackling with the bustle of physical labor and the alertness required of the mind for direction.

Autumnal Equinox (September 21-23)—The Sun on its ecliptic now crosses the celestial equator from north to south, beginning its journey to where the Earth will incline away from the Sun. Once again balance is achieved and day and night are of equal length: 12 hours each. The energy of the Harvest transforms into rejoicing. The Mental Body becomes an observant witness to the land's transformation. The happiness and sharing of the thanksgiving touches the Emotional Body, allowing sincere compassion for the turning of the seasonal wheel from life towards death.

Samhain (October 31-November 1)—As the wheel turns, the light continues to decline and life fades. Samhain is the third and final Harvest. It is the Harvest of the livestock, the season of the dead. The energy shifts into an ultrasensitive attunement with the Spirit world, and the gateway between the land of the living and the land of the dead opens. The Spirit Body is seized and fine-tuned. All senses are turned inward. This is the energy to which the Spirit Body is most sensitive.

The Shamanic tools to use this season are releasing and transformation rituals, meditation, mask-dancing/shadow-self and harvest/thanksgiving ceremonies.

Winter is the most intense energy. The shifts in this season are:

Winter Solstice (December 21-23)—The Sun has now reached its farthest distance south of the celestial equator, and the Northern Hemisphere is inclined away from the Sun. Daylight has waned and the night is longer at this midwinter time. The morning will bring the birth of the "new Sun" as once again its journey into fullness begins. The energy is laboring with the excitement of rebirthing the light of the Sun and moving through the final days of Winter. This energy agitates the Mental Body with the anticipation of rebirth in all aspects of life.

Imbolg/Candlemas (February 1-2)—The season of death and silence has ended. The "new Sun" that was birthed at the Winter Solstice has grown like a boy into manhood and reflects its light proudly on the Gaia. Now is the point of repose when the energy begins to mount as the season of Spring draws near. For the first time all Bodies (Mental, Emotional, Physical and Spiritual) merge together, filling with light while turning to nature expectantly for rebirth.

Shamanic tools that are most effective for Winter are visualizations, bone/death rituals, dreaming and trance work.

As we work with the right shamanic tools in their proper season, we receive the full effect of their magick, the magick of Mother Earth, and the magick we contain within. That is the *oneness* of life.

An Isian Winter
Solstice Decoration

deTraci Regula

Isis, in her role as a supreme mother goddess, brought forth a Sun-child, Horus, at the time of the Winter Solstice. His birth was synchronous with the return of lengthening days, the end of the decline of the hours of light. What better symbol of hope and the eventual arrival of Spring than the birth of a child? Many other faiths placed the birth of a new infant-god at this time of year, including Christianity, Mithraism and many others in the ancient world.

Throughout history there has been much sharing between religions which celebrate similar holidays at similar times. For this reason we now find "Hannukah Trees" in some Jewish households, derived from the tradition of "Christmas Trees," which were in turn derived from the tree-decorating rites of many varieties of pagan faiths. In the faith of Isis and Osiris, followers were forbidden to cut down a living tree, and the ceremony of the "Raising Up of the Djed Pillar" may have originally been tied to tree worship and the decorating of the sacred object. For those who might enjoy adding a symbol with Isian associations to the Solstice-time observances, here are instructions for creating an Isian Solstice Frond using a fan palm branch, gold paint, and Egyptian-inspired ornaments.

The ancient worship of Isis included many public processions in which sacred objects were carried to be displayed to the masses which lined the pathway of the procession through the city, much like modern parades or Mardi Gras celebrations. Gilded palms and winnowing fans were sometimes carried to symbolize rich harvests or, possibly, the life-giving Breath of Isis. Palm trees were sacred to Isis and Osiris and frequently grew in the temple gardens, providing shade and fruit. The multirayed form of the fan palm is also symbolic of the rays of the sun, appropriate here at the time of the return of the sun.

First, find a fan palm frond or, if this is not available, a large decorative winnowing fan woven of fiber. These are frequently available in basket or international shops and are usually flat and shaped like a leaf. If you do use a fan palm frond, try to use one which has fallen naturally or has dried on the tree. By all means avoid harming the tree from which it was taken. If you must cut a living frond, repay the tree with a gift of fertilizer and water.

Once you have selected the frond, use scissors to trim off any flimsy portions. Be careful doing this, as some fan palm fronds have unexpectedly sharp serrations along the edges. Trim it down far enough so that when it is held upright, the frond tips do not flop down.

Cut the stem down to about an 18" section. In the case of very woody palm stems, you may need to use a small saw. (Note: Depending on the size of your palm frond, these measurements may differ. Also, if you are using a ready-made winnowing fan, you should be able to simply gild it and hang it on the wall with a nail.) Depending on the overall flatness of the fan palm there are two methods for preparing the frond to be displayed. If you have a straight, flat frond, simply drill a hole in the middle of the fan portion about eight inches in from where the individual "fingers" separate. Paint the frond using gold paint, or, if you prefer, silver. Then attach it to a wall using a nail through the hole. Another method for displaying your frond is to take a wide-mouthed vase filled with sand or glass pebbles and insert the palm frond stem into it. The Solstice Palm can then be set against a wall if the frond is too heavy to stand alone using this method.

Once you have gilded the palm, you can paint additional designs on it using different colors of paint or you can create separate ornaments to hang on it. Usually ordinary Christmas ornament hangers can pierce the frond to attach ornaments. Small glass baubles are pretty, or you can create ornaments incorporating Egyptian symbols. Several suitable signs would be the Isis knot ⚕ , the Ankh ☥ , and the Shen ◯ , symbol of eternity. These can be painted onto store-bought ornaments or can be made of almost any material. Metallic chenille strips can be bent into almost any shape. Other symbols could be the crescent and disk headdress of Isis, the cornucopia which she often carried in classical times, and lotuses. Garlands of small glass beads can also be added, and beads strung on wire can also be formed into the symbols mentioned above.

As you make your Solstice palm, remember that in the temples of ancient Egypt the higher clergy were almost invariably accomplished, skilled artisans. Whether their talents were directed toward the creation of sacred statuary, the building of temples and shrines, or the compounding of the oils and incenses used by the temples, work of the hands was regarded as a sacred act of worship, emulating the primal creative forces exerted by the gods and goddesses themselves. Any act of creation is an act of worship, even more so when the effort is directed at creating an object to be used in the festivals of the god or goddess to whom you're devoted. This was true in ancient Egypt and is still true in the Christian communities which produce wine, embroidery, or other products for their use and for the support of their community.

The sacred frond which you have created here does not need to be restricted to the festival of the Winter Solstice. It would also be appropriate for display at the time of the *Navigium Isidis* on March 5th, when the launching of the Ship of Isis opened the season of navigation in Greco-Roman times. Due to the palm's rayed star shape, a silver one would be appropriate to display at the time of the rising of the star Sothis (known also as Sirius), which has long been sacred to Isis as the "Home of the Soul of Isis." This rising time, when the star is again visible in the night sky after long absence, will vary by latitude, but it occurs in Egypt about August 1st (in modern times). A call to a local observatory can tell you when Sothis is visible in your area.

Whenever or however you display this symbol of Isian faith, remember that the faith of Isis was renowned for its religious tolerance and support of divergent viewpoints. This frond can, from the Isian viewpoint, share space with the symbols of any other faith and need not supplant any. May all the gods and goddesses bless your Solstice celebration!

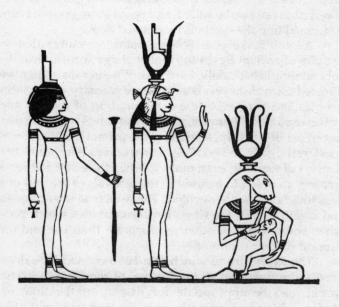

Creating Sacred Space with the Four Elements

Susan Levitt

Prior to doing ritual, meditation, or any spiritual work (such as tarot reading, rune reading, casting the I-Ching, or trance journey), spiritually purify and cleanse the place where the work will occur. This is done by utilizing the four elements: Earth, Air, Fire, and Water.

The four elements are a way to divide the cosmos, and by combining the elements to create sacred space we can transform reality. These four elements correspond to the four directions and colors: Earth is north (white), Air is east (yellow), Fire is south (red), and Water is black (west). These four colors also represent the four races of humanity. The four elements are found in many spiritual systems such as the Native American medicine wheel, the four directions of pagan ritual, the four elements of the alchemical schools of Medieval Europe, the four elements of astrology, and the four suits of tarot. The magic of alchemy is to change our base selves into gold, radiant and rare.

The feminine elements are Earth and Water, Mother Earth and Mother Ocean, the amniotic fluid from which all life emerges. The masculine elements are Fire and Air. In alchemical script, the symbol for Fire is △ and the symbol for Water is ▽ . Combined, they create the balance of the six-pointed star ✡ . The symbol for Air is △ and the symbol for Earth is ▽ , although Earth is also drawn as a circle divided into four sections ⊕ , and as a pentacle ✪ , a pentagram enclosed in a circle.

The stable, feminine element Earth represents the material

world, money, health, tangible goods and the concrete reality of the Earth Mother whom we walk upon daily. Because we are in a physical body, Earth-plane reality confronts us daily. The minotaur of ancient Crete, the golden calf, Persephone in the underworld, and the goose that laid the golden eggs are Earth myths and stories. In astrology, the Earth signs are Virgo, Capricorn, and Taurus.

The quick, masculine element Air represents the mind, mental activity, intellect, thoughts, and ideas. The Tower of Babel, the winged messenger God Hermes, and the smoke of the peace pipe are just a few of the Air myths and symbols. In astrology, the Air signs are Gemini, Libra, and Aquarius.

The nurturing, feminine element Water represents emotions, intuition, spiritual belief, faith, and love. According to the ancient Chinese, Water is the most powerful element, for it can flow around any obstacle in its path without changing essence. The quest for the fountain of youth, the mermaid, and the waters of the Holy Grail are examples of Water myths and legends. In astrology, the Water signs are Pisces, Cancer, and Scorpio.

The exciting, masculine element Fire represents will, drive, destiny, creativity, and spirit in action. Prometheus bound, Satan and his flames, the Phoenix that rises from its own ashes, and Apollo in his sun chariot are a few of the many Fire myths. The Fire signs are Sagittarius, Aries, and Leo.

Rite of Earth
Blessed Art Thou, Creatures of Earth

To create sacred space, begin with the element Earth. Physically clean and purify the Earth by sweeping or vacuuming the room where you will do spiritual work. Clean untidy messes, pick up clothes from the floor, and wash the dishes in the sink. Cleanliness is next to Goddessliness. Do not be intoxicated with drugs, alcohol, cigarettes, or caffeinated beverages. Intoxicants of any kind can cast confusion. To relax your body, you may wish to have a healing massage, a chiropractic alignment, or an acupuncture treatment the day before the spiritual work. Your physical body is your temple, so exercise, sleep, and a diet of wholesome foods are important to maintain the emotional balance and mental equilibrium so important to spiritual work.

Rite of Air
Blessed Art Thou, Creatures of Air

For the element Air, crack open a window or door and burn a purifying incense. These include frankincense and myrrh, sage, rosemary, copal, cedar, and sweetgrass. The classic incenses of frankincense and myrrh are burned on a piece of hot charcoal. Frankincense represents the Sun and myrrh represents the Moon. The two combined create a sweet smelling fragrance. Myrrh added to any incense increases its powers

If you do not have access to those resins, burn the kitchen herbs of rosemary or sage. Fragrant rosemary was used during the Middle Ages in Europe to ward off the plague and mask the stench of the dead. The kitchen herb sage is used by Native Americans as a strong purifier. Sage can be burned alone or in combination with cedar and sweetgrass.

To burn herbs, place them in an ashtray or other safe container, light them, and fan the smoldering herbs. They will burn easily if fanned. You may wish to experiment with other herbs, such as cinnamon, bay laurel leaves, and lavender. (Do not try to use charcoal in an ashtray!)

As the herbs or incenses smoke, walk through the room and fill the corners with the scented smoke, paying special attention to corners and behind doors. If there is dirt, get out the broom and sweep again. Incense is aromatherapy for spirit.

Rite of Fire
Blessed Art Thou, Creatures of Fire

For the element Fire, light a white candle for peace and serenity. After your spiritual work, either allow the candle to burn all the way down and extinguish itself or extinguish the flame yourself with wetted fingers or a candle snuffer. The benefit of a candle that burns itself out is the continuation of energy of the spiritual work as the candle burns. The benefit of the candle which is snuffed out is that it may then be used again for the next tarot card reading. Do not blow out a candle.

White candles are recommended for all magical work, for white represents purity and goodness. Colors other than white may be used consciously. A blue candle is for peace (as is white) and spiritual healing. A red candle is for strength, life, and vitality. A yellow candle is for mental clarity.

The color green is a combination of blue and yellow. Green candles are for physical healing, plant life, and prosperity. The color purple is a combination of blue and red. Purple candles are for strength and royal countenance. The color orange is a combination of red and yellow. Orange candles are used for vigor and protection.

Brown candles are for the earth. Turquoise and lavender are high spiritual colors and their candles invoke higher blessings. Pink and light-blue candles are for love. Black candles are not recommended for beginners because black invokes deep, dark, inner-womb transformations that may be difficult for the novice to grasp. A small black or gray candle may be appropriate for Winter Solstice to represent the darkest night. A black candle is burned next to an orange candle on Halloween, representing the dead and the living. If you are not familiar with candle magic, it is best to work with white candles.

Rite of Water
Blessed Art Thou, Creatures of Water

For the element Water, you may wish to bathe prior to doing spiritual work. The tub may be filled with a cup of epsom salts to draw out impurities, or filled with aromatic herbs such as comfrey, lavender, and mint.

After the bath, sprinkle around the room and in the corners seawater, holy Water, or any herbal Water you feel has purifying properties. Prepackaged liquids from stores with names such as "Peaceful Home" and "Jinx Removing" are worthless, so instead make your own herbal cleansing Waters.

You may wish to have a chalice of Water present during your spiritual work. The chalice represents the Holy Grail, the woman's womb. After your work you may wish to swim or walk by a river, lake, or ocean to flush away any energy that is not in the highest good for your growth, health, and transformation.

You may find that you gravitate towards one element, such as keeping a pristine house (Earth) like the Goddess Hestia. At different times in your life, one element may be more important than another, such as Air being most important for a graduate student. But it is in the balance of the four elements where the true healing can occur. When we honor the four elements as tools for purification, we will be blessed to find beauty in all directions.

SWORDS 1 SWORDS

△ The Ace of Swords △

A Ritual of Invoking the Four Elements of the Tarot

Chic Cicero & Sandra Tabatha Cicero

This ritual involves the use of certain Tarot cards to awaken the powers of the elements. It is based upon the Supreme Invoking Ritual of the Pentagram used by the Golden Dawn. However, there are some important differences. In the S.I.R.P. the elements are invoked in a circle, suggesting the evolution of light (sunrise, noon, sunset and night) as well as the rotation of the seasons (Spring, Summer, Fall and Winter). In this ritual, the elements are invoked in the order of the Four Worlds of the Qabalah, and the Tetragrammaton, the four-lettered name of God. The following rite expands upon the Qabalistic ideas inherent to the S.I.R.P. through the imagery of the Tarot.

(1) Prepare the temple. From a consecrated pack of Tarot cards, remove the four Aces. Put the rest of the deck aside. Place each Ace in its assigned quarter of the temple: Wands—South, Cups—West, Swords—East, Pentacles—North. You will need a Lotus Wand or similar implement used for invoking.

(2) Take a ritual bath.

(3) Perform a Ritual of Protection such as the Lesser Banishing Ritual of the Pentagram.

(4) Take up the wand and walk clockwise to the South. Trace a large circle in the air in front of the Ace of Wands. Draw the Invoking Pentagram of Spirit Active and intone the names "BITOM" (Bay-ee—toh-em) and "EHEIEH" (Eh-hay-yay). Give the LVX Signs. (L—left arm straight out from shoulder and right

arm straight up in the air; V—both arms up overhead in the shape of the letter; X—cross arms on breast).

(5) Trace the Invoking Pentagram of Fire and intone the names "OIP TEAA PEDOCE" (Oh-ee-pay, Tay-ah-ah, Pay-doe-kay) and "ELOHIM" (El-oh-heem). Give the sign of Fire (place hands palms-outward against the forehead, forming a triangle, apex upward).

(6) With the wand, trace sigil of the First Whirlings (the form of a spiral) in front of the Ace of Wands. Again vibrate the name "EHEIEH."

(7) Say, "I invoke thee, the Root of the Powers of Fire! Thou Great and Flaming Torch from which the whole of these has sprung! Thou art the Spark, the Seed, the Force, and the rushing Strength of Nature! Thou art the power of YOD from the Four-fold Name of the Eternal! Pure spiritual essence of Fire! Father of Many Flames! Initiator of the Whirl and the Lightening Bolt! Quintessence of the Powers of the South! I invoke and welcome thee to this mystic sphere!"

(8) Go to the west and stand before the Ace of Cups. Draw a large circle in front of the card. With the wand, trace the Invoking Pentagram of Spirit Passive and intone the names "HCOMA" (Hay-coh-mah) and "AGLA" (Ah-gah-lah). Give the LVX Signs.

(9) Draw the Invoking Pentagram of Water and vibrate the names "EMPEH ARSEL GAIOL" (Em-pay, Ar-sel, Gah-ee-ohl) and "ALEPH LAMED, AL" (Ah-lef, Lah-med, Ah-l). Give the sign of Water (hands together, palms inward at the level of the chest, forming a triangle, apex downward).

(10) With the wand, draw the sigil of the First Whirlings in front of the Ace of Cups and intone the name "EHEIEH."

(11) Say, "I invoke thee, the Root of the Powers of Water! Thou magnifcent Chalice of pure and limpid fluid! Thou art the Wellspring of all life and the Fountain of Creation! Thou art the Womb the Sea, the Form and the fertile Genius of Nature! Thou art the power of HEH from the Fourfold Name of the Eternal! Divine and pure essence of the Waters! Fruitful Mother of limitless forms and ideas! Embodiment of the Holy Grail! Heart of the Powers of the West! I invoke and welcome Thee to this mystic sphere!"

(12) Walk Deosil to the East. Trace a large circle in front of the Ace of Swords with the wand. Draw the Invoking Pentagram of Spirit Active and vibrate the names "EXARP" (Ex-ar-pay) and "EHEIEH." Give the LVX Signs.

(13) Trace the Invoking Pentagram of Air and intone the names "ORO IBAH AOZPI" (Or-row, Ee-bah-hey Ah-ohzohd-pee) and "YHVH" (Yode-hehvav-heh). Give the Sign of Air (both arms up and bent at the elbows, as in the position of Atlas supporting a great weight).

(14) Trace the sigil of the Whirl in front of the Ace of Swords and vibrate "EHEIEH."

(15) Say, "I invoke thee, the Root of the Powers of Air! Thou steadfast Sword of Might! Thou art the Breath, the Intellect, the Word, and the Invoked Force of the Universe! Thou art the power of VAV from the fourfold name of the Eternal! Astral essence of Air! The Reconciler! Son of the marriage of Fire and Water! Double-edged Initiator of healing through equilibrium! Thou who dost cut through the curtain of Night to bring forth

the Dawn! Base of the Powers of the East! I invoke and welcome thee to this mystic sphere !

(16) Go sunwise to the North and trace a circle in front of the Ace of Pentacles. Draw the Invoking Pentagram of Spirit Passive and intone the names "NANTA" (En-ah-en-tah) and "AGLA." Give the LVX Signs.

(17) Draw the Invoking Pentagram of Earth and vibrate the names "EMOR DIAL HECTEGA" (Ee-mor, Dee-ahl, Heck-tay-gah) and "ADONAI" (Ah-doe-nye). Give the sign of Earth (right arm straight out in a 45-degree angle fron the body, hand flat with the thumb facing up).

(18) Trace the spiral sigil of the First Whirlings and intone the name "EHEIEH."

(19) Say, "I invoke thee, the Root of the Powers of Earth! Thou magnificent Pentacle formed from the substance of the stars! Thou art the body, the temple and the physical manifestation of the Universe ! Thou art the power of the Final HEH from the Four-fold Name of the Eternal! Tangible essence of Earth! Daughter of the Three Mothers! Bride of Spirit! Celestial core of the rocks, gems, and mountains! Divine initiator into the Active World of Matter! Cornerstone of the Powers of the North! I invoke and welcome thee to this mystic sphere!"

(20) Repeat the Qabalistic Cross.

(21) At this point, the four Elements have been invoked through the Aces of the Tarot. It would now be appropriate to continue with whatever magickal operation is desired, such as a scrying, divination, healing, consecration, etc.

(22) When you are finished with the main ritual and wish to close the circle, go around counterclockwise to each quarter, starting in the South and ending in the North (as in the beginning). Trace the Banishing Pentagram of Fire in front of the Ace of Wands. In the West, trace the Banishing Pentagram of Water. East—Banishing Pentagram of Air; North—Banishing Pentagram of Earth.

(23) Perform the Lesser Banishing Ritual of the Pentagram.

(24) Say, "I now release the Root Powers of the Tarot Aces and any other spirits that may have been bound by this ceremony. Depart in peace to your abodes but be ready to come again when ye are called. Go with the blessings of YEHESHUAH YEHOVASHAH (Yeh-hay-shoe-ah, Yeh-hoh-vah-shah). I now declare this temple duly closed."

SO MOTE IT BE!

Goddess—Animal Totems

Janina Renee

Many types of animals have been manifestations, totems, or symbols of the Great Goddess at one time or another. The qualities which we identify with the Goddess, and perceive or project into animals, can represent aspects of our inner natures. By understanding the totemic essence of an animal (or our own perception thereof), we can also relate to our own personal Goddess-archetypes. Integrating the lessons of the Goddess's animal totems enables us to contact our instincts and portions of the deeper levels of the psyche.

The role of the Life-giving Mother as Lady of the Beasts has been recognized since times most ancient. Thus, virtually any living creature is Her totem. However, the following are a few of Her more familiar totems. (Note: Even though many of the following religious beliefs were long ago abandoned, I write in the present tense because Goddesses can be active as archetypes, arid also because many forgotten Goddess names are being rediscovered and reactivated by Neopagans).

BEAR: symbolically, the bear is associated with mothering and childbirth. Bear hugs and teddy bears suggest the nurturing qualities of mama bears. However, the bear also represents the aggressive and protective instincts of the mother, instincts that can invoke primal rage and fury. The bear's hibernation connects it with Earth mysteries as well as the psychological quality of introspection that brings self-renewal. The Celtic goddess Artio has been associated with a bear cult and presides over wildlife in general. Freya may have been associated with bears before cats became better known in Europe. Artemis can take the form of a bear, and some of Her rites have featured bear-masked dancers. Bear-Goddess figures are also found in Baltic and Slavic pagan cultures.

BEES, BEETLES, and other WINGED INSECTS: The efficient matriarchal organization of bees has long attracted interest. Folklorist Jakob Grimm said, "It seems natural, in connection with these bustling winged creatures, to think of the silent race of elves and dwarfs, which like them obeys a queen." The Roman goddess Mellona and the Lithuanian Austheia are associated with bees, and priestesses of Artemis have been called *Melissae* which means "bees." Bees and other helpful insects are harbingers of spring and of the earth's fertility. Many have the name "Mary" or "Lady" attached to them, showing their connection with earlier goddesses. The Ladybug has been an emblem of the Roman goddess Lucina and is sacred to Freya.

BIRDS: In folk belief, the soul is often represented as a bird, and birds can be spirit messengers. Birds symbolize thought, imagination, inspiration, intuition, and the transcendental qualities that allow the individual the personal freedom to fly belond limitations and penetrate the higher realms. Bird imagery associated with manifestations of the Goddess dates back to paleolithic cultures. More information on bird totems follows under separate captions.

BIRDS OF PREY: Birds of prey herald the Goddess as Death Wielder. Freya and Frigga take on the plumage of hawks and falcons, and the Sparrowhawk has been sacred to the Bohemians. The swiftness, power, and keenness of vision of these birds invokes awe and inspiration

CAT: The comfort-seeking ways of cats associate them with Bast and Freya, goddesses of love and patronesses of all arts and pleasures. Freya also teaches witchcraft, as does Diana, who takes the form of a cat in witch lore. Cats figure in the witch lore of the Basques, and are tied in with their cult of Saint Agato. Cats' keen night vision and their rounded eyes, which are said to become roundest at the Full Moon, give them lunar associations. Other goddesses connected with cats are Cerridwen and

Anu, and there seems to have been an oracular cat cult in Ireland. As there were no cats in Neolithic or Copper Age Europe, many of their goddess associations are more recent.

COW: The cow is connected with the very earthy aspect of the Goddess that relates to the physical conditions of existence. In the Eddas, the cow Audumbla is a primal ancestress and World Mother. The cow's sacred meanings are also tied in with the wealth of the Earth and the fertility cycles of the Moon. Goddesses associated with cows include the Hindu Lakshmi; Io and the cow-eyed Hera; Europa, who may have been a Cretan mother goddess and moon goddess; the pre-Biblical Ashtaroth; the Egyptian goddesses Isis and Hathor; and the Celtic Brigid, who is said to have been a cowherd.

CROW AND RAVEN: These birds have been manifestations of the Death Goddess. The Celtic War Goddess called the Morrigan appears on the battlefield in the guise of a crow or raven, and combines aspects of the goddesses Ana, Badb, and Macha. The Baltic Goddess Ragana also has totemic associations with crows.

DEER: The tender relationships between does and their fawns make us see them as primal mother figures, and the deer has been a totem of the Birth-Giving Goddess since early times. Artemis can take the form of a deer, and the deer also has Sumerian Goddess associations. As we become aware of the importance of healing touch, the gentleness of the doe can take on special meanings for us.

DOG: Dogs are important household guardians, and mythological dogs are companions of the dead and guardians of the Underworld in Egyptian, Greek, Mexican, and Northern European lore. Their nocturnal howling makes them heralds of the Death Goddess. One of Hecate's three heads is described as dog-like. Dog symbolism is also associated with Hel, Artemis, and Nehalennia.

DOVE: The dove is a manifestation of the fertility goddesses of Asia Minor, India, Crete, Greece, and Northern Europe. Harke, a form of Freya or Holda, flies through the air in the shape of a dove in order to make the earth fruitful. Also associated with doves are Atargatis, Tanith the Carthaginian Goddess of heaven (who is accompanied by two of them), Venus, and Hera.

FISH AND SEA MAMMALS: The watery realm is likened to the greater Unconscious and engenders and nourishes life. Because fish move through this element, they symbolize fertility and richness as well the psychological process of "becoming." An ancient Boetian amphora shows the Goddess with a fish in her womb. The fish also represents deep emotions. Among goddesses associated with fish symbolism are Atargatis the Syrian "fish mother," Artemis, Aphania, Dictynna the "Lady of the Nets," Britomartis, Sedna the Eskimo heroine who rules an undersea realm and engendered whales and seals, Venus, Myrrhine, Mara, Hecate, and Behrta.

FROGS, TOADS, and other AQUATIC CREATURES: Aquatic creatures share symbolism with fish. Frogs represent embryonic life, due to their stages of transformation. In folklore, the sounds of frogs bring the rains and the return of spring. A Frog Goddess is a characteristic motif in early Anatolia, and the Egyptian frog-headed Goddess Heket gave breath to humans at the time of creation. Toad figurines have been used as fertility charms, and toads were a portent of pregnancy to European peasants. Toads appear as witches' familiars, and are the main manifestation of the Baltic Witch Goddess Ragana.

HORSE: Horses represent personal power, both in physical and spiritual domains. The horse is one of the most favored totems in shamanic rites, carrying its rider into other dimensions. The horse is especially an emblem of Celtic goddesses, including Rigantona, Epona, Etain, and Macha. Hecate is depicted with the head of a horse, and Demeter disguised herself as a mare.

LIONESS: Big cats suggest the terrifying yet beautiful aspects of the Dark Goddess because they have great power coupled with grace. The lioness depicts the raw power and destructive fury of the Goddess. Thus, the gentle cow goddess Hathor could transform into Sekhmet the lioness, saying, "For truly, when I spill men's blood, my heart rejoices." The lioness also has symbolic affinities to the fire element. Astarte has been depicted with the head of a lioness, and Erishkegal and Bast are also able to make that transformation. Tibetan Tara and the fierce Hindu Goddess Durga are shown mounted on lions. Other goddesses accompanied by lions include Cybele and Fortuna.

OWL: Folk belief gives owls prophetic knowledge of human destiny, but also makes them birds of ill omen. Owls are emblems of Athena, Goddess of Wisdom. They are also manifestations of the Death Goddess. Owl-goddess figurines were important funeral obects through Neolithic and Megalithic times. The owl was the hieroglyph for death in ancient Egypt. The owl retains her Death-Goddess image in the Northern European legends wherein a nun is transformed into an owl and flies before the Wild Hunt, acting as Odin's herald. This is probably related to the legend of Blodeuwedd, who is transformed into an owl and pursued by Gwydion, Odin's Celtic counterpart. Signifying both wisdom and death, owls illustrate the ambivalent nature of the Crone aspect of the Goddess.

RABBIT and HARE: Though they are biologically different, rabbits and hares share some symbolism. Their sex drive and reproductive capacity is legendary. The fact that rabbits are burrowing animals connects them with the Earth mysteries, and hares have traditional associations with the Moon in both eastern and western lore. Shape-shifting witches favored the forms of hares, connecting them with the Goddess Sorcery. As symbols of the Earth's renewal, bunnies are sacred to Ostara. These creatures are also sacred to Venus, Diana, and Hecate.

SERPENT: Because snakes shed their skin, they signify self-renewal and immortality. Snakes also personify the Life Force, as their coiling forms suggest energy flow. Geomancers perceive the Earth's energy taking a serpentine course as it flows through landforms. Snakes are tied to the Earth mysteries, and their stirring in spring suggests the quickening of nature. Minoan Goddess or priestess figurines clutching snakes are admired art objects. Serpent effigies have been cult objects associated with Brigid, whose domination of life energies makes her patroness of healing arts. One of Hecate's heads is serpentine.

Coatlicue the five-fold Goddess of the Aztecs is serpent-skirted, and Ix-Chel, Mayan Goddess of water, the Moon, childbirth, and weaving also has snake symbolism. Snake Goddess figurines in household shrines of Old Europe show Her as household guardian. Other goddesses depicted as handling serpents or having them as totems include Rhea, Athena, Demeter, Hera, Britomartis, and Brehkina.

SPIDER: Spider symbolism shows the Goddess as the matrix of life, binding all destinies together. This is evident in the descriptions of the Mayan Goddess Ix-Chel, called Lady-Unique-All-Embracing, and of whom it is said that the world is her web and she is at its center. Spider Grandmother is important in southwestern lore. To the Zuni and Hopi she is an Earth Goddess and mother of the twin War Gods. To the Kiowa she is a culture heroine who continues to help her people. The spider also appears as a benevolent figure in Ukrainian folklore.

SOW: The sow represents two very different aspects of the Goddess. Her fast-growing, rounded body symbolizes pregnancy and the Earth's fertility. Representations of the sow as Grain Goddess date to the 7th millenium B.C.E. It's good luck to exchange pig figurines on New Year's Day, and pig-shaped cookies were sacrificial offerings. On the other hand, swine have a reputation for eating any of their young that are flawed. This is a dark aspect of Nature, who is not a doting mother and does not tolerate weakness or incompetence. The sow is a prime manifestation of the White Goddess, whose names include Demeter, Cerridwen, Henwen, and Freya.

WATERBIRDS: Because of the richness of marshes, rivers, and ponds in engendering life, the birds and animals dwelling in them symbolize fertility and transformation. Thus we have a belief that the stork brings babies. Waterbirds were significant to Goddess worship early on, and anthropomorphic waterbird figures from the Upper Paleolithic attest to this. Diving birds also symbolize unconscious knowledge because of their ability to penetrate the depths. Swans are seen to glide between the worlds and are a symbol of Brigid in Gaelic Scotland, and norns and valkyries often take their forms. Swans are also sacred to

Venus, as are ducks.

WOLF: For the Romans, the she-wolf was a primal ancestress, having nursed the founders of their great city. The howling of wolves associates them with Moon Goddesses and Death Goddesses—such as Diana, Hecate, and Hel. In Scandinavian lore, sorceresses ride wolves, and old women living alone in the forest are called "wolf mothers" and give shelter to wolves when they are hunted.

A Charm

Take of English earth as much
As either hand may rightly clutch.
In the taking of it breathe
Prayer for all who lie beneath.
Not the great nor well-bespoke,
But the mere uncounted folk
Of whose life and death is none
Report or lamentation.
Lay that earth upon thy heart
And thy sickness shall depart!
It shall sweeten and make whole
Fevered breath and festered soul.
It shall mightily restrain
Over-busied hand and brain.
It shall ease thy mortal strife
'Gainst the immortal woe of life,
Till thyself, restored, shall prove
 By what grace the Heavens do move.
Take of English flowers these—
Spring's full-faced primroses
Summer's wild wide-hearted rose,
Autumn's wall-flower of the close,
And, thy darkness to illume,
Winter's bee-thronged ivy-bloom.
Seek and serve them where they bide
From Candlemas to Christmas-tide,
For these simples, used aright,
Can restore a failing sight.
These shall cleanse and purify
Webbed and inward-turning eye;
These shall show thee treasure hid
Thy familiar fields amid;
And reveal (which is thy need)
Every man a King indeed!

—Rudyard Kipling

Phases of the Moon

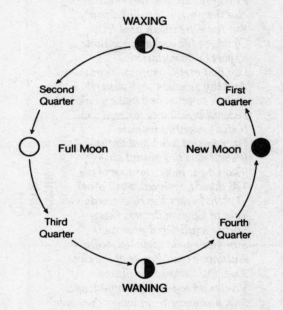

1st Quarter: begins when the Sun and Moon are conjunct, just after the New Moon.

2nd Quarter: begins halfway between the New Moon and Full Moon. The Sun and Moon are at 90° or squaring each other.

3rd Quarter: begins with the Full Moon when the Sun and Moon are in opposition.

4th Quarter: begins halfway between the Full Moon and New Moon when the Sun and Moon are again squaring each other.

TABLE OF TERMS REFERRING TO LUNAR QUARTERS (PHASES)

Sun-Moon Angle	MAGICKAL ALMANAC TERM	Common Terms		Division by:	
		2	4	8	
0-90° after Conjunction	First Quarter	Increasing Waxing Light New	New Moon	New Moon	
				Crescent	
90-180°	Second Quarter		First Quarter	First Quarter	
				Gibbous	
180-270°	Third Quarter	Decreasing Waning Dark Old	Full Moon	Full Moon	
				Disseminating	
270-360°	Fourth Quarter		Last Quarter	Last Quarter	
				Balsamic	

The Planetary Hours

The selection of an auspicious time for starting any affair is an important matter. The ancients paid special attention to determining a favorable time for the erection of important edifices, and many of these structures are still standing today as a constant source of wonder and admiration.

When a thing is once commenced, its existence tends to be of a nature corresponding to the conditions under which it was begun. Not only should you select the appropriate date but when possible you should also start the affair under an appropriate *Planetary Hour*.

Each hour of the day is ruled by a planet, and so the nature of any time during the day corresponds to the nature of the planet ruling it. Not only can you start important matters according to the appropriate planetary hour, but you can judge the nature of a matter (say, a letter you receive) from the planetary hour in which you are first aware of it or when it is first brought into contact with you.

The nature of the planetary hours is the same as the description of each of the planets, except that you will not need to refer to the descriptions for Uranus, Neptune and Pluto as they are considered here as higher octaves of Mercury, Venus and Mars, respectively. If something is ruled by Uranus, you can use the hour of Mercury.

The only other factor you need to know to use the Planetary Hours is the time of your local Sunrise and Sunset for any given day. This is given in the chart following the planetary hour grids.

Having determined the times of Sunrise and Sunset, you merely divide the daylight hours, and then the nighttime hours, into 12 equal parts. They will only once in awhile turn out to be periods of 60 minutes in length, for during our summertime there is more daylight than night, and during the winter, more night than day. Having charted the times when each of these 12 night periods and 12 day periods occurs, refer to the table and ascribe to each such period the planetary rulership in the order listed.

SUNRISE

Hour	Sun	Mon	Tues	Wed	Thur	Fri	Sat
1	☉	☽	♂	☿	♃	♀	♄
2	♀	♄	☉	☽	♂	☿	♃
3	☿	♃	♀	♄	☉	☽	♂
4	☽	♂	☿	♃	♀	♄	☉
5	♄	☉	☽	♂	☿	♃	♀
6	♃	♀	♄	☉	☽	♂	☿
7	♂	☿	♃	♀	♄	☉	☽
8	☉	☽	♂	☿	♃	♀	♄
9	♀	♄	☉	☽	♂	☿	♃
10	☿	♃	♀	♄	☉	☽	♂
11	☽	♂	☿	♃	♀	♄	☉
12	♄	☉	☽	♂	☿	♃	♀

SUNSET

Hour	Sun	Mon	Tues	Wed	Thur	Fri	Sat
1	♃	♀	♄	☉	☽	♂	☿
2	♂	☿	♃	♀	♄	☉	☽
3	☉	☽	♂	☿	♃	♀	♄
4	♀	♄	☉	☽	♂	☿	♃
5	☿	♃	♀	♄	☉	☽	♂
6	☽	♂	☿	♃	♀	♄	☉
7	♄	☉	☽	♂	☿	♃	♀
8	♃	♀	♄	☉	☽	♂	☿
9	♂	☿	♃	♀	♄	☉	☽
10	☉	☽	♂	☿	♃	♀	♄
11	♀	♄	☉	☽	♂	☿	♃
12	☿	♃	♀	♄	☉	☽	♂

☉ Sun; ☿ Mercury; ♄ Saturn; ♂ Mars; ♀ Venus; ☽ Moon; ♃ Jupiter.

SUNRISE

UNIVERSAL TIME FOR MERIDIAN OF GREENWICH

LAT		+10°	+20°	+30°	+40°	+42°	+46°	+50°
		h m	h m	h m	h m	h m	h m	h m
JAN	2	6 16	6 34	6 55	7 21	7 28	7 42	7 58
	14	6 21	6 38	6 57	7 21	7 26	7 39	7 54
	26	6 23	6 37	6 54	7 14	7 19	7 30	7 42
FEB	7	6 22	6 34	6 47	7 03	7 07	7 15	7 25
	19	6 19	6 27	6 37	6 49	6 51	6 57	7 04
	27	6 16	6 22	6 29	6 37	6 39	6 44	6 49
MAR	7	6 12	6 16	6 20	6 25	6 26	6 29	6 32
	19	6 05	6 06	6 06	6 06	6 06	6 06	6 06
	27	6 01	5 59	5 56	5 53	5 52	5 51	5 49
APR	12	5 52	5 45	5 37	5 28	5 26	5 21	5 15
	20	5 48	5 39	5 29	5 16	5 13	5 06	4 58
	28	5 44	5 33	5 21	5 05	5 01	4 53	4 43
MAY	6	5 41	5 28	5 13	4 55	4 50	4 41	4 29
	18	5 38	5 23	5 05	4 43	4 37	4 25	4 11
	26	5 38	5 21	5 01	4 37	4 31	4 17	4 02
JUN	3	5 38	5 20	4 59	4 33	4 26	4 12	3 55
	15	5 39	5 20	4 58	4 30	4 24	4 09	3 50
	23	5 41	5 22	5 00	4 32	4 25	4 09	3 51
JUL	1	5 43	5 24	5 02	4 34	4 28	4 13	3 55
	9	5 45	5 27	5 06	4 39	4 33	4 18	4 01
	17	5 47	5 30	5 10	4 45	4 39	4 25	4 09
	25	5 48	5 33	5 14	4 51	4 46	4 34	4 19
AUG	2	5 50	5 36	5 19	4 59	4 54	4 43	4 30
	10	5 51	5 38	5 24	5 06	5 02	4 52	4 41
	18	5 51	5 41	5 29	5 14	5 10	5 02	4 53
	26	5 51	5 43	5 33	5 21	5 19	5 12	5 05
SEP	3	5 51	5 45	5 38	5 29	5 27	5 22	5 17
	11	5 50	5 46	5 42	5 36	5 35	5 32	5 29
	19	5 49	5 48	5 46	5 44	5 43	5 42	5 41
	27	5 49	5 50	5 51	5 52	5 52	5 52	5 53
OCT	13	5 48	5 54	6 00	6 08	6 09	6 13	6 18
	21	5 49	5 57	6 05	6 16	6 19	6 24	6 31
	29	5 50	6 00	6 11	6 25	6 28	6 35	6 44
NOV	6	5 52	6 04	6 17	6 34	6 38	6 47	6 57
	14	5 54	6 08	6 24	6 43	6 48	6 58	7 10
	22	5 57	6 13	6 30	6 52	6 58	7 09	7 23
	30	6 01	6 18	6 37	7 01	7 07	7 19	7 35
DEC	8	6 05	6 23	6 43	7 09	7 15	7 28	7 45
	16	6 09	6 27	6 49	7 15	7 21	7 35	7 52
	24	6 13	6 32	6 53	7 19	7 26	7 40	7 57
	30	6 17	6 35	6 56	7 22	7 28	7 42	7 59

SUNSET

UNIVERSAL TIME FOR MERIDIAN OF GREENWICH

LAT		+10°	+20°	+30°	+40°	+42°	+46°	+50°
		h m	h m	h m	h m	h m	h m	h m
JAN	2	17 48	17 30	17 09	16 43	16 36	16 22	16 06
	14	17 57	17 40	17 21	16 57	16 52	16 39	16 24
	26	18 02	17 48	17 32	17 11	17 06	16 56	16 43
FEB	7	18 07	17 55	17 42	17 26	17 22	17 13	17 04
	19	18 09	18 01	17 51	17 40	17 37	17 31	17 24
	27	18 10	18 04	17 57	17 49	17 47	17 43	17 38
MAR	7	18 11	18 07	18 03	17 58	17 57	17 54	17 51
	19	18 11	18 11	18 10	18 10	18 10	18 10	18 10
	27	18 11	18 13	18 15	18 19	18 19	18 21	18 23
APR	12	18 10	18 17	18 25	18 35	18 37	18 42	18 48
	20	18 11	18 20	18 30	18 43	18 46	18 53	19 01
	28	18 11	18 22	18 35	18 51	18 55	19 03	19 13
MAY	6	18 12	18 25	18 40	18 59	19 04	19 14	19 25
	18	18 14	18 30	18 48	19 11	19 16	19 28	19 43
	26	18 16	18 33	18 53	19 18	19 24	19 37	19 53
JUN	3	18 18	18 36	18 57	19 24	19 30	19 45	20 02
	15	18 22	18 40	19 02	19 30	19 37	19 52	20 11
	23	18 23	18 42	19 04	19 33	19 39	19 55	20 13
JUL	1	18 25	18 43	19 05	19 33	19 39	19 55	20 13
	9	18 25	18 43	19 04	19 31	19 37	19 52	20 09
	17	18 25	18 42	19 02	19 27	19 33	19 46	20 02
	25	18 25	18 40	18 58	19 21	19 27	19 39	19 53
AUG	2	18 23	18 37	18 53	19 13	19 18	19 29	19 42
	10	18 20	18 32	18 46	19 04	19 08	19 18	19 29
	18	18 17	18 27	18 39	18 53	18 57	19 05	19 14
	26	18 13	18 21	18 30	18 42	18 45	18 51	18 58
SEP	3	18 08	18 14	18 21	18 29	18 31	18 36	18 41
	11	18 03	18 07	18 11	18 16	18 18	18 20	18 24
	19	17 58	18 00	18 01	18 03	18 04	18 05	18 06
	27	17 53	17 52	17 51	17 50	17 50	17 49	17 49
OCT	13	17 44	17 39	17 32	17 24	17 23	17 19	17 14
	21	17 40	17 33	17 24	17 13	17 10	17 05	16 58
	29	17 38	17 27	17 16	17 02	16 59	16 52	16 43
NOV	6	17 36	17 23	17 10	16 53	16 49	16 40	16 30
	14	17 35	17 21	17 05	16 45	16 40	16 30	16 18
	22	17 35	17 19	17 01	16 39	16 34	16 22	16 09
	30	17 36	17 19	17 00	16 36	16 30	16 17	16 02
DEC	8	17 39	17 21	17 00	16 35	16 28	16 15	15 59
	16	17 42	17 23	17 02	16 36	16 29	16 15	15 58
	24	17 46	17 27	17 06	16 39	16 33	16 19	16 02
	30	17 50	17 32	17 11	16 45	16 39	16 25	16 08

MOONRISE

UNIVERSAL TIME FOR MERIDIAN OF GREENWICH

LAT		+10°	+20°	+30°	+40°	+42°	+46°	+50°
		h m	h m	h m	h m	h m	h m	h m
JAN	2	19 51	19 37	19 22	19 03	18 58	18 48	18 36
	14	5 05	5 26	5 51	6 22	6 30	6 47	7 08
	26	14 16	13 54	13 28	12 55	12 47	12 30	12 08
FEB	7	0 26	0 46	1 08	1 36	1 43	1 58	2 16
	19	9 27	9 15	9 01	8 45	8 41	8 32	8 22
	27	17 10	17 02	16 52	16 39	16 36	16 30	16 22
MAR	7	.. ..	.. ..	.. ..	0 22	0 29	0 46	1 06
	19	8 12	7 58	7 41	7 20	7 15	7 04	6 51
	27	15 54	15 49	15 42	15 34	15 32	15 28	15 23
APR	12	3 50	3 51	3 52	3 53	3 54	3 54	3 55
	20	11 01	10 41	10 19	9 51	9 44	9 29	9 10
	28	17 59	18 14	18 31	18 52	18 58	19 09	19 23
MAY	6	.. ..	.. ..	0 14	0 35	0 40	0 51	1 03
	18	9 52	9 35	9 16	8 51	8 45	8 32	8 16
	26	16 45	17 02	17 22	17 47	17 53	18 06	18 22
JUN	3	23 00	23 09	23 18	23 30	23 33	23 39	23 46
	15	8 39	8 24	8 08	7 47	7 42	7 30	7 17
	23	15 33	15 51	16 13	16 41	16 48	17 03	17 21
JUL	1	21 38	21 44	21 51	21 59	22 01	22 05	22 09
	9	3 01	2 40	2 16	1 45	1 38	1 21	1 01
	17	10 57	11 04	11 12	11 22	11 25	11 30	11 36
	25	17 35	17 53	18 13	18 39	18 45	18 58	19 14
AUG	2	23 02	22 48	22 32	22 12	22 08	21 58	21 46
	10	6 02	5 52	5 41	5 26	5 23	5 15	5 07
	18	13 05	13 26	13 51	14 22	14 30	14 47	15 07
	26	18 56	18 56	18 56	18 56	18 56	18 57	18 57
SEP	3	0 40	0 19	.. ..	.. ..	.. ..	.. ..	23 51
	11	8 18	8 30	8 43	9 00	9 04	9 12	9 23
	19	14 54	15 08	15 23	15 42	15 47	15 57	16 09
	27	20 38	20 20	19 59	19 32	19 26	19 12	18 55
OCT	13	10 30	10 51	11 15	11 46	11 53	12 10	12 30
	21	16 09	16 04	15 58	15 51	15 49	15 46	15 41
	29	23 31	23 16	23 00	22 38	22 33	22 22	22 09
NOV	6	5 42	5 57	6 15	6 38	6 44	6 56	7 10
	14	12 04	12 13	12 24	12 36	12 39	12 45	12 53
	22	18 13	17 52	17 28	16 58	16 51	16 35	16 15
	30	1 03	1 05	1 07	1 10	1 11	1 13	1 15
DEC	8	7 53	8 12	8 34	9 02	9 08	9 23	9 41
	16	13 17	13 07	12 56	12 42	12 39	12 32	12 24
	24	21 09	21 00	20 50	20 37	20 34	20 28	20 20
	30	1 32	1 46	2 01	2 21	2 25	2 36	2 48

(.. ..) INDICATES PHENOMENON WILL OCCUR THE NEXT DAY.

MOONSET

UNIVERSAL TIME FOR MERIDIAN OF GREENWICH

LAT		+10°	+20°	+30°	+40°	+42°	+46°	+50°
		h m	h m	h m	h m	h m	h m	h m
JAN	2	7 48	8 04	8 21	8 43	8 48	8 59	9 13
	14	16 50	16 29	16 05	15 34	15 27	15 10	14 50
	26	2 24	2 46	3 11	3 43	3 51	4 09	4 30
FEB	7	12 13	11 53	11 30	11 01	10 54	10 38	10 19
	19	22 17	22 31	22 48	23 09	23 14	23 25	23 38
	27	5 02	5 13	5 25	5 40	5 43	5 51	6 00
MAR	7	10 54	10 33	10 08	9 37	9 30	9 13	8 53
	19	21 09	21 26	21 45	22 10	22 16	22 29	22 45
	27	3 42	3 50	3 59	4 10	4 12	4 18	4 24
APR	12	16 12	16 14	16 15	16 17	16 18	16 19	16 20
	20	.. ..	.. ..	.. ..	0 19	0 27	0 42	1 01
	28	5 09	4 56	4 41	4 23	4 19	4 10	3 59
MAY	6	11 38	11 25	11 09	10 51	10 46	10 36	10 24
	18	22 49	23 04	23 21	23 41	23 46	23 57	.. ..
	26	3 50	3 35	3 17	2 56	2 51	2 39	2 26
JUN	3	10 20	10 09	9 57	9 42	9 38	9 30	9 21
	15	21 30	21 43	21 56	22 13	22 17	22 26	22 36
	23	2 33	2 16	1 56	1 31	1 25	1 12	0 56
JUL	1	9 04	8 56	8 47	8 35	8 33	8 27	8 20
	9	16 12	16 34	16 59	17 31	17 39	17 56	18 17
	17	23 04	22 55	22 45	22 32	22 29	22 23	22 15
	25	4 36	4 17	3 55	3 27	3 20	3 05	2 47
AUG	2	11 00	11 13	11 27	11 44	11 48	11 57	12 08
	10	18 44	18 51	18 59	19 09	19 12	19 17	19 23
	18	0 00	.. ..	.. ..	23 32	23 25	23 07	22 46
	26	6 32	6 29	6 27	6 24	6 23	6 21	6 19
SEP	3	13 49	14 09	14 33	15 03	15 10	15 26	15 45
	11	20 18	20 05	19 49	19 30	19 26	19 16	19 05
	19	2 04	1 48	1 30	1 08	1 03	0 51	0 37
	27	8 42	9 00	9 19	9 44	9 50	10 04	10 20
OCT	13	22 16	21 55	21 31	21 01	20 54	20 37	20 17
	21	3 53	3 56	3 59	4 03	4 04	4 07	4 09
	29	11 31	11 47	12 06	12 29	12 35	12 47	13 01
NOV	6	17 35	17 18	16 59	16 34	16 29	16 16	16 00
	14	.. ..	.. ..	23 54	23 44	23 42	23 36	23 30
	22	6 18	6 38	7 01	7 31	7 38	7 54	8 13
	30	13 19	13 15	13 10	13 04	13 02	12 59	12 56
DEC	8	19 41	19 23	19 02	18 36	18 29	18 15	17 58
	16	1 09	1 16	1 25	1 36	1 39	1 45	1 52
	24	8 59	9 10	9 23	9 38	9 42	9 50	9 59
	30	13 29	13 14	12 57	12 35	12 30	12 19	12 06

(.. ..) INDICATES PHENOMENON WILL OCCUR NEXT DAY.

Tables of Spirits and Planets

Angels and Planets Ruling:

Hours NIGHT	SUNDAY	MONDAY	TUESDAY	WEDNESDAY	THURSDAY	FRIDAY	SATURDAY
1	♃ Sachiel	♀ Anael	♄ Cassiel	☉ Michael	☽ Gabriel	♂ Samael	☿ Raphael
2	♂ Samael	☿ Raphael	♃ Sachiel	♀ Anael	♄ Cassiel	☉ Michael	☽ Gabriel
3	☉ Michael	☽ Gabriel	♂ Samael	☿ Raphael	♃ Sachiel	♀ Anael	♄ Cassiel
4	♀ Anael	♄ Cassiel	☉ Michael	☽ Gabriel	♂ Samael	☿ Raphael	♃ Sachiel
5	☿ Raphael	♃ Sachiel	♀ Anael	♄ Cassiel	☉ Michael	☽ Gabriel	♂ Samael
6	☽ Gabriel	♂ Samael	☿ Raphael	♃ Sachiel	♀ Anael	♄ Cassiel	☉ Michael
7	♄ Cassiel	☉ Michael	☽ Gabriel	♂ Samael	☿ Raphael	♃ Sachiel	♀ Anael
8	♃ Sachiel	♀ Anael	♄ Cassiel	☉ Michael	☽ Gabriel	♂ Samael	☿ Raphael
9	♂ Samael	☿ Raphael	♃ Sachiel	♀ Anael	♄ Cassiel	☉ Michael	☽ Gabriel
10	☉ Michael	☽ Gabriel	♂ Samael	☿ Raphael	♃ Sachiel	♀ Anael	♄ Cassiel
11	♀ Anael	♄ Cassiel	☉ Michael	☽ Gabriel	♂ Samael	☿ Raphael	♃ Sachiel
12	☿ Raphael	♃ Sachiel	♀ Anael	♄ Cassiel	☉ Michael	☽ Gabriel	♂ Samael

Angels and Planets Ruling:

Hours DAY	SUNDAY	MONDAY	TUESDAY	WEDNESDAY	THURSDAY	FRIDAY	SATURDAY
1	☉ Michael	☽ Gabriel	♂ Samael	☿ Raphael	♃ Sachiel	♀ Anael	♄ Cassiel
2	♀ Anael	♄ Cassiel	☉ Michael	☽ Gabriel	♂ Samael	☿ Raphael	♃ Sachiel
3	☿ Raphael	♃ Sachiel	♀ Anael	♄ Cassiel	☉ Michael	☽ Gabriel	♂ Samael
4	☽ Gabriel	♂ Samael	☿ Raphael	♃ Sachiel	♀ Anael	♄ Cassiel	☉ Michael
5	♄ Cassiel	☉ Michael	☽ Gabriel	♂ Samael	☿ Raphael	♃ Sachiel	♀ Anael
6	♃ Sachiel	♀ Anael	♄ Cassiel	☉ Michael	☽ Gabriel	♂ Samael	☿ Raphael
7	♂ Samael	☿ Raphael	♃ Sachiel	♀ Anael	♄ Cassiel	☉ Michael	☽ Gabriel
8	☉ Michael	☽ Gabriel	♂ Samael	☿ Raphael	♃ Sachiel	♀ Anael	♄ Cassiel
9	♀ Anael	♄ Cassiel	☉ Michael	☽ Gabriel	♂ Samael	☿ Raphael	♃ Sachiel
10	☿ Raphael	♃ Sachiel	♀ Anael	♄ Cassiel	☉ Michael	☽ Gabriel	♂ Samael
11	☽ Gabriel	♂ Samael	☿ Raphael	♃ Sachiel	♀ Anael	♄ Cassiel	☉ Michael
12	♄ Cassiel	☉ Michael	☽ Gabriel	♂ Samael	☿ Raphael	♃ Sachiel	♀ Anael

Almanac Pages

Raymond Buckland

The almanac pages give information important to many aspects of working magick. For example, in many magickal systems, the phases of the Moon are strictly adhered to, along with the times of the Moon's rising and setting. The times for sunrise and sunset are likewise frequently necessary. (Where there are local variations in time, these must be taken into account. Most local newspapers give exact times for different geographical areas.)

The PHASES of the Moon are especially important. Constructive magick must be done in the waxing phase, while destructive magick (*e.g.* to get rid of something, such as a bad habit) is carried out in the waning phase.

The ASTROLOGICAL SIGN of the Moon is also included in the date pages along with the time (figured in Central Standard Time—adjust if necessary) of the Moon's ingress into the following sign.

Many FESTIVALS, and the dates they are celebrated, are included in the almanac. If your favorite is not there, please let us know so that we may include it in future issues.

The TAROT CARD associated with each particular day is also listed. This is used by many people as a focus for daily meditation. You don't have to use the card given, if you prefer another. The order we use is based on an old Romany tradition which starts the first of the year with The Lovers and follows through from there. A daily ritual can be constructed using the tarot card, the INCENSE (which, again, is a suggestion only, based on traditional use) and the COLOR, applied to the candle being burned.

As with the tarot card and incense, the HERB listed is a suggestion, based on tradition. This can be another basis for meditation, or for study. To take one herb a day and study its many uses can be a wonderful way to build up a knowledge of herbal lore, and the look, feel and smell of an herb can inspire moving meditations.

Each of the Full Moons traditionally is named to reflect the time of the year at which it occurs, starting with the WOLF Moon. This is named for the time, in Europe, when the wolves would be especially prominent and dangerous because of the scarcity of food. They were frequently credited with preternatural cunning and are featured in many old tales and legends. The next Moon is the STORM Moon, which occurs at a time often markled by turbulent weather. The CHASTE Moon symbolizes the purity of the new Spring, while the following SEED Moon marks the sowing season.

The hare was a sacred animal, frequently associated with the Moon. Witches were once thought to be able to turn themselves into hares when meeting at the full of the Moon. April's Moon carries the name HARE. May's is the DYAD Moon, the Latin word for "a pair," marking the Moon of the astrological sign of Gemini. Then there is the MEAD Moon, which some people attribute to the honey wine aptly described as "the nectar of the gods," yet others ascribe it to the meadows and their readiness for mowing.

The WORT Moon is named from the old Anglo-Saxon word *wyrt*, meaning "plant." This was the time when the *wyrts* would be gathered and stored. In late August/early September there was the barley harvest, hence the BARLEY Moon. The BLOOD Moon reflected the time for sacrifice; domestic animals were slaughtered to prepare for winter food storage, and the wild animals were thinned out for the coming season. The SNOW Moon tied-in with the coming of the first snow, and the OAK Moon with the sacred tree of the Druids.

Monday

DECEMBER 1991

S	M	T	W	T	F	S
1	2	3	4	5	6	7
8	9	10	11	12	13	14
15	16	17	18	19	20	21
22	23	24	25	26	27	28
29	30	31				

Tuesday

JANUARY 1992

S	M	T	W	T	F	S
			1	2	3	4
5	6	7	8	9	10	11
12	13	14	15	16	17	18
19	20	21	22	23	24	25
26	27	28	29	30	31	

1

Wednesday

Moon Phase: 4th Quarter
        Waning
Moon enters Sagittarius 1:31 a.m.
Festivals: San-ga-nichi [Jap.] (first day)
        Good Luck Day
        First Footing [Scot.]

Moon Sign: Scorpio
Tarot Card: The Lovers
Herb: Almond
Incense: Sandalwood
Color: Purple

2

Thursday

Moon Phase: 4th Quarter
        Waning
Festivals: Advent of Isis [Egypt.]
        Nativity of Our Lady Inanna
        [Sum.]

Moon Sign: Sagittarius
Tarot Card: The Chariot
Herb: Asparagus
Incense: Myrrh
Color: Blue

3
Friday

Moon Phase: 4th Quarter
Waning
Moon enters Capricorn 1:10 p.m.
Festivals: San-ga-nichi—(last day)

Moon Sign: Sagittarius
Tarot Card: Justice
Herb: Bilberry
Incense: Jasmine
Color: Green

4
Saturday

Moon Phase: New Moon
Festivals: New Moon Greeting [Brit.]

Moon Sign: Capricorn
Tarot Card: The Hermit
Herb: Bird's Tongue
Incense: Benzoin or Cedar
Color: Black

5
Sunday

Moon Phase: 1st Quarter
Waxing
Festivals: Pagan Feast of Epiphany
Good Luck Day

Moon Sign: Capricorn
Tarot Card: Wheel of Fortune
Herb: Bloodroot
Incense: Pine
Color: Yellow

JANUARY 1992

S	M	T	W	T	F	S
			1	2	3	4
5	6	7	8	9	10	11
12	13	14	15	16	17	18
19	20	21	22	23	24	25
26	27	28	29	30	31	

6 *Monday*

Moon Phase: 1st Quarter
            Waxing
Moon enters Aquarius 2:00 p.m.
Festivals: Twelfth Night
           Epiphany of Kore [Grk.]
           Haxey Hood [Eng.]

Moon Sign: Capricorn
Tarot Card: Strength
Herb: Buckthorn
Incense: Cinnamon
Color: White

7 *Tuesday*

Moon Phase: 1st Quarter
            Waxing
Festivals: Distaff Day [Brit.]
           Seven Herbs Festival [Jap.]

Moon Sign: Aquarius
Tarot Card: The Hanged Man
Herb: Cat's Foot
Incense: Frankincense
Color: Red

8 *Wednesday*

Moon Phase: 1st Quarter
            Waxing
Moon enters Pisces 2:53 p.m.

Moon Sign: Aquarius
Tarot Card: Death
Herb: Coltsfoot
Incense: Sandalwood
Color: Purple

9 *Thursday*

Moon Phase: 1st Quarter
            Waxing

Moon Sign: Pisces
Tarot Card: Temperance
Herb: Cyclamen
Incense: Myrrh
Color: Blue

10

Friday

Moon Phase: 1st Quarter
           Waxing

Moon Sign Pisces:
Tarot Card: The Devil
Herb: Elecampane
Incense: Jasmine
Color: Green

11

Saturday

Moon Phase: 1st Quarter
           Waxing
Moon enters Aries 2:23 a.m.
Festivals: Burning the Clavie [Scot.]

Moon Sign: Pisces
Tarot Card: The Tower
Herb: Ferula
Incense: Benzoin or Cedar
Color: Black

12

Sunday

Moon Phase: 2nd Quarter
           Waxing
Festivals: Compitalia [Rom.]
          Nez Percé War Dances
          [NW Am.]

Moon Sign: Aries
Tarot Card: The Star
Herb: Garden Violet
Incense: Pine
Color: Yellow

JANUARY 1992

S	M	T	W	T	F	S
			1	2	3	4
5	6	7	8	9	10	11
12	13	14	15	16	17	18
19	20	21	22	23	24	25
26	27	28	29	30	31	

13   *Monday*

Moon Phase: 2nd Quarter
          Waxing
Moon enters Taurus 11:01 a.m.
Festivals: Plough Monday [Brit.]

Moon Sign: Aries
Tarot Card: The Moon
Herb: Hawthorn
Incense: Cinnamon
Color: White

14   *Tuesday*

Moon Phase: 2nd Quarter
          Waxing
Festivals: Makar Sankrati [Hin.]

Moon Sign: Taurus
Tarot Card: The Sun
Herb: Hepatica
Incense: Frankincense
Color: Red

15   *Wednesday*

Moon Phase: 2nd Quarter
          Waxing
Moon enters Gemini 3:56 p.m.
Festivals: Carmentalia [Rom.]

Moon Sign: Taurus
Tarot Card: Judgement
Herb: Hound's-Tongue
Incense: Sandalwood
Color: Purple

16   *Thursday*

Moon Phase: 2nd Quarter
          Waxing

Moon Sign: Gemini
Tarot Card: The World
Herb: Jasmine
Incense: Myrrh
Color: Blue

17   *Friday*

Moon Phase: 2nd Quarter
             Waxing
Moon enters Cancer 5:27 p.m.

Moon Sign: Gemini
Tarot Card: The Fool
Herb: Lavender
Incense: Jasmine
Color: Green

18   *Saturday*

Moon Phase: 2nd Quarter
             Waxing

Moon Sign: Cancer
Tarot Card: Ace of Swords
Herb: Magnolia
Incense: Benzoin or Cedar
Color: Black

19   *Sunday*

Moon Phase: Full Moon (Wolf)
Moon enters Leo 4:58 p.m.

Moon Sign: Cancer
Tarot Card: Two of Swords
Herb: Mexican Damiana
Incense: Pine
Color: Yellow

JANUARY 1992

S	M	T	W	T	F	S
			1	2	3	4
5	6	7	8	9	10	11
12	13	14	15	16	17	18
19	20	21	22	23	24	25
26	27	28	29	30	31	

20 *Monday*

Moon Phase: 3rd Quarter
       Waning
Sun enters Aquarius 1:34 p.m.
Festivals: Eve of St. Agnes [Rom.]

Moon Sign: Leo
Tarot Card: Three of Swords
Herb: Cross Mint
Incense: Cinnamon
Color: White

21 *Tuesday*

Moon Phase: 3rd Quarter
       Waning
Moon enters Virgo 4:23 p.m.
Festivals: St. Agnes Day [Rom.]

Moon Sign: Leo
Tarot Card: Four of Swords
Herb: Black Mulberry
Incense: Frankincense
Color: Red

22 *Wednesday*

Moon Phase: 3rd Quarter
       Waning
Festivals: St. Vincent's Day

Moon Sign: Virgo
Tarot Card: Five of Swords
Herb: Bittersweet
Incense: Sandalwood
Color: Purple

23 *Thursday*

Moon Phase: 3rd Quarter
       Waning
Moon enters Libra 5:43 p.m.
Festivals: Buffalo and Comanche Dances
       [Southwest Amerindian]

Moon Sign: Virgo
Tarot Card: Six of Swords
Herb: Heart's Ease
Incense: Myrrh
Color: Blue

24
Friday

Moon Phase: 3rd Quarter
Waning
Festivals: Start of Burgeoning Time
[Kelt.]

Moon Sign: Libra
Tarot Card: Seven of Swords
Herb: Pilewort
Incense: Jasmine
Color: Green

25
Saturday

Moon Phase: 3rd Quarter
Waning
Moon enters Scorpio 10:33 p.m.
Festivals: Burns Night [Scot.]

Moon Sign: Libra
Tarot Card: Eight of Swords
Herb: Pokeweed
Incense: Benzoin or Cedar
Color: Black

26
Sunday

Moon Phase: 4th Quarter
Waxing

Moon Sign: Scorpio
Tarot Card: Nine of Swords
Herb: Butter Rose
Incense: Pine
Color: Yellow

DECEMBER 1991

S	M	T	W	T	F	S
1	2	3	4	5	6	7
8	9	10	11	12	13	14
15	16	17	18	19	20	21
22	23	24	25	26	27	28
29	30	31				

JANUARY

S	M	T	W	T	F	S
			1	2	3	4
5	6	7	8	9	10	11
12	13	14	15	16	17	18
19	20	21	22	23	24	25
26	27	28	29	30	31	

27 *Monday*

Moon Phase: 4th Quarter
Waning

Moon Sign: Scorpio
Tarot Card: Ten of Swords
Herb: Compass Plant
Incense: Cinnamon
Color: White

28 *Tuesday*

Moon Phase: 4th Quarter
Waning
Moon enters Sagittarius 7:21 a.m.
Festivals: Upelly-Aa [Scot.]

Moon Sign: Scorpio
Tarot Card: Page of Swords
Herb: Rhatany
Incense: Frankincense
Color: Red

29 *Wednesday*

Moon Phase: 4th Quarter
Waning
Festivals: Peace [Rom.]

Moon Sign: Sagittarius
Tarot Card: Knight of Swords
Herb: Sanicle
Incense: Sandalwood
Color: Purple

30 *Thursday*

Moon Phase: 4th Quarter
Waning
Moon enters Capricorn 7:08 p.m.

Moon Sign: Sagittarius
Tarot Card: Queen of Swords
Herb: Shepherd's-purse
Incense: Myrrh
Color:Blue

31   *Friday*

Moon Phase: 4th Quarter
             Waning
Festivals: Hecate's Feast [Gr./Rom.]
            Eve of Brighde [Ir.]

Moon Sign: Capricorn
Tarot Card: King of Swords
Herb: Aloe
Incense: Jasmine
Color: Green

1   *Saturday*

Moon Phase: 4th Quarter
             Waning
Festivals: Brighde [Ir.]
            Oimelc/Imbolc
            Eleusinian Lesser Mysteries
            [Gk.] (first day)
            Fire Festival

Moon Sign: Capricorn
Tarot Card: Ace of Wands
Herb: Balm
Incense: Benzoin or Cedar
Color: Black

2   *Sunday*

Moon Phase: 4th Quarter
            Waxing
Moon enters Aquarius 8:09 a.m.
Festivals: Candlemas
           Forty Shillings Day [Eng.]
           The Wives' Feast Day [Eng.]
           Cradle Rocking [Eng.]

Moon Sign: Capricorn
Tarot Card: Two of Wands
Herb: Birthroot
Incense: Pine
Color: Yellow

FEBRUARY

S	M	T	W	T	F	S
						1
2	3	4	5	6	7	8
9	10	11	12	13	14	15
16	17	18	19	20	21	22
23	24	25	26	27	28	29

3   *Monday*

Moon Phase: 4th Quarter   Moon Sign: Aquarius
            Waning   Tarot Card: Three of Wands
Festivals: Eleusinian Lesser Mysteries   Herb: Blue Cohosh
           (last day)   Incense: Cinnamon
           Chinese New Years Day Color: White
           Blaze Day

4   *Tuesday*

Moon Phase: New Moon   Moon Sign: Aquarius
Moon enters Pisces 8:51 p.m.   Tarot Card: Four of Wands
                                  Herb: Burdock
                                  Incense: Frankincense
                                  Color: Red

5   *Wednesday*

Moon Phase: 1st Quarter   Moon Sign: Pisces
            Waxing   Tarot Card: Five of Wands
Festivals: Isis Festival [Egypt.]   Herb: Cayenne
           St. Agatha's Day   Incense: Sandalwood
                                  Color: Purple

6   *Thursday*

Moon Phase: 1st Quarter   Moon Sign: Pisces
            Waxing   Tarot Card: Six of Wands
                                  Herb: Columbine
                                  Incense: Myrrh
                                  Color: Blue

7
Friday

Moon Phase: 1st Quarter
Waxing
Moon enters Aries 8:16 a.m.

Moon Sign: Pisces
Tarot Card: Seven of Wands
Herb: Dandelion
Incense: Jasmine
Color: Green

8
Saturday

Moon Phase: 1st Quarter
Waxing
Festivals: Brighde Octave [Ir.]

Moon Sign: Aries
Tarot Card: Eight of Wands
Herb: Elm
Incense: Benzoin or Cedar
Color: Black

9
Sunday

Moon Phase: 1st Quarter
Waxing
Moon enters Taurus 5:37 p.m.
Festivals: St. Apollonia's Dau

Moon Sign: Aries
Tarot Card: Nine of Wands
Herb: Asafetida
Incense: Pine
Color: Yellow

FEBRUARY

S	M	T	W	T	F	S
						1
2	3	4	5	6	7	8
9	10	11	12	13	14	15
16	17	18	19	20	21	22
23	24	25	26	27	28	29

10
Monday

Moon Phase: 1st Quarter
Waxing

Moon Sign: Pisces
Tarot Card: Ten of Wands
Herb: Garlic
Incense: Cinnamon
Color: White

11
Tuesday

Moon Phase: 2nd Quarter
Waxing
Festivals: Gyro Night [Scot.]

Moon Sign: Taurus
Tarot Card: Page of Wands
Herb: Heather
Incense: Frankincense
Color: Red

12
Wednesday

Moon Phase: 2nd Quarter
Waxing
Moon enters Gemini 12:09 a.m.

Moon Sign: Taurus
Tarot Card: Knight of Wands
Herb: Heart Liverleaf
Incense: Sandalwood
Color: Purple

13
Thursday

Moon Phase: 2nd Quarter
Waxing
Festivals: Parentalia [Rom.] (first day)

Moon Sign: Gemini
Tarot Card: Queen of Wands
Herb: Virgin Mouse-ear
Incense: Myrrh
Color: Blue

14 *Friday*

Moon Phase: 2nd Quarter
          Waxing
Moon enters Cancer 3:32 a.m.
Festivals: Lupercalia Eve [Rom.]
          Valentine's Day

Moon Sign: Gemini
Tarot Card: King of Wands
Herb: Jimsonweed
Incense: Jasmine
Color: Green

15 *Saturday*

Moon Phase: 2nd Quarter
          Waxing
Festivals: Lupercalia [Rom.]

Moon Sign: Cancer
Tarot Card: Ace of Cups
Herb: Leek
Incense: Benzoin or Cedar
Color: Black

16 *Sunday*

Moon Phase: 2nd Quarter
          Waxing
Moon enters Leo 4:16 a.m.

Moon Sign: Cancer
Tarot Card: Two of Cups
Herb: Maindenhair
Incense: Pine
Color: Yellow

FEBRUARY

S	M	T	W	T	F	S
						1
2	3	4	5	6	7	8
9	10	11	12	13	14	15
16	17	18	19	20	21	22
23	24	25	26	27	28	29

17 *Monday*

Moon Phase: 2nd Quarter
             Waxing

Moon Sign: Leo
Tarot Card: Three of Cups
Herb: Mezereon
Incense: Cinnamon
Color: White

18 *Tuesday*

Moon Phase: Full Moon (Storm)
Moon enters Virgo 3:48 a.m.

Moon Sign: Leo
Tarot Card: Four of Cups
Herb: Water Mint
Incense: Frankincense
Color: Red

19 *Wednesday*

Moon Phase: 3rd Quarter
             Waning
Sun enters Pisces 3:45 a.m.

Moon Sign: Virgo
Tarot Card: Five of Cups
Herb: Mullein
Incense: Sandalwood
Color: Purple

20 *Thursday*

Moon Phase: 3rd Quarter
             Waning
Moon enters Libra 4:05 a.m.
Festivals: Seminole Powwow [SE Am.]—
             (first day)

Moon Sign: Virgo
Tarot Card: Six of Cups
Herb: Violet Bloom
Incense: Myrrh
Color: Blue

21

Friday

Moon Phase: 3rd Quarter
           Waning
Festivals: Parentalia—last day
           Festival of the Dead [Rom.]

Moon Sign: Libra
Tarot Card: Seven of Cups
Herb: Papaya
Incense: Jasmine
Color: Green

22

Saturday

Moon Phase: 3rd Quarter
           Waning
Moon enters Scorpio 7:12 a.m.
Festivals: Charistia [Rom.] (Goodwill)
           Seminole Powwow—last day

Moon Sign: Libra
Tarot Card: Eight of Cups
Herb: Pimpernel
Incense: Benzoin or Cedar
Color: Black

23

Sunday

Moon Phase: 3rd Quarter
           Waning

Moon Sign: Scorpio
Tarot Card: Nine of Cups
Herb: Winter Fern
Incense: Pine
Color: Yellow

FEBRUARY

S	M	T	W	T	F	S
						1
2	3	4	5	6	7	8
9	10	11	12	13	14	15
16	17	18	19	20	21	22
23	24	25	26	27	28	29

24 *Monday*

Moon Phase: 3rd Quarter
          Waning
Moon enters Sagittarius 2:27 p.m.
Festivals: St. Matthias's Day

Moon Sign: Scorpio
Tarot Card: Ten of Cups
Herb: Primrose
Incense: Cinnamon
Color: White

25 *Tuesday*

Moon Phase: 4th Quarter
          Waning

Moon Sign: Sagittarius
Tarot Card: Page of Cups
Herb: Ragwort
Incense: Frankincense
Color: Red

26 *Wednesday*

Moon Phase: 4th Quarter
          Waning

Moon Sign: Sagittarius
Tarot Card: Knight of Cups
Herb: Rockrose
Incense: Sandalwood
Color: Purple

27 *Thursday*

Moon Phase: 4th Quarter
          Waning
Moon enters Capricorn 1:34 a.m.

Moon Sign: Sagittarius
Tarot Card: Queen of Cups
Herb: Sarsaparilla
Incense: Myrrh
Color: Blue

28   *Friday*

Moon Phase: 4th Quarter
             Waning

Moon Sign: Capricorn
Tarot Card: King of Cups
Herb: Shinleaf
Incense: Jasmine
Color: Green

29   *Saturday*

Moon Phase: 4th Quarter
             Waning
Moon enters Aquarius 2:35 p.m.
Festivals: Job's Day
            Leap Year Day

Moon Sign: Carpricorn
Tarot Card: Ace of Pentacles
Herb: Star Anice
Incense: Benzoin or Cedar
Color: Black

1   *Sunday*

Moon Phase: 4th Quarter
             Waxing
Festivals: Matronalia [Rom.]
           Whuppity Stourie [Scot.]
           St. David's Day

Moon Sign: Aquarius
Tarot Card: Two of Pentacles
Herb: Wild Hyssop
Incense: Pine
Color: Yellow

MARCH

S	M	T	W	T	F	S
						1
1	2	3	4	5	6	7
8	9	10	11	12	13	14
15	16	17	18	19	20	21
22	23	24	25	26	27	28
29	30	31				

2　　*Monday*

Moon Phase: 4th Quarter
　　　　　Waning
Festivals: St. Chad's Day

Moon Sign: Aquarius
Tarot Card: Three of Pentacles
Herb: Althea
Incense: Cinnamon
Color: White

3　　*Tuesday*

Moon Phase:　4th Quarter
　　　　　Waning
Moon enters Pisces 3:12 a.m.
Festivals: Girls' Festival [Jap.]
　　　　St. Winnold's Day

Moon Sign: Aquarius
Tarot Card: Four of Pentacles
Herb: Barberry
Incense: Frankincense
Color: Red

4　　*Wednesday*

Moon Phase:　New Moon
Festivals: Ash Wednesday

Moon Sign: Pisces
Tarot Card: Five of Pentacles
Herb: Birthwort
Incense: Sandalwood
Color: Purple

5　　*Thursday*

Moon Phase:　1st Quarter
　　　　　Waxing
Moon enters Aries 2:08 p.m
Festivals: Ship of Isis [Egypt.]

Moon Sign: Pisces
Tarot Card: Six of Pentacles
Herb: Blue Flag
Incense: Myrrh
Color: Blue

6

Friday

Moon Phase: 1st Quarter
          Waxing
Festivals: Start of Flowering Time [Kelt.]

Moon Sign: Aries
Tarot Card: Seven of Pentacles
Herb: Buttercup
Incense: Jasmine
Color: Green

7

Saturday

Moon Phase: 1st Quarter
          Waxing
Moon enters Taurus 11:06 p.m.
Festivals: Junonalia [Rom.]

Moon Sign: Aries
Tarot Card: Eight of Pentacles
Herb: Celandine
Incense:Benzoin or Cedar
Color: Black

8

Sunday

Moon Phase: 1st Quarter
          Waxing

Moon Sign: Taurus
Tarot Card: Nine of Pentacles
Herb: Comfrey
Incense: Pine
Color: Yellow

MARCH

S	M	T	W	T	F	S
1	2	3	4	5	6	7
8	9	10	11	12	13	14
15	16	17	18	19	20	21
22	23	24	25	26	27	28
29	30	31				

9
Monday

Moon Phase: 1st Quarter
            Waxing
Festivals: Collop Monday [Brit.]

Moon Sign: Taurus
Tarot Card: Ten of Pentacles
Herb: Desert Tea
Incense: Cinnamon
Color: White

10
Tuesday

Moon Phase: 1st Quarter
            Waxing
Moon enters Gemini 6:04 a.m.
Festivals: Shrove Tuesday
        Nos Ynyd [Welsh]
        Favardigan [Pers.] (first day)

Moon Sign: Taurus
Tarot Card: Page of Pentacles
Herb: English Ivy
Incense: Frankincense
Color: Red

11
Wednesday

Moon Phase: 2nd Quarter
            Waxing
Festivals: Ash Wednesday
        Start of Marbles Season [Brit.]

Moon Sign: Gemini
Tarot Card: Knight of Pentacles
Herb: Feverfew
Incense: Sandalwood
Color: Purple

12
Thursday

Moon Phase: 2nd Quarter
            Waxing
Moon enters Cancer 10:51 a.m.
Festivals: Hypatia [Alex.]
        St. Gregory's Day

Moon Sign: Gemini
Tarot Card: Queen of Pentacles
Herb: Ginger
Incense: Myrrh
Color: Blue

13 *Friday*

Moon Phase: 2nd Quarter
Waxing
Festivals: Kissing Friday [Eng.]

Moon Sign: Cancer
Tarot Card: King of Pentacles
Herb: Hedge Bindweed
Incense: Jasmine
Color: Green

14 *Saturday*

Moon Phase: 2nd Quarter
Waxing
Moon enters Leo 1:21 p.m.

Moon Sign: Cancer
Tarot Card: The Magician
Herb: Herb Robert
Incense: Benzoin or Cedar
Color: Black

15 *Sunday*

Moon Phase: 2nd Quarter
Waxing
Festivals: Anna Perenna [Rom.]

Moon Sign: Leo
Tarot Card: High Priestess
Herb: Houseleek
Incense: Pine
Color: Yellow

MARCH

S	M	T	W	T	F	S
1	2	3	4	5	6	7
8	9	10	11	12	13	14
15	16	17	18	19	20	21
22	23	24	25	26	27	28
29	30	31				

16 *Monday*

Moon Phase: 2nd Quarter
             Waning
Moon enters Virgo 2:14 p.m.
Festivals: Sixth Gahambar [Zoroastrian]

Moon Sign: Leo
Tarot Card: The Empress
Herb: Juniper
Incense: Cinnamon
Color: White

17 *Tuesday*

Moon Phase: 2nd Quarter
             Waxing
Festivals: Liberlia [Rom.]
           Higan [Jap.] (first day)
           St. Patrick's Day

Moon Sign: Virgo
Tarot Card: The Emperor
Herb: Lemon
Incense: Frankincense
Color: Red

18 *Wednesday*

Moon Phase: Full Moon (Chaste)
Moon enters Libra 2:58 p.m.

Moon Sign: Virgo
Tarot Card: The Hierophant
Herb: Mallow
Incense: Sandalwood
Color: Purple

19 *Thursday*

Moon Phase: 3rd Quarter
             Waning
Festivals: Lesser Panathenea [Grk.]
           Minerva's Birthday [Rom.]
           St. Joseph's Day

Moon Sign: Libra
Tarot Card: The Lovers
Herb: Milfoil
Incense: Myrrh
Color: Blue

20 *Friday*

Moon Phase: 3rd Quarter
         Waning
Sun enters Aries 2:49 a.m.
Moon enters Scorpio 5:21 p.m.
Festivals: Vernal Equinox
         Persian New Year's Day
         Favardigan (last day)

Moon Sign: Libra
Tarot Card: The Chariot
Herb: Mistletoe
Incense: Jasmine
Color: Green

21 *Saturday*

Moon Phase: 3rd Quarter
         Waning

Moon Sign: Scorpio
Tarot Card: Justice
Herb: Shepherd's Club
Incense: Benzoin or Cedar
Color: Black

22 *Sunday*

Moon Phase: 3rd Quarter
         Waning
Moon enters Sagittarius 11:14 p.m.

Moon Sign: Scorpio
Tarot Card: The Hermit
Herb: Nutmeg
Incense: Pine
Color: Yellow

MARCH

S	M	T	W	T	F	S
	1	2	3	4	5	6	7
8	9	10	11	12	13	14
15	16	17	18	19	20	21
22	23	24	25	26	27	28
29	30	31				

23
Monday

Moon Phase: 3rd Quarter
           Waning
Festivals: Higan (last day)

Moon Sign: Sagittarius
Tarot Card: Wheel of Fortune
Herb: Pawpaw
Incense: Cinnamon
Color: White

24
Tuesday

Moon Phase: 3rd Quarter
              Waning
Festivals: St. Gabriel's Day

Moon Sign: Sagittarius
Tarot Card: Strength
Herb: Pinkroot
Incense: Frankincense
Color: Red

25
Wednesday

Moon Phase: 4th Quarter
              Waning
Moon enters Capricorn 9:09 a.m.
Festivals: Annunciacion
           Festival of Joy
           Lady Day
           Old New Year's Day [Eng.]

Moon Sign: Sagittarius
Tarot Card: The Hanged Man
Herb: Poison Parsley
Incense: Sandalwood
Color: Purple

26
Thursday

Moon Phase: 4th Quarter
              Waning
Festivals: Fercula

Moon Sign: Capricorn
Tarot Card: Death
Herb: Privet
Incense: Myrrh
Color: Blue

27　　　　　　　　　　　　　　　　*Friday*

Moon Phase:　4th Quarter
　　　　　　　Waning
Moon enters Aquarius 9:45 p.m.

Moon Sign: Capricorn
Tarot Card: Temperance
Herb: Cocash Weed
Incense: Jasmine
Color: Green

28　　　　　　　　　　　　　　　*Saturday*

Moon Phase:　4th Quarter
　　　　　　　Waning

Moon Sign: Aquarius
Tarot Card: The Devil
Herb: Rosemary
Incense: Benzoin or Cedar
Color: Black

29　　　　　　　　　　　　　　　　*Sunday*

Moon Phase:　4th Quarter
　　　　　　　Waning
Festivals: First of the Borrowing Days
　　　　　　　[Brit.]

Moon Sign: Aquarius
Tarot Card: The Tower
Herb: Sassafras
Incense: Pine
Color: Yellow

MARCH						
S	M	T	W	T	F	S
1	2	3	4	5	6	7
8	9	10	11	12	13	14
15	16	17	18	19	20	21
22	23	24	25	26	27	28
29	30	31				

30   *Monday*

Moon Phase: 4th Quarter
         Waning
Moon enters Pisces 10:24 a.m.

Moon Sign: Aquarius
Tarot Card: The Star
Herb: Skullcap
Incense: Cinnamon
Color: White

31   *Tuesday*

Moon Phase: 4th Quarter
         Waning
Festivals: Oranges and Lemons [Eng.]
         Last of the Borrowing Days

Moon Sign: Pisces
Tarot Card: The Moon
Herb: Sticklewort
Incense: Frankincense
Color: Red

1   *Wednesday*

Moon Phase: 4th Quarter
         Waning
Moon enters Aries 9:05 p.m.
Festivals: All Fool's Day
         Ceres [Rom.]
         Huli Festival

Moon Sign: Pisces
Tarot Card: The Sun
Herb: Wax Myrtle
Incense: Sandalwood
Color: Purple

2   *Thursday*

Moon Phase: New Moon
Festivals: Taily Day [Scot.]
         No Ruz—Zoroastrian
         New Year
         St. Urban's Day

Moon Sign: Aries
Tarot Card: Judgement
Herb: Amaranth
Incense: Myrrh
Color: Blue

3
Friday

Moon Phase: 1st Quarter
Waxing
Moon enters Taurus 5:19 a.m.

Moon Sign: Aries
Tarot Card: The World
Herb: Basil
Incense: Jasmine
Color: Green

4
Saturday

Moon Phase: 1st Quarter
Waxing
Festivals: Megalesia [Phryg.] (first day)
Festival of the Great Mother
[Rom.]

Moon Sign: Taurus
Tarot Card: The Fool
Herb: Bistort
Incense:Benzoin or Cedar
Color: Black

5
Sunday

Moon Phase: 1st Quarter
Waxing

Moon Sign: Taurus
Tarot Card: Ace of Swords
Herb: Blue Vervain
Incense: Pine
Color: Yellow

APRIL

S	M	T	W	T	F	S
			1	2	3	4
5	6	7	8	9	10	11
12	13	14	15	16	17	18
19	20	21	22	23	24	25
26	27	28	29	30		

6 *Monday*

Moon Phase: 1st Quarter
Waxing
Moon enters Gemini 11:34 a.m.

Moon Sign: Taurus
Tarot Card: Two of Swords
Herb: Calendula
Incense: Cinnamon
Color: White

7 *Tuesday*

Moon Phase: 1st Quarter
Waxing

Moon Sign: Gemini
Tarot Card: Three of Swords
Herb: Celery
Incense: Frankincense
Color: Red

8 *Wednesday*

Moon Phase: 1st Quarter
Waxing
Moon enters Cancer 4:19 p.m.
Festivals: Hana Matsuri [Jap.]

Moon Sign: Gemini
Tarot Card: Four of Swords
Herb: Coralroot
Incense: Sandalwood
Color: Purple

9 *Thursday*

Moon Phase: 1st Quarter
Waxing

Moon Sign: Cancer
Tarot Card: Five of Swords
Herb: Majuang
Incense: Myrrh
Color: Blue

10   *Friday*

Moon Phase: 2nd Quarter
           Waxing
Moon enters Leo 7:47 p.m.
Festivals: Megalesia (last day)

Moon Sign: Cancer
Tarot Card: Six of Swords
Herb: Ergot
Incense: Jasmine
Color: Green

11   *Saturday*

Moon Phase: 2nd Quarter
           Waxing

Moon Sign: Leo
Tarot Card: Seven of Swords
Herb: Feverweed
Incense: Benzoin or Cedar
Color: Black

12   *Sunday*

Moon Phase: 2nd Quarter
           Waxing
Moon enters Virgo 10:10 p.m.
Festivals: Cerealia [Rom.] (first day)
           Palm Sunday

Moon Sign: Leo
Tarot Card: Eight of Swords
Herb: Ginseng
Incense: Pine
Color: Yellow

APRIL

S	M	T	W	T	F	S
			1	2	3	4
5	6	7	8	9	10	11
12	13	14	15	16	17	18
19	20	21	22	23	24	25
26	27	28	29	30		

13 Monday

Moon Phase: 2nd Quarter
Waxing
Festivals: Vaisakhi [Sikh]

Moon Sign: Virgo
Tarot Card: Nine of Swords
Herb: Hedge Garlic
Incense: Cinnamon
Color: White

14 Tuesday

Moon Phase: 2nd Quarter
Waxing

Moon Sign: Virgo
Tarot Card: Ten of Swords
Herb: Hibiscus
Incense: Frankincense
Color: Red

15 Wednesday

Moon Phase: 2nd Quarter
Waxing
Moon enters Libra 12:11 a.m.

Moon Sign: Virgo
Tarot Card: Page of Swords
Herb: Hyssop
Incense: Sandalwood
Color: Purple

16 Thursday

Moon Phase: Full Moon (Seed)

Moon Sign: Libra
Tarot Card: Knight of Swords
Herb: Khus-khus
Incense: Myrrh
Color: Blue

17 *Friday*

Moon Phase: 3rd Quarter
            Waning
Moon enters Scorpio 3:11 a.m.
Festivals: Good Friday
        End of Marbles Season [Brit.]

Moon Sign: Libra
Tarot Card: Queen of Swords
Herb: Lettuce
Incense: Jasmine
Color: Green

18 *Saturday*

Moon Phase: 3rd Quarter
            Waning

Moon Sign: Scorpio
Tarot Card: King of Swords
Herb: Mandrake
Incense: Benzoin or Cedar
Color: Black

19 *Sunday*

Moon Phase: 3rd Quarter
            Waning
Sun enters Taurus 1:58 p.m.
Moon enters Sagittarius 8:41 a.m.
Festivals: Easter Sunday
        Cerealia (last day)

Moon Sign: Scorpio
Tarot Card: Ace of Wands
Herb: Milk Thistle
Incense: Pine
Color: Yellow

APRIL

S	M	T	W	T	F	S
			1	2	3	4
5	6	7	8	9	10	11
12	13	14	15	16	17	18
19	20	21	22	23	24	25
26	27	28	29	30		

20 *Monday*

Moon Phase: 3rd Quarter
    Waning
Festivals: Egg Rolling [Brit.]
   Yaqui Pageant [SW Am.]

Moon Sign: Sagittarius
Tarot Card: Two of Wands
Herb: Golden Bough
Incense: Cinnamon
Color: White

21 *Tuesday*

Moon Phase: 3rd Quarter
    Waning
Moon enters Capricorn at 5:41 p.m.

Moon Sign: Sagittarius
Tarot Card: Three of Wands
Herb: Velvet Dock
Incense: Frankincense
Color: Red

22 *Wednesday*

Moon Phase: 3rd Quarter
    Waning

Moon Sign: Capricorn
Tarot Card: Four of Wands
Herb: White Oak
Incense: Sandalwood
Color: Purple

23 *Thursday*

Moon Phase: 3rd Quarter
    Waning
Festivals: St. George's Day [Eng.]
   San Jorge Feast Day
   Shakespeare Day [Eng.]

Moon Sign: Capricorn
Tarot Card: Five of Wands
Herb: Parsley
Incense: Myrrh
Color: Blue

24
Friday

Moon Phase: 4th Quarter
Waning
Moon enters Aquarius 5:39 a.m.

Moon Sign: Capricorn
Tarot Card: Six of Wands
Herb: Pipissewa
Incense: Jasmine
Color: Green

25
Saturday

Moon Phase: 4th Quarter
Waning
Festivals: St. Mark's Day

Moon Sign: Aquarius
Tarot Card: Seven of Wands
Herb: Pokeweed
Incense: Benzoin or Cedar
Color: Black

26
Sunday

Moon Phase: 4th Quarter
Waning
Moon enters Pisces 6:21 p.m.

Moon Sign: Aquarius
Tarot Card: Eight of Wands
Herb: Primwort
Incense: Pine
Color: Yellow

APRIL

S	M	T	W	T	F	S
			1	2	3	4
5	6	7	8	9	10	11
12	13	14	15	16	17	18
19	20	21	22	23	24	25
26	27	28	29	30		

27   *Monday*

Moon Phase: 4th Quarter
           Waning
Festivals: Hocktide [Eng.]

Moon Sign: Pisces
Tarot Card: Nine of Wands
Herb: Life Root
Incense: Cinnamon
Color: White

28   *Tuesday*

Moon Phase: 4th Quarter
           Waning
Festivals: Hochtide [Eng.]
           Floralia [Rom.] (first day)

Moon Sign: Pisces
Tarot Card: Ten of Wands
Herb: Rowan
Incense: Frankincense
Color: Red

29   *Wednesday*

Moon Phase: 4th Quarter
           Waning
Moon enters Aries 5:14 a.m.

Moon Sign: Pisces
Tarot Card: Page of Wands
Herb: Savory
Incense: Sandalwood
Color: Purple

30   *Thursday*

Moon Phase: 4th Quarter
           Waning
Festivals: Laurentialia
          Oidhche Bhealtaine [Kelt.]—
          Beltane Eve.
          Walpurgisnacht [Ger.]
          First Gahambar [Zoroastrian]

Moon Sign: Aries
Tarot Card: Knight of Wands
Herb: Skunk Cabbage
Incense: Myrrh
Color: Blue

1 *Friday*

Moon Phase: 4th Quarter
Waning
Moon enters Taurus 1:10 p.m.
Festivals: Beltane/Caedamh [Kelt.]
May Day/Maid Marian Day
[Eng.]
Bona Dea [Rom.]
Fire Festival

Moon Sign: Aries
Tarot Card: Queen of Wands
Herb: Queen's Root
Incense: Jasmine
Color: Green

2 *Saturday*

Moon Phase: New Moon

Moon Sign: Taurus
Tarot Card: King of Wands
Herb: Centaury
Incense: Benzoin or Cedar
Color: Black

3 *Sunday*

Moon Phase: 1st Quarter
Waxing
Moon enters Gemini 6:29 p.m.
Festivals: Floralia (last day)
Corn Festival [SW Am.]

Moon Sign: Taurus
Tarot Card: Ace of Cups
Herb: Bearberry
Incense: Pine
Color: Yellow

MAY

S	M	T	W	T	F	S
					1	2
3	4	5	6	7	8	9
10	11	12	13	14	15	16
17	18	19	20	21	22	23
24	25	26	27	28	29	30
31						

4

Moon Phase: 1st Quarter
            Waxing

Moon Sign: Gemini
Tarot Card: Two of Cups
Herb: Black Alder
Incense: Cinnamon
Color: White

5

Moon Phase: 1st Quarter
            Waxing
Moon enters Cancer 10:11 p.m.

Moon Sign: Gemini
Tarot Card: Three of Cups
Herb: Boneset
Incense: Frankincense
Color: Red

6

Moon Phase: 1st Quarter
            Wxning

Moon Sign: Cancer
Tarot Card: Four of Cups
Herb: Chamomile
Incense: Sandalwood
Color: Purple

7

Moon Phase: 1st Quarter
            Waxing

Moon Sign: Cancer
Tarot Card: Five of Cups
Herb: Chervil
Incense: Myrrh
Color: Blue

8 — *Friday*

Moon Phase: 1st Quarter
　　　　Waxing
Moon enters Leo 1:08 a.m.
Festivals: Furry Dance [Eng.]
　　　　Robin Hood May Games [Eng.]

Moon Sign: Cancer
Tarot Card: Six of Cups
Herb: Coriander
Incense: Jasmine
Color: Green

9 — *Saturday*

Moon Phase: 2nd Quarter
　　　　Waxing
Festivals: Lémuria [Rom.] (first day)

Moon Sign: Leo
Tarot Card: Seven of Cups
Herb: Dill
Incense: Benzoin or Cedar
Color: Black

10 — *Sunday*

Moon Phase: 2nd Quarter
　　　　Waxing
Moon enters Virgo 3:57 a.m.

Moon Sign: Leo
Tarot Card: Eight of Cups
Herb: Eucalyptus
Incense: Pine
Color: Yellow

MAY

S	M	T	W	T	F	S
					1	2
3	4	5	6	7	8	9
10	11	12	13	14	15	16
17	18	19	20	21	22	23
24	25	26	27	28	29	30
31						

11   *Monday*

Moon Phase: 2nd Quarter
            Waxing

Moon Sign: Virgo
Tarot Card: Nine of Cups
Herb: Figwort
Incense: Cinnamon
Color: White

12   *Tuesday*

Moon Phase: 2nd Quarter
            Waxing
Moon enters Libra 7:06 a.m.
Festivals: St. Pancrass Day

Moon Sign: Virgo
Tarot Card: Ten of Cups
Herb: Goat's Rue
Incense: Frankincense
Color: Red

13   *Wednesday*

Moon Phase: 2nd Quarter
            Waxing
Festivals: Garland Day [Brit.]

Moon Sign: Libra
Tarot Card: Page of Cups
Herb: Hedge Hyssop
Incense: Sandalwood
Color: Purple

14   *Thursday*

Moon Phase: 2nd Quarter
            Waxing
Moon enters Scorpio 11:16 a.m.

Moon Sign: Libra
Tarot Card: Knight of Cups
Herb: Musk Mallow
Incense: Myrrh
Color: Blue

15
Friday

Moon Phase: 2nd Quarter
                    Waxing

Moon Sign: Scorpio
Tarot Card: Queen of Cups
Herb: Iceland Moss
Incense: Jasmine
Color: Green

16
Saturday

Moon Phase: Full Moon (Hare)
Moon enters Sagittarius 5:23 p.m.

Moon Sign: Scorpio
Tarot Card: King of Cups
Herb: Kidney Vetch
Incense: Benzoin or Cedar
Color: Black

17
Sunday

Moon Phase: 3rd Quarter
                    Waning
Festivals: Start of Ripening Time [Kelt.]

Moon Sign: Sagittarius
Tarot Card: Ace of Pentacles
Herb: Licorice
Incense: Pine
Color: Yellow

MAY

S	M	T	W	T	F	S
					1	2
3	4	5	6	7	8	9
10	11	12	13	14	15	16
17	18	19	20	21	22	23
24	25	26	27	28	29	30
31						

18   *Monday*

Moon Phase: 3rd Quarter
         Waning

Moon Sign: Sagittarius
Tarot Card: Two of Pentacles
Herb: Marjoram
Incense: Cinnamon
Color: White

19   *Tuesday*

Moon Phase: 3rd Quarter
         Waning
Moon enters Capricorn 2:13 a.m.

Moon Sign: Sagittarius
Tarot Card: Three of Pentacles
Herb: Milkweed
Incense: Frankincense
Color: Red

20   *Wednesday*

Moon Phase: 3rd Quarter
         Waning
Sun enters Gemini 1:13 p.m.
Festivals: Okinaga-Tarashi-Hime [Jap.]

Moon Sign: Capricorn
Tarot Card: Four of Pentacles
Herb: All-heal
Incense: Sandalwood
Color: Purple

21   *Thursday*

Moon Phase: 3rd Quarter
         Waning
Moon enters Aquarius 1:44 p.m.

Moon Sign: Capricorn
Tarot Card: Five of Pentacles
Herb: Candlewick
Incense: Myrrh
Color: Blue

22   *Friday*

Moon Phase: 3rd Quarter
             Waning

Moon Sign: Aquarius
Tarot Card: Six of Pentacles
Herb: Red Oak
Incense: Jasmine
Color: Green

23   *Saturday*

Moon Phase: 3rd Quarter
             Waning
Festivals: Rosalia [Rom.]

Moon Sign: Aquarius
Tarot Card: Seven of Pentacles
Herb: Pasque Flower
Incense: Benzoin or Cedar
Color: Black

24   *Sunday*

Moon Phase: 4th Quarter
             Waning
Moon enters Pisces 2:26 a.m.
Festivals: Les-Saintes-Maries-de-la-Mer
           [Romany]

Moon Sign: Aquarius
Tarot Card: Eight of Pentacles
Herb: Wintergreen
Incense: Pine
Color: Yellow

MAY

S	M	T	W	T	F	S
					1	2
3	4	5	6	7	8	9
10	11	12	13	14	15	16
17	18	19	20	21	22	23
24	25	26	27	28	29	30
31						

25 *Monday*

Moon Phase: 4th Quarter
          Waning
Festivals: Rogationtide/Beating the
          Bounds [Eng.]
          Anthea's Day

Moon Sign: Pisces
Tarot Card: Nine of Pentacles
Herb: Pomegranate
Incense: Cinnamon
Color: White

26 *Tuesday*

Moon Phase: 4th Quarter
          Waning
Moon enters Aries 1:53 p.m.

Moon Sign: Pisces
Tarot Card: Ten of Pentacles
Herb: Quassia
Incense: Frankincense
Color: Red

27 *Wednesday*

Moon Phase: 4th Quarter
          Waning

Moon Sign: Aries
Tarot Card: Page of Pentacles
Herb: Raspberry
Incense: Sandalwood
Color: Purple

28 *Thursday*

Moon Phase: 4th Quarter
          Waning
Moon enters Taurus 10:17 p.m.
Festivals: Holy Thursday/Ascension Day
          Wicken Love Feast [Eng.]

Moon Sign: Aries
Tarot Card: Knight of Pentacles
Herb: Mountain Ash
Incense: Myrrh
Color: Blue

29   *Friday*

Moon Phase: 4th Quarter
         Waning
Festivals: Arbor Day [Eng.]
        Ambarvalia [Rom.]
        Oak Apple Day [Eng.]

Moon Sign: Taurus
Tarot Card: Queen of Pentacles
Herb: Saw Palmetto
Incense: Jasmine
Color: Green

30   *Saturday*

Moon Phase: 4th Quarter
         Waning

Moon Sign: Taurus
Tarot Card: King of Pentacles
Herb: Soapwort
Incense: Benzoin or Cedar
Color: Black

31   *Sunday*

Moon Phase: New Moon
Moon enters Gemini 3:20 a.m.
Festivals: Secula Games[Rom.] (first day)

Moon Sign: Taurus
Tarot Card: The Magician
Herb: Hardhack
Incense: Pine
Color: Yellow

			MAY			
S	M	T	W	T	F	S
					1	2
3	4	5	6	7	8	9
10	11	12	13	14	15	16
17	18	19	20	21	22	23
24	25	26	27	28	29	30
31						

1
Monday

Moon Phase: 1st Quarter
          Waxing
Festivals: Carna [Rom.]

Moon Sign: Gemini
Tarot Card: High Priestess
Herb: Bitter Ash
Incense: Cinnamon
Color: White

2
Tuesday

Moon Phase: 1st Quarter
          Waxing
Moon enters Cancer 5:59 a.m.
Festivals: St. Elmo's Day

Moon Sign: Gemini
Tarot Card: The Empress
Herb: Hellebore
Incense: Frankincense
Color: Red

3
Wednesday

Moon Phase: 1st Quarter
          Waxing

Moon Sign: Cancer
Tarot Card: The Emperor
Herb: Bearded Darnel
Incense: Sandalwood
Color: Purple

4
Thursday

Moon Phase: 1st Quarter
          Waxing
Moon enters Leo 7:36 a.m.

Moon Sign: Cancer
Tarot Card: The Hierophant
Herb: Red Alder
Incense: Myrrh
Color: Blue

5
Friday

Moon Phase: 1st Quarter
Waxing
Festivals: Domnu/Sheela-na-Gig [Ir.]

Moon Sign: Leo
Tarot Card: The Lovers
Herb: Borage
Incense: Jasmine
Color: Green

6
Saturday

Moon Phase: 1st Quarter
Waxing
Moon enters Virgo 9:29 a.m.

Moon Sign: Leo
Tarot Card: The Chariot
Herb: Cannabis
Incense: Benzoin or Cedar
Color: Black

7
Sunday

Moon Phase: 2nd Quarter
Waxing

Moon Sign: Virgo
Tarot Card: Justice
Herb: Chickweed
Incense: Pine
Color: Yellow

JUNE

S	M	T	W	T	F	S
	1	2	3	4	5	6
7	8	9	10	11	12	13
14	15	16	17	18	19	20
21	22	23	24	25	26	27
28	29	30				

8 *Monday*

Moon Phase: 2nd Quarter
            Waxing
Moon enters Libra 12:34 p.m.

Moon Sign: Virgo
Tarot Card: The Hermit
Herb: Cornflower
Incense: Cinnamon
Color: White

9 *Tuesday*

Moon Phase: 2nd Quarter
            Waxing
Festivals: Vestalia [Rom.]
           St. Columba's Day

Moon Sign: Libra
Tarot Card: Wheel of Fortune
Herb: Dogbane
Incense: Frankincense
Color: Red

10 *Wednesday*

Moon Phase: 2nd Quarter
            Waxing
Moon enters Scorpio 5:28 p.m.
Festivals: Appleby Horse Fair
           [Eng. Romany]

Moon Sign: Libra
Tarot Card: Strength
Herb: European Centaury
Incense: Sandalwood
Color: Purple

11 *Thursday*

Moon Phase: 2nd Quarter
            Waxing
Festivals: St. Barnabas's Day

Moon Sign: Scorpio
Tarot Card: The Hanged Man
Herb: Flax
Incense: Myrrh
Color: Blue

12

Friday

Moon Phase: 2nd Quarter
            Waxing

Moon Sign: Scorpio
Tarot Card: Death
Herb: Goldenrod
Incense: Jasmine
Color: Green

13

Saturday

Moon Phase: 2nd Quarter
            Waxing
Moon enters Sagittarius 12:30 a.m.
Festivals: Tibetan All Soul's Day
           San Antonio de Padua

Moon Sign: Scorpio
Tarot Card: Temperance
Herb: Hedge Mustard
Incense: Benzoin or Cedar
Color: Black

14

Sunday

Moon Phase: Full Moon (Dyad)
            Lunar Eclipse

Moon Sign: Sagittarius
Tarot Card: The Devil
Herb: Holly
Incense: Pine
Color: Yellow

JUNE

S	M	T	W	T	F	S
		1	2	3	4	5	6
7	8	9	10	11	12	13
14	15	16	17	18	19	20
21	22	23	24	25	26	27
28	29	30				

15   *Monday*

Moon Phase: 3rd Quarter
            Waning
Moon enters Capricorn 9:51 a.m.
Festivals: St. Vitus's Day
           Apache Ceremonials start
           [SW Am.]

Moon Sign: Sagittarius
Tarot Card: The Tower
Herb: Imperial Masterwort
Incense: Cinnamon
Color: White

16   *Tuesday*

Moon Phase: 3rd Quarter
             Waning

Moon Sign: Capricorn
Tarot Card: The Star
Herb: Knotweed
Incense: Frankincense
Color: Red

17   *Wednesday*

Moon Phase: 3rd Quarter
             Waning
Moon enters Aquarius 9:20 p.m.

Moon Sign: Capricorn
Tarot Card: The Moon
Herb: Linden
Incense: Sandalwood
Color: Purple

18   *Thursday*

Moon Phase: 3rd Quarter
             Waning

Moon Sign: Aquarius
Tarot Card: The Sun
Herb: Marsh Tea
Incense: Myrrh
Color: Blue

19   *Friday*

Moon Phase: 3rd Quarter   Moon Sign: Aquarius
            Waning   Tarot Card: Judgement
Festivals: Waa-laa [NW Am] (first day)   Herb: Milkwort
                                   Incense: Jasmine
                                   Color: Green

20   *Saturday*

Moon Phase: 3rd Quarter   Moon Sign: Aquarius
            Waning   Tarot Card: The World
Sun enters Cancer 9:15 p.m.   Herb: Monarda
Moon enters Pisces 10:01 a.m.   Incense: Benzoin or Cedar
Festivals: Summer Solstice   Color: Black

21   *Sunday*

Moon Phase: 3rd Quarter   Moon Sign: Pisces
            Waning   Tarot Card: The Fool
Festivals: Feast of San Aloisio   Herb: Feltwort
            Waa-laa (last day)   Incense: Pine
                                   Color: Yellow

JUNE

S	M	T	W	T	F	S
	1	2	3	4	5	6
7	8	9	10	11	12	13
14	15	16	17	18	19	20
21	22	23	24	25	26	27
28	29	30				

22
Monday

Moon Phase: 3rd Quarter
          Waning
Moon enters Aries 10:04 p.m.

Moon Sign: Pisces
Tarot Card: Ace of Swords
Herb: Black Oak
Incense: Cinnamon
Color: White

23
Tuesday

Moon Phase: 4th Quarter
          Waning
Festivals: Midsummer Eve
          Ishtar [Bab.]
          Noche de San Juan Bautista
          Fire Festival

Moon Sign: Aries
Tarot Card: Two of Swords
Herb: Passion Flower
Incense: Frankincense
Color: Red

24
Wednesday

Moon Phase: 4th Quarter
          Waning
Festivals: Midsummer Day
          Neith and Isis [Egypt.]
          Midsummer Bride [Scan.]

Moon Sign: Aries
Tarot Card: Three of Swords
Herb: Pitcher Plant
Incense: Sandalwood
Color: Purple

25
Thursday

Moon Phase: 4th Quarter
          Waning
Moon enters Taurus 7:29 a.m.
Festivals: Well-Dressing [Brit.]

Moon Sign: Aries
Tarot Card: Four of Swords
Herb: Quaking Aspen
Incense: Myrrh
Color: Blue

26
Friday

Moon Phase: 4th Quarter
Waning

Moon Sign: Taurus
Tarot Card: Five of Swords
Herb: Bitter Ash
Incense: Jasmine
Color: Green

27
Saturday

Moon Phase: 4th Quarter
Waning
Moon enters Gemini 1:15 p.m.

Moon Sign: Taurus
Tarot Card: Six of Swords
Herb: Rattlesnake Plantain
Incense: Benzoin or Cedar
Color: Black

28
Sunday

Moon Phase: 4th Quarter
Waning

Moon Sign: Gemini
Tarot Card: Seven of Swords
Herb: Rue
Incense: Pine
Color: Yellow

JUNE

S	M	T	W	T	F	S
	1	2	3	4	5	6
7	8	9	10	11	12	13
14	15	16	17	18	19	20
21	22	23	24	25	26	27
28	29	30				

29 *Monday*

Moon Phase: 4th Quarter
          Waning
Moon enters Cancer 3:43 p.m.
Festivals: Second Gahambar [Zoroastrian]
          Rush Bearing [Eng.]
          St Peter's Day

Moon Sign: Gemini
Tarot Card: Eight of Swords
Herb: Scotch Broom
Incense: Cinnamon
Color: White

30 *Tuesday*

Moon Phase: New Moon

Moon Sign: Cancer
Tarot Card: Nine of Swords
Herb: Solomon's Seal
Incense: Frankincense
Color: Red

1 *Wednesday*

Moon Phase: 1st Quarter
          Waxing
Moon enters Leo 4:16 p.m.

Moon Sign: Cancer
Tarot Card: Ten of Swords
Herb: Woundwort
Incense: Sandalwood
Color: Purple

2 *Thursday*

Moon Phase: 1st Quarter
          Waxing

Moon Sign: Leo
Tarot Card: Page of Swords
Herb: Ivy
Incense: Myrrh
Color: Blue

3 *Friday*

Moon Phase: 1st Quarter
Waxing
Moon enters Virgo 4:30 p.m.
Festivals: Dog Days begin
Sothis [Egypt.]
Canicula [Rom.]

Moon Sign: Leo
Tarot Card: Knight of Swords
Herb: Bear's Garlic
Incense: Jasmine
Color: Green

4 *Saturday*

Moon Phase: 1st Quarter
Waxing
Festivals: Old Midsummer Eve
Waterfall Ceremony [SW Am]
Powwow [NW Am]

Moon Sign: Virgo
Tarot Card: Queen of Swords
Herb: Smooth Alder
Incense: Benzoin or Cedar
Color: Black

5 *Sunday*

Moon Phase: 1st Quarter
Waxing
Moon enters Libra 6:28 p.m.
Festivals: Old Midsummer Day
Manx Tynwald

Moon Sign: Virgo
Tarot Card: King of Swords
Herb: Boxwood
Incense: Pine
Color: Yellow

JULY

S	M	T	W	T	F	S
			1	2	3	4
5	6	7	8	9	10	11
12	13	14	15	16	17	18
19	20	21	22	23	24	25
26	27	28	29	30	31	

6 — *Monday*

Moon Phase: 2nd Quarter
                        Waxing

Moon Sign: Libra
Tarot Card: Ace of Wands
Herb: Caraway
Incense: Cinnamon
Color: White

7 — *Tuesday*

Moon Phase: 2nd Quarter
                      Waxing
Moon enters Scorpip 10:54 p.m.
Festivals: Tanabata [Jap.]
                  Chih-Nu [Chin.]

Moon Sign: Libra
Tarot Card: Two of Wands
Herb: Chicory
Incense: Frankincense
Color: Red

8 — *Wednesday*

Moon Phase: 2nd Quarter
                      Waxing

Moon Sign: Scorpio
Tarot Card: Three of Wands
Herb: Corydalis
Incense: Sandalwood
Color: Purple

9 — *Thursday*

Moon Phase: 2nd Quarter
                      Waxing

Moon Sign: Scorpio
Tarot Card: Four of Wands
Herb: Dog Poison
Incense: Myrrh
Color: Blue

10
Friday

Moon Phase: 2nd Quarter
          Waxing
Moon enters Sagittarius 6:18 a.m.

Moon Sign: Scorpio
Tarot Card: Five of Wands
Herb: European Vervain
Incense: Jasmine
Color: Green

11
Saturday

Moon Phase: 2nd Quarter
          Waxing

Moon Sign: Sagittarius
Tarot Card: Six of Wands
Herb: Foxglove
Incense: Benzoin or Cedar
Color: Black

12
Sunday

Moon Phase: 2nd Quarter
          Waxing
Moon enters Capricorn 4:16 p.m.

Moon Sign: Sagittarius
Tarot Card: Seven of Wands
Herb: Golden Seal
Incense: Pine
Color: Yellow

JULY

S	M	T	W	T	F	S
			1	2	3	4
5	6	7	8	9	10	11
12	13	14	15	16	17	18
19	20	21	22	23	24	25
26	27	28	29	30	31	

13

Moon Phase: 2nd Quarter
        Waxing
Festivals: Bon [Jap.]—Feast of Lanterns

Moon Sign: Capricorn
Tarot Card: Eight of Wands
Herb: Hellebore
Incense: Cinnamon
Color: White

14

Moon Phase: Full Moon (Mead)

Moon Sign: Capricorn
Tarot Card: Nine of Wands
Herb: Hollyhock
Incense: Frankincense
Color: Red

15

Moon Phase: 3rd Quarter
        Waning
Moon enters Aquarius 4:04 a.m.
Festivals: St. Swithin's Day

Moon Sign: Capricorn
Tarot Card: Ten of Wands
Herb: Indian Corn
Incense: Sandalwood
Color: Purple

16

Moon Phase: 3rd Quarter
        Waning

Moon Sign: Aquarius
Tarot Card: Page of Wands
Herb: Kola
Incense: Myrrh
Color: Blue

17 — *Friday*

Moon Phase: 3rd Quarter
Waning
Moon enters Pisces 4:45 p.m.
Festivals: Ama-Terasu-O-Mi-Kami
[Jap.]—Sun Goddess

Moon Sign: Aquarius
Tarot Card: Knight of Wands
Herb: Lion's Foot
Incense: Jasmine
Color: Green

18 — *Saturday*

Moon Phase: 3rd Quarter
Waning

Moon Sign: Pisces
Tarot Card: Queen of Wands
Herb: Masterwort
Incense: Benzoin or Cedar
Color: Black

19 — *Sunday*

Moon Phase: 3rd Quarter
Waning
Festivals: Opet [Egypt.]

Moon Sign: Pisces
Tarot Card: King of Wands
Herb: Mint
Incense: Pine
Color: Yellow

JULY

S	M	T	W	T	F	S
			1	2	3	4
5	6	7	8	9	10	11
12	13	14	15	16	17	18
19	20	21	22	23	24	25
26	27	28	29	30	31	

20
Monday

Moon Phase: 3rd Quarter
Waning
Moon enters Aries 12:45 a.m.
Festivals: St. Wilgefortis's Day

Moon Sign: Pisces
Tarot Card: Ace of Cups
Herb: Mountain Balm
Incense: Cinnamon
Color: White

21
Tuesday

Moon Phase: 3rd Quarter
Waning

Moon Sign: Aries
Tarot Card: Two of Cups
Herb: Mustard
Incense: Frankincense
Color: Red

22
Wednesday

Moon Phase: 4th Quarter
Waning
Sun enters Leo 8:10 a.m.
Moon enters Taurus 3:37 p.m.
Festivals: St. Mary Magdalen's Day
Choctaw Festival [SE Am]
(first day)

Moon Sign: Aries
Tarot Card: Three of Cups
Herb: Oat
Incense: Sandalwood
Color: Purple

23
Thursday

Moon Phase: 4th Quarter
Waning
Festivals: Star of Isis [Egypt.]

Moon Sign: Taurus
Tarot Card: Four of Cups
Herb: Pennyroyal
Incense: Myrrh
Color: Blue

1992 *July* 1992

24   *Friday*

Moon Phase: 4th Quarter
        Waning
Moon enters Gemini 10:45 p.m.

Moon Sign: Taurus
Tarot Card: Five of Cups
Herb: Plantain
Incense: Jasmine
Color: Green

25   *Saturday*

Moon Phase: 4th Quarter
        Waning
Festivals: Furrinalia [Rom.]
       Horn Fair [Eng.]
       Corn Dance [SW Am]
       Choctaw Festival (last day)

Moon Sign: Gemini
Tarot Card: Six of Cups
Herb: Tacamahac
Incense: Benzoin or Cedar
Color: Black

26   *Sunday*

Moon Phase: 4th Quarter
        Waning
Festivals: St. Anne's Day

Moon Sign: Gemini
Tarot Card: Seven of Cups
Herb: Bitter Wood
Incense: Pine
Color: Yellow

JULY

S	M	T	W	T	F	S
			1	2	3	4
5	6	7	8	9	10	11
12	13	14	15	16	17	18
19	20	21	22	23	24	25
26	27	28	29	30	31	

27   *Monday*

Moon Phase: 4th Quarter
             Waning
Moon enters Cancer 2:09 a.m.
Festivals: Hatshepsut [Egypt.]
           Swan-Upping [Eng.]

Moon Sign: Gemini
Tarot Card: Eight of Cups
Herb: Adder's Violet
Incense: Cinnamon
Color: White

28   *Tuesday*

Moon Phase: 4th Quarter
             Waning
Festivals: Start of Gathering Time [Kelt.]

Moon Sign: Cancer
Tarot Card: Nine of Cups
Herb: Safflower
Incense: Frankincense
Color: Red

29   *Wednesday*

Moon Phase: New Moon
Moon enters Leo 2:40 a.m.

Moon Sign: Cancer
Tarot Card: Ten of Cups
Herb: Scurvy Grass
Incense: Sandalwood
Color: Purple

30   *Thursday*

Moon Phase: 1st Quarter
             Waxing

Moon Sign: Leo
Tarot Card: Page of Cups
Herb: Sorrel
Incense: Myrrh
Color: Blue

31
Friday

Moon Phase: 1st Quarter
         Waxing
Moon enters Virgo 2:02 a.m.
Festivals: Lughnasad Eve [Kelt.]
         Fire Festival

Moon Sign: Leo
Tarot Card: Knight of Cups
Herb: Wormwood
Incense: Jasmine
Color: Green

1
Saturday

Moon Phase: 1st Quarter
         Waxing
Festivals: Lughnasas [Kelt.]
         Carman [Ir.]
         Lughnasa [Ir.]

Moon Sign: Virgo
Tarot Card: Queen of Cups
Herb: Sweet Flag
Incense: Benzoin or Cedar
Color: Black

2
Sunday

Moon Phase: 1st Quarter
         Waxing
Moon enters Libra 2:18 a.m.

Moon Sign: Virgo
Tarot Card: King of Cups
Herb: Acacia
Incense: Pine
Color: Yellow

AUGUST

S	M	T	W	T	F	S
						1
2	3	4	5	6	7	8
9	10	11	12	13	14	15
16	17	18	19	20	21	22
23	24	25	26	27	28	29
30	31					

3 *Monday*

Moon Phase: 1st Quarter
                Waxing

Moon Sign: Libra
Tarot Card: Ace of Pentacles
Herb: Angelica
Incense: Cinnamon
Color: White

4 *Tuesday*

Moon Phase: 1st Quarter
                Waxing
Moon enters Scorpio 5:17 a.m.

Moon Sign: Libra
Tarot Card: Two of Pentacles
Herb: Bedstraw
Incense: Frankincense
Color: Red

5 *Wednesday*

Moon Phase: 2nd Quarter
                Waxing
Festivals: St. James's Day
          Shoshone-Bannock [NW Am.]
          (first day)

Moon Sign: Scorpio
Tarot Card: Three of Pentacles
Herb: Blackberry
Incense: Sandalwood
Color: Purple

6 *Thursday*

Moon Phase: 2nd Quarter
                Waxing
Moon enters Sagittarius 11:58 a.m.

Moon Sign: Scorpio
Tarot Card: Four of Pentacles
Herb: Briar Hip
Incense: Myrrh
Color: Blue

7
Friday

Moon Phase: 2nd Quarter
Waxing

Moon Sign: Sagittarius
Tarot Card: Five of Pentacles
Herb: Cardamon
Incense: Jasmine
Color: Green

8
Saturday

Moon Phase: 2nd Quarter
Waxing
Moon enters Capricorn 10:01 p.m.
Festivals: Shoshone-Bannock (last day)

Moon Sign: Sagittarius
Tarot Card: Six of Pentacles
Herb: Chive
Incense: Benzoin or Cedar
Color: Black

9
Sunday

Moon Phase: 2nd Quarter
Waxing

Moon Sign: Capricorn
Tarot Card: Seven of Pentacles
Herb: Cotton
Incense: Pine
Color: Yellow

AUGUST

S	M	T	W	T	F	S
						1
2	3	4	5	6	7	8
9	10	11	12	13	14	15
16	17	18	19	20	21	22
23	24	25	26	27	28	29
30	31					

10   *Monday*

Moon Phase: 2nd Quarter
       Waxing
Festivals: St. Lawrence's Day

Moon Sign: Capricorn
Tarot Card: Eight of Pentacles
Herb: Dog's Mercury
Incense: Cinnamon
Color: White

11   *Tuesday*

Moon Phase: 2nd Quarter
       Waxing
Moon enters Aquarius 10:07 a.m.

Moon Sign: Capricorn
Tarot Card: Nine of Pentacles
Herb: Evening Primrose
Incense: Frankincense
Color: Red

12   *Wednesday*

Moon Phase: 2nd Quarter
       Waxing

Moon Sign: Aquarius
Tarot Card: Ten of Pentacles
Herb: Fragrant Valerian
Incense: Sandalwood
Color: Purple

13   *Thursday*

Moon Phase: Full Moon (Wort)
Moon enters Pisces 10:52 p.m.
Festivals: St. Cassian's Day

Moon Sign: Aquarius
Tarot Card: Page of Pentacles
Herb: Goldthread
Incense: Myrrh
Color: Blue

14
Friday

Moon Phase: 3rd Quarter
       Waning

Moon Sign: Pisces
Tarot Card: Knight of Pentacles
Herb: Hemlock Spruce
Incense: Jasmine
Color: Green

15
Saturday

Moon Phase: 3rd Quarter
       Waning
Festivals: Dog Days end
       Old Lammas
       Asuncion

Moon Sign: Pisces
Tarot Card: Queen of Pentacles
Herb: Hops
Incense: Benzoin or Cedar
Color: Black

16
Sunday

Moon Phase: 3rd Quarter
       Waning
Moon enters Aries 11:12 a.m.
Festivals: St. Roch's Day

Moon Sign: Pisces
Tarot Card: King of Pentacles
Herb: Indian Pipe
Incense: Pine
Color: Yellow

AUGUST

S	M	T	W	T	F	S
						1
2	3	4	5	6	7	8
9	10	11	12	13	14	15
16	17	18	19	20	21	22
23	24	25	26	27	28	29
30	31					

17 *Monday*

Moon Phase: 3rd Quarter
Waning
Festivals: Amenartus [Egypt.]

Moon Sign: Aries
Tarot Card: The Magician
Herb: Kousso
Incense: Cinnamon
Color: White

18 *Tuesday*

Moon Phase: 3rd Quarter
Waning
Moon enters Taurus 10:11 p.m.
Festivals: St. Helena's Day

Moon Sign: Aries
Tarot Card: High Priestess
Herb: Lobelia
Incense: Frankincense
Color: Red

19 *Wednesday*

Moon Phase: 3rd Quarter
Waning
Festivals: Vinalia [Rom.]

Moon Sign: Taurus
Tarot Card: The Empress
Herb: Matico
Incense: Sandalwood
Color: Purple

20 *Thursday*

Moon Phase: 3rd Quarter
Waning

Moon Sign: Taurus
Tarot Card: The Emperor
Herb: Peppermint
Incense: Myrrh
Color: Blue

21

Moon Phase: 4th Quarter
                    Waning
Moon enters Gemini 6:37 a.m.

Moon Sign: Taurus
Tarot Card: The Hierophant
Herb: Monkshood
Incense: Jasmine
Color: Green

22

Moon Phase: 4th Quarter
                    Waning
Sun enters Virgo 3:11 p.m.

Moon Sign: Gemini
Tarot Card: The Lovers
Herb: Nasturtium
Incense: Benzoin or Cedar
Color: Black

23

Moon Phase: 4th Quarter
                    Waning
Moon enters Cancer 11:37 a.m.
Festivals: Moira's Day [Grk.]

Moon Sign: Gemini
Tarot Card: The Chariot
Herb: Olive
Incense: Pine
Color: Yellow

AUGUST

S	M	T	W	T	F	S
						1
2	3	4	5	6	7	8
9	10	11	12	13	14	15
16	17	18	19	20	21	22
23	24	25	26	27	28	29
30	31					

24
Monday

Moon Phase: 4th Quarter
Waning
Festivals: St. Bartholomew's Day

Moon Sign: Cancer
Tarot Card: Justice
Herb: Squaw Balm
Incense: Cinnamon
Color: White

25
Tuesday

Moon Phase: 4th Quarter
Waning
Moon enters Leo 1:16 p.m.
Festivals: Paryushana-Parva [Jain][Hindu]

Moon Sign: Cancer
Tarot Card: The Hermit
Herb: Ribwort
Incense: Frankincense
Color: Red

26
Wednesday

Moon Phase: 4th Quarter
Waning
Festivals: Ilmatar [Fin.]

Moon Sign: Leo
Tarot Card: Wheel of Fortune
Herb: Prickly Ash
Incense: Sandalwood
Color: Purple

27
Thursday

Moon Phase: New Moon
Moon enters Virgo 12:47 p.m.

Moon Sign: Leo
Tarot Card: Strength
Herb: Queen of the Meadow
Incense: Myrrh
Color: Blue

28
Friday

Moon Phase: 1st Quarter
               Waxing

Moon Sign: Virgo
Tarot Card: The Hanged Man
Herb: Red Eyebright
Incense: Jasmine
Color: Green

29
Saturday

Moon Phase: 1st Quarter
               Waxing
Moon enters Libra 12:12 p.m.

Moon Sign: Virgo
Tarot Card: Death
Herb:Saffron
Incense: Benzoin or Cedar
Color: Black

30
Sunday

Moon Phase: 1st Quarter
               Waxing

Moon Sign: Libra
Tarot Card: Temperance
Herb: Senega Snakeroot
Incense: Pine
Color: Yellow

AUGUST

S	M	T	W	T	F	S
						1
2	3	4	5	6	7	8
9	10	11	12	13	14	15
16	17	18	19	20	21	22
23	24	25	26	27	28	29
30	31					

31 *Monday*

Moon Phase: 1st Quarter
           Waxing
Moon enters Scorpio 1:39 p.m.

Moon Sign: Libra
Tarot Card: The Devil
Herb: Speedwell
Incense: Cinnamon
Color: White

1 *Tuesday*

Moon Phase: 1st Quarter
           Waxing

Moon Sign: Scorpio
Tarot Card: The Tower
Herb: Woodruff
Incense: Frankincense
Color: Red

2 *Wednesday*

Moon Phase: 1st Quarter
           Waxing
Moon enters Sagittarius 6:51 p.m.

Moon Sign: Scorpio
Tarot Card: The Star
Herb: Adder's Tongue
Incense: Sandalwood
Color: Purple

3 *Thursday*

Moon Phase: 2nd Quarter
           Waxing
Festivals: Cromwell's Day [Eng.]

Moon Sign: Sagittarius
Tarot Card: The Moon
Herb: Anise
Incense: Myrrh
Color: Blue

4
Friday

Moon Phase: 2nd Quarter
               Waxing

Moon Sign: Sagittarius
Tarot Card: The Sun
Herb: Beechdrops
Incense: Jasmine
Color: Green

5
Saturday

Moon Phase: 2nd Quarter
               Waxing
Moon enters Capricorn 4:07 a.m.

Moon Sign: Sagittarius
Tarot Card: Judgement
Herb: Black Cohosh
Incense: Benzoin or Cedar
Color: Black

6
Sunday

Moon Phase: 2nd Quarter
               Waxing

Moon Sign: Capricorn
Tarot Card: The World
Herb: Brooklime
Incense: Pine
Color: Yellow

SEPTEMBER

S	M	T	W	T	F	S
		1	2	3	4	5
6	7	8	9	10	11	12
13	14	15	16	17	18	19
20	21	22	23	24	25	26
27	28	29	30			

7   *Monday*

Moon Phase: 2nd Quarter
           Waxing
Moon enters Aquarius 4:09 p.m.
Festivals: Abbuts Bromley Horn Dance
           [Eng.]

Moon Sign: Capricorn
Tarot Card: The Fool
Herb: Carline Thistle
Incense: Cinnamon
Color: White

8   *Tuesday*

Moon Phase: 2nd Quarter
           Waxing
Festivals: Navidad de la Virgen
           Pinnhut Festival [SW Am]

Moon Sign: Aquarius
Tarot Card: Ace of Swords
Herb: Cinquefoil
Incense: Frankincense
Color: Red

9   *Wednesday*

Moon Phase: 2nd Quarter
           Waxing
Festivals: Kiku no Sekku [Jap.]

Moon Sign: Aquarius
Tarot Card: Two of Swords
Herb: Cowslip
Incense: Sandalwood
Color: Purple

10   *Thursday*

Moon Phase: 2nd Quarter
           Waxing
Moon enters Pisces 4:57 a.m.

Moon Sign: Aquarius
Tarot Card: Three of Swords
Herb: Dogwood
Incense: Myrrh
Color: Blue

11
Friday

Moon Phase: Full Moon (Barley)

Moon Sign: Pisces
Tarot Card: Four of Swords
Herb: Everlasting
Incense: Jasmine
Color: Green

12
Saturday

Moon Phase: 3rd Quarter
                    Waning
Moon enters Aries 5:03 p.m.
Festivals: Third Gahambar [Zoroastrian]

Moon Sign: Pisces
Tarot Card: Five of Swords
Herb: Fraxinella
Incense: Benzoin or Cedar
Color: Black

13
Sunday

Moon Phase: 3rd Quarter
                    Waning
Festivals: Lighting the Fire [Egypt.]
              Lectisternium [Rom.]

Moon Sign: Aries
Tarot Card: Six of Swords
Herb: Great Burnet
Incense: Pine
Color: Yellow

SEPTEMBER

S	M	T	W	T	F	S
		1	2	3	4	5
6	7	8	9	10	11	12
13	14	15	16	17	18	19
20	21	22	23	24	25	26
27	28	29	30			

14
Monday

Moon Phase: 3rd Quarter
             Waning
Moon enters Taurus 3:68 a.m.
Festivals: Holy Rood Day

Moon Sign: Aries
Tarot Card: Seven of Swords
Herb: Hemp Agrimony
Incense: Cinnamon
Color: White

15
Tuesday

Moon Phase: 3rd Quarter
             Waning
Moon enters Taurus 3:48 a.m.
Festivals: Acorn Festival [SW Am]

Moon Sign: Aries
Tarot Card: Eight of Swords
Herb: Horehound
Incense: Frankincense
Color: Red

16
Wednesday

Moon Phase: 3rd Quarter
             Waning
Festivals: St. Ninian's Day

Moon Sign: Taurus
Tarot Card: Nine of Swords
Herb: Indian Turnip
Incense: Sandalwood
Color: Purple

17
Thursday

Moon Phase: 3rd Quarter
             Waning
Moon enters Gemini 12:41 p.m.

Moon Sign: Taurus
Tarot Card: Ten of Swords
Herb: Lady's Mantle
Incense: Myrrh
Color: Blue

18 *Friday*

Moon Phase: 3rd Quarter
Waning

Moon Sign: Gemini
Tarot Card: Page of Swords
Herb: Loosestrife
Incense: Jasmine
Color: Green

19 *Saturday*

Moon Phase: 4th Quarter
Waning
Moon enters Cancer 7:00 p.m.

Moon Sign: Gemini
Tarot Card: Knight of Swords
Herb: Meadow Saffron
Incense: Benzoin or Cedar
Color: Black

20 *Sunday*

Moon Phase: 4th Quarter
Waning

Moon Sign: Cancer
Tarot Card: Queen of Swords
Herb: Brandy Mint
Incense: Pine
Color: Yellow

SEPTEMBER

S	M	T	W	T	F	S
		1	2	3	4	5
6	7	8	9	10	11	12
13	14	15	16	17	18	19
20	21	22	23	24	25	26
27	28	29	30			

21   *Monday*

Moon Phase: 4th Quarter
           Waning
Moon enters Leo 10:20 p.m.
Festivals: Feast of Divine Life
            Fire Festival
            St. Matthew's Day

Moon Sign: Cancer
Tarot Card: King of Swords
Herb: Motherwort
Incense: Cinnamon
Color: White

22   *Tuesday*

Moon Phase: 4th Quarter
           Waning
 Sun enters Libra 12:44 p.m.
Festivals: Autumnal Equinox

Moon Sign: Leo
Tarot Card: Ace of Wands
Herb: Nerve Root
Incense: Frankincense
Color: Red

23   *Wednesday*

Moon Phase: 4th Quarter
           Waning
Moon enters Virgo 11:09 p.m.
Festivals: Greater Eleusinian Mysteries
           [Grk.] (first day)

Moon Sign: Leo
Tarot Card: Two of Wands
Herb: Onion
Incense: Sandalwood
Color: Purple

24   *Thursday*

Moon Phase: 4th Quarter
           Waning

Moon Sign: Virgo
Tarot Card: Three of Wands
Herb: Peony
Incense: Myrrh
Color: Blue

25 *Friday*

Moon Phase: 4th Quarter
                Waning
Moon enters Libra 10:58 p.m.

Moon Sign: Virgo
Tarot Card: Four of Wands
Herb: Ripple Grass
Incense: Jasmine
Color: Green

26 *Saturday*

Moon Phase: New Moon

Moon Sign: Libra
Tarot Card: Five of Wands
Herb: Yellow Wood
Incense: Benzoin or Cedar
Color: Black

27 *Sunday*

Moon Phase: 1st Quarter
                Waxing
Moon enters Scorpio 11:45 p.m.
Festivals: St. Cosmas and
                St. Damian's Day

Moon Sign: Libra
Tarot Card: Six of Wands
Herb: Gravelroot
Incense: Pine
Color: Yellow

SEPTEMBER

S	M	T	W	T	F	S
		1	2	3	4	5
6	7	8	9	10	11	12
13	14	15	16	17	18	19
20	21	22	23	24	25	26
27	28	29	30			

28 *Monday*

Moon Phase: 1st Quarter
     Waxing

Moon Sign: Scorpio
Tarot Card: Seven of Wands
Herb: Euphrasy
Incense: Cinnamon
Color: White

29 *Tuesday*

Moon Phase: 1st Quarter
     Waxing
Festivals: Michelmas

Moon Sign: Scorpio
Tarot Card: Eight of Wands
Herb: Sage
Incense: Frankincense
Color: Red

30 *Wednesday*

Moon Phase: 1st Quarter
     Waxing
Moon enters Sagittarius 3:34 a.m.

Moon Sign: Scorpio
Tarot Card: Nine of Wands
Herb: Agave
Incense: Sandalwood
Color: Purple

1 *Thursday*

Moon Phase: 1st Quarter
     Waxing
Festivals: Hsia Yuan [Chin.]
     Greater Eleusinian Mysteries
     (last day)

Moon Sign: Sagittarius
Tarot Card: Ten of Wands
Herb: Arnica
Incense: Myrrh
Color: Blue

2
Friday

Moon Phase: 1st Quarter
        Waxing
Moon enters Capricorn 11:30 a.m.
Festivals: Angeles Guardianes
        Old Man's Day [Eng.]

Moon Sign: Sagittarius
Tarot Card: Page of Wands
Herb: Belladonna
Incense: Jasmine
Color: Green

3
Saturday

Moon Phase: 2nd Quarter
        Waxing
Festivals: Mihr Jashan [Jap.] (first day)

Moon Sign: Capricorn
Tarot Card: Knight of Wands
Herb: Black Root
Incense: Benzoin or Cedar
Color: Black

4
Sunday

Moon Phase: 2nd Quarter
        Waxing
Moon enters Aquarius 10:54 p.m.
Festivals: St. Francis's Day
        Elk Festival [SW Am.]

Moon Sign: Capricorn
Tarot Card: Queen of Wands
Herb: Bryony
Incense: Pine
Color: Yellow

OCTOBER

S	M	T	W	T	F	S
				1	2	3
4	5	6	7	8	9	10
11	12	13	14	15	16	17
18	19	20	21	22	23	24
25	26	27	28	29	30	31

5 Monday

Moon Phase: 2nd Quarter
      Waxing

Moon Sign: Aquarius
Tarot Card: King of Wands
Herb: Carrot
Incense: Cinnamon
Color: White

6 Tuesday

Moon Phase: 2nd Quarter
      Waxing
Festivals: St. Faith's Day

Moon Sign: Aquarius
Tarot Card: Ace of Cups
Herb: Clove
Incense: Frankincense
Color: Red

7 Wednesday

Moon Phase: 2nd Quarter
      Waxing
Moon enters Pisces 11:38 a.m.
Festivals: Mihr Jashan (last day)

Moon Sign: Aquarius
Tarot Card:Two of Cups
Herb: Cubeb
Incense: Sandalwood
Color: Purple

8 Thursday

Moon Phase: 2nd Quarter
      Waxing
Festivals: Start of Fading Time [Kelt.]

Moon Sign: Pisces
Tarot Card: Three of Cups
Herb: Dyer's Broom
Incense: Myrrh
Color: Blue

9   *Friday*

Moon Phase: 2nd Quarter
         Waxing
Moon enters Aries 11:37 p.m.
Festivals: St. Denis's Day

Moon Sign: Pisces
Tarot Card: Four of Cups
Herb: Fennel
Incense: Jasmine
Color: Green

10   *Saturday*

Moon Phase: 2nd Quarter
         Waxing
Festivals: Inoko [Jap.]

Moon Sign: Aries
Tarot Card: Five of Cups
Herb: Fringe Tree
Incense: Benzoin or Cedar
Color: Black

11   *Sunday*

Moon Phase: Full Moon (Blood)

Moon Sign: Aries
Tarot Card: Six of Cups
Herb: Ground Ivy
Incense: Pine
Color: Yellow

OCTOBER

S	M	T	W	T	F	S
				1	2	3
4	5	6	7	8	9	10
11	12	13	14	15	16	17
18	19	20	21	22	23	24
25	26	27	28	29	30	31

12 *Monday*

Moon Phase: 3rd Quarter
         Waning
Moon enter Taurus 9:49 a.m.
Festivals: Fourth Gahamar [Zoroastrian]

Moon Sign: Aries
Tarot Card: Seven of Cups
Herb: Hemp Nettle
Incense: Cinnamon
Color: White

13 *Tuesday*

Moon Phase: 3rd Quarter
         Waning
Festivals: Fontinalia [Rom.]
      St Edward the Confessor's Day

Moon Sign: Taurus
Tarot Card: Eight of Cups
Herb: Horse Chestnut
Incense: Frankincense
Color: Red

14 *Wednesday*

Moon Phase: 3rd Quarter
         Waning
Moon enters Gemini 8:09 p.m.

Moon Sign: Taurus
Tarot Card: Nine of Cups
Herb: Irish Moss
Incense: Sandalwood
Color: Purple

15 *Thursday*

Moon Phase: 3rd Quarter
         Waning

Moon Sign: Gemini
Tarot Card: Ten of Cups
Herb: Larch
Incense: Myrrh
Color: Blue

16

Moon Phase: 3rd Quarter
Waning
Festivals: Cera [Ir.]

Moon Sign: Gemini
Tarot Card: Page of Cups
Herb: Lovage
Incense: Jasmine
Color: Green

17

Moon Phase: 3rd Quarter
Waning
Moon enters Cancer 12:37 a.m.
Festivals: Festival of Departed Worthies
[Tib.]
Shinto Deities [Jap.]

Moon Sign: Gemini
Tarot Card: Knight of Cups
Herb: Meadowsweet
Incense: Benzoin or Cedar
Color: Black

18

Moon Phase: 4th Quarter
Waning
Festivals: St. Luke's Day

Moon Sign: Cancer
Tarot Card: Queen of Cups
Herb: Lamb Mint
Incense: Pine
Color: Yellow

OCTOBER

S	M	T	W	T	F	S
				1	2	3
4	5	6	7	8	9	10
11	12	13	14	15	16	17
18	19	20	21	22	23	24
25	26	27	28	29	30	31

19 *Monday*

Moon Phase: 4th Quarter
Waning
Moon enters Leo 5:02 a.m.

Moon Sign: Cancer
Tarot Card: King of Cups
Herb: Mountain Laurel
Incense: Cinnamon
Color: White

20 *Tuesday*

Moon Phase: 4th Quarter
Waning

Moon Sign: Leo
Tarot Card: Ace of Pentacles
Herb: Nettle
Incense: Frankincense
Color: Red

21 *Wednesday*

Moon Phase: 4th Quarter
Waning
Moon enters Virgo 7:29 a.m.
Festivals: St. Ursula's Day

Moon Sign: Leo
Tarot Card: Two of Pentacles
Herb: Periwinkle
Incense: Sandalwood
Color: Purple

22 *Thursday*

Moon Phase: 4th Quarter
Waning
Sun enters Scorpio 9:58 p.m.

Moon Sign: Virgo
Tarot Card: Three of Pentacles
Herb: Periwinkle
Incense: Myrrh
Color: Blue

23
Friday

Moon Phase: 4th Quarter
             Waning
Moon enters Libra 8:40 a.m.

Moon Sign: Virgo
Tarot Card: Four of Pentacles
Herb: Pleurisy Root
Incense: Jasmine
Color: Green

24
Saturday

Moon Phase: 4th Quarter
             Waning

Moon Sign: Libra
Tarot Card: Fiove of Pentacles
Herb: Pride of China
Incense: Benzoin or Cedar
Color: Black

25
Sunday

Moon Phase: New Moon
Moon enters Scorpio 10:05 a.m.
Festivals: St. Crispin's Day

Moon Sign: Libra
Tarot Card: Six of Pentacles
Herb: Purple Boneset
Incense: Pine
Color: Yellow

OCTOBER

S	M	T	W	T	F	S
				1	2	3
4	5	6	7	8	9	10
11	12	13	14	15	16	17
18	19	20	21	22	23	24
25	26	27	28	29	30	31

26 *Monday*

Moon Phase: 1st Quarter
Waxing
Festivals: Aban Jashan [Jap.]

Moon Sign: Scorpio
Tarot Card: Seven of Pentacles
Herb: Red Pimpernel
Incense: Cinnamon
Color: White

27 *Tuesday*

Moon Phase: 1st Quarter
Waxing
Moon enters Sagittarius 1:30 p.m.
Festivals: Kashikiya–Hime [Jap.]

Moon Sign: Scorpio
Tarot Card: Eight of Pentacles
Herb: Blessed Thistle
Incense: Frankincense
Color: Red

28 *Wednesday*

Moon Phase: 1st Quarter
Waxing
Festivals: St. Simon and St. Jude's Day

Moon Sign: Sagittarius
Tarot Card: Nine of Pentacles
Herb: Senna
Incense: Sandalwood
Color: Purple

29 *Thursday*

Moon Phase: 1st Quarter
Waxing
Moon enters Capricorn 8:19 p.m.

Moon Sign: Sagittarius
Tarot Card: Ten of Pentacles
Herb: Spikenard
Incense: Myrrh
Color: Blue

1992 *Oct./Nov.* 1992

30 — Friday

Moon Phase: 1st Quarter
Waxing

Moon Sign: Capricorn
Tarot Card: Page of Pentacles
Herb: Witch Hazel
Incense: Jasmine
Color: Green

31 — Saturday

Moon Phase: 1st Quarter
Waxing

Moon Sign: Capricorn
Tarot Card: Knight of Pentacles
Herb: Alfalfa
Incense: Benzoin or Cedar
Color: Black

1 — Sunday

Moon Phase: 1st Quarter
Waxing
Moon enters Aquarius 6:44 a.m.
Festivals: All Saint's Day
Assembly of Tara [Kelt.]

Moon Sign: Capricorn
Tarot Card: Queen of Pentacles
Herb: Arum
Incense: Pine
Color: Yellow

NOVEMBER

S	M	T	W	T	F	S
1	2	3	4	5	6	7
8	9	10	11	12	13	14
15	16	17	18	19	20	21
22	23	24	25	26	27	28
29	30					

2 *Monday*

Moon Phase: 2nd Quarter
            Waxing
Festivals: Samhain (last day)
           All Soul's Day

Moon Sign: Aquarius
Tarot Card: King of Pentacles
Herb: Bennet
Incense: Cinnamon
Color: White

3 *Tuesday*

Moon Phase: 2nd Quarter
            Waxing
Moon enters Pisces 7:13 p.m.
Festivals: Gaelic New Year

Moon Sign: Aquarius
Tarot Card: The Magician
Herb: Blazing Star
Incense: Frankincense
Color: Red

4 *Wednesday*

Moon Phase: 2nd Quarter
            Waxing

Moon Sign: Pisces
Tarot Card: High Priestess
Herb: Buchu
Incense: Sandalwood
Color: Purple

5 *Thursday*

Moon Phase: 2nd Quarter
            Waxing

Moon Sign: Pisces
Tarot Card: The Empress
Herb: Castor Bean
Incense: Myrrh
Color: Blue

6
Friday

Moon Phase: 2nd Quarter
     Waxing
Moon enters Aries 7:20 a.m.

Moon Sign: Pisces
Tarot Card: The Emperor
Herb: Club Moss
Incense: Jasmine
Color: Green

7
Saturday

Moon Phase: 2nd Quarter
     Waxing

Moon Sign: Aries
Tarot Card: The Hierophant
Herb: Cucumber
Incense: Benzoin or Cedar
Color: Black

8
Sunday

Moon Phase: 2nd Quarter
     Waxing
Moon enters Taurus 5:20 p.m.

Moon Sign: Aries
Tarot Card: The Lovers
Herb: Echinacea
Incense: Pine
Color: Yellow

NOVEMBER

S	M	T	W	T	F	S
1	2	3	4	5	6	7
8	9	10	11	12	13	14
15	16	17	18	19	20	21
22	23	24	25	26	27	28
29	30					

9   *Monday*

Moon Phase: 2nd Quarter
               Waxing

Moon Sign: Taurus
Tarot Card: The Chariot
Herb: Fenugreek
Incense: Cinnamon
Color: White

10   *Tuesday*

Moon Phase: Full Moon (Snow)

Moon Sign: Taurus
Tarot Card: Justice
Herb: Fumitory
Incense: Frankincense
Color: Red

11   *Wednesday*

Moon Phase: 3rd Quarter
               Waning
Moon enters Gemini 12:50 a.m.
Festivals: Old November Day [Kelt.]

Moon Sign: Taurus
Tarot Card: The Hermit
Herb: Guaiac
Incense: Sandalwood
Color: Purple

12   *Thursday*

Moon Phase: 3rd Quarter
               Waning

Moon Sign: Gemini
Tarot Card: Wheel of Fortune
Herb: Henbane
Incense: Myrrh
Color: Blue

13
Friday

Moon Phase: 3rd Quarter
            Waning
Moon enters Cancer 6:20 a.m.

Moon Sign: Gemini
Tarot Card: Strength
Herb: Horseradish
Incense: Jasmine
Color: Green

14
Saturday

Moon Phase: 3rd Quarter
            Waning

Moon Sign: Cancer
Tarot Card: The Hanged Man
Herb: Ironweed
Incense: Benzoin or Cedar
Color: Black

15
Sunday

Moon Phase: 3rd Quarter
            Waning
Moon enters Leo 10:24 a.m.

Moon Sign: Cancer
Tarot Card: Death
Herb: Larkspur
Incense: Pine
Color: Yellow

NOVEMBER

S	M	T	W	T	F	S
1	2	3	4	5	6	7
8	9	10	11	12	13	14
15	16	17	18	19	20	21
22	23	24	25	26	27	28
29	30					

16 *Monday*

Moon Phase: 3rd Quarter
            Waning

Moon Sign: Leo
Tarot Card: Temperance
Herb: Lungwort
Incense: Cinnamon
Color: White

17 *Tuesday*

Moon Phase: 4th Quarter
            Waning
Moon enters Virgo 1:29 p.m.

Moon Sign: Leo
Tarot Card: The Devil
Herb: Droppwort
Incense: Frankincense
Color: Red

18 *Wednesday*

Moon Phase: 4th Quarter
            Waning

Moon Sign: Virgo
Tarot Card: The Tower
Herb: Spearmint
Incense: Sandalwood
Color: Purple

19 *Thursday*

Moon Phase: 4th Quarter
            Waning
Moon enters Libra 4:04 p.m.

Moon Sign: Virgo
Tarot Card: The Star
Herb: Mouse Ear
Incense: Myrrh
Color: Blue

20 *Friday*

Moon Phase: 4th Quarter
Waning
Festivals: St. Edmund's Day

Moon Sign: Libra
Tarot Card: The Moon
Herb: Dwarf Nettle
Incense: Jasmine
Color: Green

21 *Saturday*

Moon Phase: 4th Quarter
Waning
Sun enters Sagittarius 7:27 p.m.
Moon enters Scorpio 6:53 p.m.

Moon Sign: Libra
Tarot Card: The Sun
Herb: Orrisroot
Incense: Benzoin or Cedar
Color: Black

22 *Sunday*

Moon Phase: 4th Quarter
Waning

Moon Sign: Scorpio
Tarot Card: Judgement
Herb: Peruvian Bark
Incense: Pine
Color: Yellow

NOVEMBER

S	M	T	W	T	F	S
1	2	3	4	5	6	7
8	9	10	11	12	13	14
15	16	17	18	19	20	21
22	23	24	25	26	27	28
29	30					

23
Monday

Moon Phase: 4th Quarter
       Waning
Moon enters Sagittarius 11:02 p.m.
Festivals: Shinjosai [Jap.]
       St. Clement's Day

Moon Sign: Scorpio
Tarot Card: The World
Herb: Blackthorn
Incense: Cinnamon
Color: White

24
Tuesday

Moon Phase: New Moon
Festivals: Adar Jashan [Jap.]

Moon Sign: Sagittarius
Tarot Card: The Fool
Herb: Hagbrush
Incense: Frankincense
Color: Red

25
Wednesday

Moon Phase: 1st Quarter
       Waxing
Festivals: Santa Catalina de Alejandría
       St. Catherine's Day

Moon Sign: Sagittarius
Tarot Card: Ace of Swords
Herb: Radish
Incense: Sandalwood
Color: Purple

26
Thursday

Moon Phase: 1st Quarter
       Waxing
Moon enters Capricorn 5:39 a.m.

Moon Sign: Sagittarius
Tarot Card: Two of Swords
Herb: Red Sedge
Incense: Myrrh
Color: Blue

27 *Friday*

Moon Phase: 1st Quarter
             Waxing

Moon Sign: Capricorn
Tarot Card: Three of Swords
Herb: St. John's Wort
Incense: Jasmine
Color: Green

28 *Saturday*

Moon Phase: 1st Quarter
             Waxing
Moon enters Aquarius 3:20 p.m.

Moon Sign: Capricorn
Tarot Card: Four of Swords
Herb: Seven Barks
Incense: Benzoin or Cedar
Color: Black

29 *Sunday*

Moon Phase: 1st Quarter
             Waxing

Moon Sign: Aquarius
Tarot Card: Five of Swords
Herb: Cypress Spurge
Incense: Pine
Color: Yellow

NOVEMBER

S	M	T	W	T	F	S
1	2	3	4	5	6	7
8	9	10	11	12	13	14
15	16	17	18	19	20	21
22	23	24	25	26	27	28
29	30					

30   *Monday*

Moon Phase: 1st Quarter
        Waxing
Festivals: St. Andrew's Day

Moon Sign: Aquarius
Tarot Card: Six of Swords
Herb: Allspice
Incense: Cinnamon
Color: White

1   *Tuesday*

Moon Phase: 1st Quarter
        Waxing
Moon enters Pisces 3:24 a.m.

Moon Sign: Aquarius
Tarot Card: Seven of Swords
Herb: Asarum
Incense: Frankincense
Color: Red

2   *Wednesday*

Moon Phase: 2nd Quarter
        Waxing

Moon Sign: Pisces
Tarot Card: Eight of Swords
Herb: Betony
Incense: Sandalwood
Color: Purple

3   *Thursday*

Moon Phase: 2nd Quarter
        Waxing
Moon enters Aries 3:50 p.m.

Moon Sign: Pisces
Tarot Card: Nine of Swords
Herb: Blind Nettle
Incense: Myrrh
Color: Blue

4   *Friday*

Moon Phase: 2nd Quarter
              Waxing
Festivals: St. Barbara's Day

Moon Sign: Aries
Tarot Card: Ten of Swords
Herb: Buckbean
Incense: Jasmine
Color: Green

5   *Saturday*

Moon Phase: 2nd Quarter
              Waxing

Moon Sign: Aries
Tarot Card: Page of Swords
Herb: Catnip
Incense: Benzoin or Cedar
Color: Black

6   *Sunday*

Moon Phase: 2nd Quarter
              Waxing
Moon enters Taurus 2:17 a.m.
Festivals: St. Nicholas's Day

Moon Sign: Aries
Tarot Card: Knight of Swords
Herb: Colombo
Incense: Pine
Color: Yellow

DECEMBER

S	M	T	W	T	F	S
		1	2	3	4	5
6	7	8	9	10	11	12
13	14	15	16	17	18	19
20	21	22	23	24	25	26
27	28	29	30	31		

7 *Monday*

Moon Phase: 2nd Quarter
    Waxing

Moon Sign: Taurus
Tarot Card: Queen of Swords
Herb: Black Currant
Incense: Cinnamon
Color: White

8 *Tuesday*

Moon Phase: 2nd Quarter
    Waxing
Moon enters Gemini 9:38 a.m.
Festivals: Nuestra Senora Guadalupe

Moon Sign: Taurus
Tarot Card: King of Swords
Herb: Elder
Incense: Frankincense
Color: Red

9 *Wednesday*

Moon Phase: Full Moon (Oak)
    Lunar Eclipse
Festivals: Tonantzin [Mex.]

Moon Sign: Gemini
Tarot Card: Ace of Wands
Herb: Fern
Incense: Sandalwood
Color: Purple

10 *Thursday*

Moon Phase: 3rd Quarter
    Waning
Moon enters Cancer 2:06 p.m.

Moon Sign: Gemini
Tarot Card: Two of Wands
Herb: Galangal
Incense: Myrrh
Color: Blue

11   *Friday*

Moon Phase: 3rd Quarter
           Waning

Moon Sign: Cancer
Tarot Card: Three of Wands
Herb: Gum Plant
Incense: Jasmine
Color: Green

12   *Saturday*

Moon Phase: 3rd Quarter
           Waning
Moon enters Leo 4:48 p.m.
Festivals: Sada [Zoroastrian]
         St. Finnian's Day

Moon Sign: Cancer
Tarot Card: Four of Wands
Herb: Henna
Incense: Benzoin or Cedar
Color: Black

13   *Sunday*

Moon Phase: 3rd Quarter
           Waning
Festivals: St. Lucy's Day

Moon Sign: Leo
Tarot Card: Five of Wands
Herb: Horseweed
Incense: Pine
Color: Yellow

DECEMBER

S	M	T	W	T	F	S
		1	2	3	4	5
6	7	8	9	10	11	12
13	14	15	16	17	18	19
20	21	22	23	24	25	26
27	28	29	30	31		

14 *Monday*

Moon Phase: 3rd Quarter
Waning
Moon enters Virgo 6:57 p.m.

Moon Sign: Leo
Tarot Card: Six of Wands
Herb: Jalap
Incense: Cinnamon
Color: White

15 *Tuesday*

Moon Phase: 3rd Quarter
Waning
Festivals: Halcyon Days begin [Grk.]

Moon Sign: Virgo
Tarot Card: Seven of Wands
Herb: Laurel
Incense: Frankincense
Color: Red

16 *Wednesday*

Moon Phase: 4th Quarter
Waning
Moon enters Libra 9:34 p.m.

Moon Sign: Virgo
Tarot Card: Eight of Wands
Herb: Madder
Incense: Sandalwood
Color: Purple

17 *Thursday*

Moon Phase: 4th Quarter
Waning
Festivals: Saturnalia [Rom.] (first day)

Moon Sign: Libra
Tarot Card: Nine of Wands
Herb: Goatsbeard
Incense: Myrrh
Color: Blue

18
Friday

Moon Phase: 4th Quarter
               Waning

Moon Sign: Libra
Tarot Card: Ten of Wands
Herb: Curled Mint
Incense: Jasmine
Color: Green

19
Saturday

Moon Phase: 4th Quarter
               Waning
Moon enters Scorpio 1:21 a.m.
Festivals: Start of Sorrowing Time [Kelt.]

Moon Sign: Libra
Tarot Card: Page of Wands
Herb: Mugwort
Incense: Benzoin or Cedar
Color: Black

20
Sunday

Moon Phase: 4th Quarter
               Waning

Moon Sign: Scorpio
Tarot Card: Knight of Wands
Herb: New Jersey Tea
Incense: Pine
Color: Yellow

DECEMBER

S	M	T	W	T	F	S
		1	2	3	4	5
6	7	8	9	10	11	12
13	14	15	16	17	18	19
20	21	22	23	24	25	26
27	28	29	30	31		

21 *Monday*

Moon Phase: 4th Quarter
        Waning
Sun enters Capricorn 8:45 a.m.
Moon enters Sagittarius 6:43 a.m.
Festivals: Winter Solstice
        St. Thomas's Day

Moon Sign: Scorpio
Tarot Card: Queen of Wands
Herb: Nightshade
Incense: Cinnamon
Color: White

22 *Tuesday*

Moon Phase: 4th Quarter
        Waning
Festivals: Yule (first day)
        Fire Festival

Moon Sign: Sagittarius
Tarot Card: King of Wands
Herb: Pansy
Incense: Frankincense
Color: Red

23 *Wednesday*

Moon Phase: New Moon
Moon enters Capricorn 2:05 p.m.
Festivals: Laurentalia [Rom.]
        Saturnalia (last day)

Moon Sign: Sagittarius
Tarot Card: Ace of Cups
Herb: Peyote
Incense: Sandalwood
Color: Purple

24 *Thursday*

Moon Phase: 1st Quarter
        Waxing
Festivals: Juvenalia [Rom.]

Moon Sign: Capricorn
Tarot Card: Two of Cups
Herb: Poison Hemlock
Incense: Myrrh
Color: Blue

25

Moon Phase: 1st Quarter
          Waxing
Moon enters Aquarius 11:44 p.m.
Festivals: Christmas

Moon Sign: Capricorn
Tarot Card: Three of Cups
Herb: English Cowslip
Incense: Jasmine
Color: Green

26

Moon Phase: 1st Quarter
          Waxing
Festivals: Boxing Day [Brit.]
          St. Stephen's Day
          Turtle Dance [SW Am.]

Moon Sign: Aquarius
Tarot Card: Four of Cups
Herb: Ragged Cup
Incense: Benzoin or Cedar
Color: Black

27

Moon Phase: 1st Quarter
          Waxing
Festivals: St. John's Day
          Deer Dance [SW Am.]

Moon Sign: Aquarius
Tarot Card: Five of Cups
Herb: Restharrow
Incense: Pine
Color: Yellow

JANUARY 1993

S	M	T	W	T	F	S
					1	2
3	4	5	6	7	8	9
10	11	12	13	14	15	16
17	18	19	20	21	22	23
24	25	26	27	28	29	30
31						

28 *Monday*

Moon Phase: 1st Quarter
         Waxing
Moon enters Pisces 11:29 a.m.
Festivals: End of Halcyon Days

Moon Sign: Aquarius
Tarot Card: Six of Cups
Herb: Share Grass
Incense: Cinnamon
Color: White

29 *Tuesday*

Moon Phase: 1st Quarter
         Waxing
Festivals: St. Thomas of Canterbury's Day

Moon Sign: Pisces
Tarot Card: Seven of Cups
Herb: Milk-purslane
Incense: Frankincense
Color: Red

30 *Wednesday*

Moon Phase: 1st Quarter
         Waxing

Moon Sign: Pisces
Tarot Card: Eight of Cups
Herb: Sandalwood
Incense: Sandalwood
Color: Purple

31 *Thursday*

Moon Phase: 2nd Quarter
         Waxing
Moon enters Aries 12:08 a.m.
Festivals: Hogmanay [Scot.]
         Fifth Gahambar [Zoroastrian]

Moon Sign: Pisces
Tarot Card: Nine of Cups
Herb: Petty Spurge
Incense: Myrrh
Color: Blue

Notes

Celestial Phenomena for 1992

VISIBILITY OF PLANETS

Planets are referenced to the constellations, not to the zodiac signs. Information on Uranus and Neptune assumes use of a telescope. Resource: *Astronomical Phenomena for the Year 1992*, prepared by the U.S. Naval Observatory and the Royal Greenwich Observatory.

MERCURY, due to its proximity to the Sun, can be seen only in the east just before sunrise and in the west just after sunset. *Morning visibility:* 1/1-30, 4/3-5/24, 8/11-9/6, 11/28-12/31, brighter at the end of each of these periods. *Best morning visibility:* in the low northern latitudes for a few days in early January and during the third week in August; in the northern latitudes for the first three weeks of December; in the southern latitudes from the second week of April to mid-May. *Evening visibility:* 2/23-3/19, 6/8-7/26, 9/27-11/16, brighter at the beginning of each period. *Best evening visibility:* in the northern latitudes during the first half of March; in the southern latitudes from the third week of June to the third week of July and from the second week of October until just before mid-November.

VENUS, until the second week of May, is brilliant in the morning sky. At that point it moves too close to the Sun for observation until mid-July, when it reappears for the rest of the year in the evening sky. Venus conjoins Mars on 2/19; Saturn on 2/28 and 12/21; Mercury on 4/6 and 7/26; Jupiter on 8/22.

MARS is visible in the constellation Ophiuchus in the morning sky at the very beginning of January. From there it passes through the constellations Sagittarius, Capricornus, Aquarius, Pisces, briefly into Cetus and back into Pisces, then on to Aries, Taurus, and Gemini, visible more than half the night by this time. It goes into Cancer, then by mid-December and for the rest of the year back into Gemini. Mars conjoins Mercury on 1/10; Venus on 2/19; Saturn on 3/6; is 5° north of *Aldebaran* on 8/11; is 5° south of *Pollux* on 11/4.

JUPITER is visible in January for more than half the night in the constellation Leo. On 2/28 it is opposed to the Sun and is visible throughout the night. Waning from opposition, by early June Jupiter is visible only in the evening twilight sky, and by September it is too close to the Sun for observation. In the beginning of October it reappears in the east at sunrise in the constellation Virgo, where it remains for the rest of the year. Jupiter conjoins Venus on 8/22.

SATURN is visible in the evening twilight sky in the constellation Capricornus until mid-January. It is too close to the Sun for observation until mid-February, reappearing in the morning sky, still in Capricornus, where it remains for the rest of the year. On 8/7 Saturn is opposed to the Sun and is visible all night. From early November on, it can be seen only in the evening twilight sky. Saturn conjoins Venus on 2/28 and 12/21; Mars on 3/6.

URANUS is too close to the Sun for observation until late January, at which point it appears shortly before sunrise in Sagittarius, where it remains for the rest of the year. On 7/7 it is opposed to the Sun and is visible throughout the night. By early October, Uranus is visible only in the evening twilight sky and by the second half of December is once again too close to the Sun for observation.

NEPTUNE is too close to the Sun for observation until late January, at which point it appears in the morning sky shortly before sunrise in Sagittarius, where it remains for the rest of the year. On 7/9 it opposes the Sun and is visible throughout the night. By mid-October and until mid-December it can be seen only in the evening twilight sky, after which it is once again too close to the Sun for observation.

ECLIPSES, 1992

There are five eclipses, three of the Sun and two of the Moon. Times are given in Eastern Standard and, in **bold typeface**, Pacific Standard. Seconds are expressed as decimal fractions of minutes. The exact time of an eclipse generally differs from the exact time of a New or Full Moon (as the case may be). The "central phase" of a Solar Eclipse is the geographical path described by the Sun's apparent path across the moving Earth as viewed through the Moon; the "greatest eclipse" occurs either at the Moon's maximum obscuration of the Sun for a Solar Eclipse, or when the Moon lies at the centermost point in its journey through the Earth's shadow for a Lunar Eclipse. Data reference: *Astronomical Phenomena for the Year 1992*, prepared jointly by the United States Naval Observatory and the Royal Greenwich Observatory.

JANUARY 4, ANNULAR ECLIPSE OF THE SUN: 13° ♑ 51'
Eclipse begins .... 3:03.6 p.m. **12:03.6 p.m.**
Central phase begins .... 4:16.0 p.m. **1:16.0 p.m.**
Greatest eclipse .... 6:04.9 p.m. **3:04.9 p.m.**
Central phase ends .... 7:53.1 p.m. **4:53.1 p.m.**
Eclipse ends .... 9:05.6 p.m. **6:05.6 p.m.**

JUNE 14-15, PARTIAL ECLIPSE OF THE MOON: 24° ♐ 20'
Moon enters penumbra .... 9:09.1 p.m. **6:09.1 p.m.**
Moon enters umbra .... 10:26.6 p.m. **7:26.6 p.m.**
Greatest eclipse .... 11:57.0 p.m. **8:57.0 p.m.**
Moon leaves umbra .... 1:27.2 a.m. **10:27.2 p.m.**
Moon leaves penumbra .... 2:44.9 a.m. **11:44.9 p.m.**
Visibility: South, Central and North America, southeastern Canada, Antarctica, the South Pacific Ocean, the southeastern North Pacific Ocean, extreme Western Europe, Africa (except the northeast), the Atlantic Ocean, New Zealand, Hawaii.

JUNE 30, TOTAL ECLIPSE OF THE SUN: 8° ♋ 57'
Eclipse begins .... 4:50.9 a.m. **1:50.9 a.m.**
Central phase begins .... 6:01.7 a.m. **3:01.7 a.m.**
Greatest eclipse .... 7:03.7 a.m. **4:03.7 a.m.**
Central phase ends .... 8:18.9 a.m. **5:18.9 a.m.**
Eclipse ends .... 9:29.7 a.m. **6:29.7 a.m.**

DECEMBER 9, TOTAL ECLIPSE OF THE MOON: 18° ♊ 10′
Moon enters penumbra . . . . 3:55.4 p.m. **12:55.4 p.m.**
Moon enters umbra . . . . 4:59.4 p.m. **1:59.4 p.m.**
Moon enters totality . . . . 6:06.8 p.m. **3:06.8 p.m.**
Greatest eclipse . . . . 6:44.1 p.m. **3:44.1 p.m.**
Moon leaves totality . . . . 7:21.5 p.m. **4:21.5 p.m.**
Moon leaves umbra . . . . 8:28.8 p.m. **5:28.8 p.m.**
Moon leaves penumbra . . . . 9:32.7 p.m. **6:32.7 p.m.**
Visibility: South and Central America, most of North America, Greenland, the Arctic regions, Africa, Europe, most of Asia, most of the Atlantic Ocean, the eastern Pacific Ocean, the Indian Ocean.

DECEMBER 23, PARTIAL ECLIPSE OF THE SUN: 2° ♑ 28′
Eclipse begins . . . . 5:20.7 p.m. **2:20.7 p.m.**
Greatest eclipse . . . . 7:30.7 p.m. **4:30.7 p.m.**
Eclipse ends . . . . 9:40.7 p.m. **6:40.7 p.m.**

Magical Events
Throughout the Year

   We would like to include a calendar and listing of magickal events throughout the year, across the country (and abroad, if possible), together with a reference list of organizations offering magickal training, seminars, etc. Inclusion of Renaissance Fairs, generally beloved by magickal folk, might be considered also. If you are the organizer of any of the above, *and have definite dates ahead of time*, please let us have full details for this section of the almanac. Deadline is January 1, 1992, for the *1993 Magickal Almanac.*

Wiccan/Pagan Sabbat, Esbat and Moon Festivals

ARKANSAS—Ozark Pagan Ecumenical Council, Box 605, Springdale AR 72764

CALIFORNIA—NROOGD, Box 360607, Milpitas CA 95035

COLORADO—D.A.W.N., Box 11202, Englewood CO 80151

FLORIDA—Garden of the Faerie Faith, Box 12941, Lake Park FL 33403

INDIANA—Aquarius Spiritus Templum, Bristol IN (219) 848-7539

ILLINOIS—Coven of the Sacred Stone, Chicago IL (312) 525-9194

MARYLAND—Ecumenicon, Box 302, Wheaton MD 20902

MASSACHUSETTS—EarthSpirit Community, Box 365, Medford MA 02155

NEW YORK—Temple of the Eternal Light, 928 E 5th St., Brooklyn NY 11230

—Open Circle, Box 4538, Sunnyside NY 11104

OHIO—Muses' Loom, Box 14902, Columbus OH 43214

—Lairus & Nema, Newark OH (614) 345-5288

OREGON—Oregon Pagan Council, Box 1012, Oregon City OR 97045

RHODE ISLAND—Our Lady of the Roses, Box 5967, Providence RI 02903

TEXAS—Judy Haskell, 5920 Bissonnet #113, Houston TX 77081

VIRGINIA—Vision Weavers' Circle, Box 3653, Fairfax VA 22038

—Wiccan Exploration, Box 807, Merrifeld VA 22116

WASHINGTON—Aquarian Tabernacle, Box 85507, Seattle WA 98145

WISCONSIN—Circle, Box 219, Mt. Horeb WI 53572

Native American Gatherings

FLORIDA—Pan-American Indian Association, Nocatee FL 33864

NEW YORK—Enchantments, 341 E 9th St., New York NY 10003

—Lone Wolf, Long Island NY (516) 821-0981

OHIO—Centre for Human Development, 4310 Mayfield Rd., S. Euclid OH 44121

—Ohio Wolf Clan Teaching Lodge, 2891 Southern Road, Richfield OH 44286

TENNESSEE—XAT Medicine Society, Nashville TN (615) 889-5759

Annual Seminars, Gatherings

FLORIDA—Medicine Wheel Gathering, Bear Tribe, Box 9167, Spokane WA 99209 (November)

—Winter Rainbow Gathering, Box 773, Gainesville FL 32601 (February)

MARYLAND—Ecumenicon, Box 302, Wheaton MD 20902 (July)

MASSACHUSETTS—Halloween Ball, WPLA, Box 8736, Salem MA 01971 (October)

NEW JERSEY—Esotericon, Box 22775, Newark, NJ 07101 (January)

OHIO—Starwood, A.C.E., 1643 Lee Rd. #9, Cleveland Heights OH 44118 (July)

   —Winterstar, A.C.E. (February)

TENNESSEE—Samhain Gathering, Cerren Ered, Box 936, Gatlinburg TN 37738 (October)

VIRGINIA—Fortfest, INFO, Box 367, Arlington VA 22210 (November)

WISCONSIN—Int'l Pagan Spirit Gathering, Circle, Box 219, Mt. Horeb WI 53572 (June)

Classes, Rituals

CALIFORNIA—Seekers' Circle, Box 16025, N. Hollywood CA 91615

   —Hermes Camp, O.T.O., 249 N. Brand Blvd. #482, Glendale CA 91203

COLORADO—High Plains Church of Wicca, 2049 S. Federal Blvd. #286, Denver CO 80219

   —Church of Seven Arrows, Box 185, Wheatridge CO 80034

GEORGIA—Y Tylwyth Teg, Box 674884, Marietta GA 30067

INDIANA—TGG, Box 219, Galveston IN 46932

MARYLAND—The Turning Wheel, 8039A Ritchie Hwy., Pasadena MD 21122

OHIO—A.C.E., 1643 Lee Rd. #9, Cleveland Heights OH 44118

"Let there be light"

Which Book Was That In?

A generation or two ago children had the books of the Bible drummed into their heads through the use of rhyme. Here is the rhyme for the books of the Old Testament:

In GENESIS the world was made by God's Almighty hand,
In EXODUS the Hebrews marched to gain the Promised Land.
LEVITICUS contains the Law—holy and just and good;
NUMBERS records the tribes enrolled, all sons of Abraham's blood.

Moses, in DEUTERONOMY, extols God's mighty deeds,
Brave JOSHUA into Canaan's land the host of Israel leads.
In JUDGES their rebellion oft provokes the Lord to smite,
But RUTH records the faith of one well pleasing in His sight.

The First and Second SAMUEL of Jesse's son we read,
Ten tribes in First and Second KINGS revolted from his seed;
The First and Second Chronicles see Judah captive made,
But EZRA leads a remnant back by princely Cyrus's aid.

The city walls of Zion NEHEMIAH builds again,
While ESTHER saves her people from the plots of wicked men.
In JOB we read how faith will live beneath affliction's rod,
Whilst David's PSALMS are precious songs to every child of God.

The PROVERBS like a goodly string of choicest pearls appear;

ECCLESIASTES teaches men how vain are all things here.
The mystic SONG OF SOLOMON extols sweet Sharon's rose,
Whilst Christ the Savior and the King the rapt ISAIAH shows.

The warning JEREMIAH apostate Israel scorns,
His plaintive LAMENTATIONS their awful downfall mourns.
EZEKIEL tells in wondrous words of dazzling mysteries,
Whilst kings and empires yet to come DANIEL in vision sees.

Of justice and of mercy HOSEA loves to tell;
JOEL recalls the blessed days when God with man shall dwell.
Among Tekoa's herdsmen AMOS received his call.
And OBADIAH prophesies of Edom's final fall.

JONAH enshrines a wondrous type of Christ our risen Lord;
MICAH pronounces Judah lost—lost, but again restored.
NAHUM declares on Ninevah just judgement shall be poured,
A view of Chaldea's coming doom HABBAKUK's visions give,
Whilst ZEPHANIAH warns the Jews to turn, repent and live.

HAGGAI wrote to those who saw the temple built again,
And ZECHARIAH prophesies of Christ's triumphant reign;
MALACHI was the last who touched the high prophetic chord—
His final notes sublimely show the coming of the Lord.

Words of Power
in Ancient Egypt

Brian Crowley

Egypt has long been regarded as a land of marvel and mystery and the acknowledged home of gods, men and magicians who used words of power or *hekau* to create specified natural and supernatural effects.

The famous Egyptian *Book of the Dead* contains entire chapters devoted to spells and charms of influence and command to be used on the physical and metaphysical planes. There was even the belief that words were concrete things. If any individual's personal words of power were stolen, that person would become vulnerable to all manner of abuse and attack.

The power of sound was with the Egyptians from the beginning of time. Hieroglyphic texts reveal several references to a Supreme Deity who first created for himself a place in which to dwell by uttering his own name *as a word of power*, and then created the heavens, the celestial bodies, the gods, Earth, people, animals, birds and other creatures, as concepts in his own mind.

The ibis-headed god Thoth, reputed inventor of *meduneter* or hieroglyphic writing (the "words of god") is said to have translated into words these divine thoughts or ideas. According to the *Book of the Dead*, when Thoth spoke the following *hekau* or "words of power," creation commenced:

Kheper medet nebt Tem
("There came [or come] into being the words of Temu.")

To the Egyptians ritual magic, or *za*, was regarded as an exact science that permeated all aspects of life, including in particular the areas of medicine, healing and prophecy. All gods,

The ibis-headed god Thoth, reputed inventor of Medu-Neter, or hieroglyphic writing. The hieroglyphs top right read Medu-Neter, literally "Words of God."

people, creatures and objects were considered to be imbued with a definable spiritual force that was at once contactable and controllable—when the correct words of command were utilized. By simply uttering the name of a being or an inanimate object, that being or object could be called into existence, thus paralleling the very act of original creation.

The reigning pharaoh would preface any new decree with the words "I am the Great Word," indicating that he was capable of conferring life. A magician would begin all spells with the words *peret herou*, literally "that which comes forth at the voice."

Utterance of a specified incantation could lead to power over wind, rain, storm and tempest, and even over the motions of river and sea. Correctly intoned *hekau* might also produce food for the hungry, banish illness and provide protection from all manner of dangers and disasters, and sometimes even death. For the Egyptians life on Earth was considered as merely a prelude to the hereafter and spells and incantations took on a particular significance when used by the deceased to negotiate safely the many pitfalls encountered beyond the threshold of death.

Even the gods themselves were obliged to abide by words of power uttered by any mortal. Every Egyptian received two names, the great name and little name, of which only the second was ever made public. Knowledge of the secret name of any god, devil or person was considered to be the key to true mastery over that being or individual, and a name was considered as important as the *Ka* of a person, the soul itself.

The worst fate that could befall any being was to see his or her name misused or destroyed, for it could be as much the object of a curse as it could of a blessing.

The very letters of a name carried their own force. When an Egyptian magician spoke, he used sound like an artist, creating a word picture of marvelous strength and influence. It followed naturally that magical writing in hieroglyphs was considered to carry a power of its own, and because of the symbols used (animals, plants, parts of the human body), this form of writing was considered of a timeless nature.

To assist in the perfection of the spirit-souls of those who had moved into the Realm of the Dead, it was customary for the still-living Egyptians to recite the names of the gods at funerals and other feasts. Sixty-six such names are listed in the Theban Recension of the *Book of the Dead*, beginning with Osiris-Kenti-Amenti, one of the many appellations of Osiris, the Egyptian "savior" and most significant of all Egyptian deities.

Having himself been resurrected from the dead, thanks to the dedicated efforts of his consort and sister, the goddess Isis, Osiris is clearly equated with the concept of eternal life. It can be said that the legend of Osiris, and that of his spouse Isis and son Horus, is the story of all creatures on Earth: birth, life, death and rebirth.

Isis, whose name literally means "seat," was the devoted sister-wife of Osiris. As the most popular goddess in the Egyptian pantheon, she was also a role model for many later Mediterranean and Middle-Eastern goddesses, and even possibly for the Tibetan Buddhist Avalokitesvara or Chinese Kuan Yin.

More importantly, Isis or Ast is hailed in various ancient Egyptian texts as "the woman of magical spells" and "the mistress of words of power, or enchantments" who is described as having turned aside countless calamities with the "magical power of her mouth."

One passage describes how "the words which she stringeth together destroy diseases, and they make to live those whose throats are stopped up [i.e., the dead]." As goddess of both earth and moon, sister-wife of Osiris and mother of Horus, Isis was said to hold sway over earth, sea and heavens, and even in the underworld. As goddess of birth, she decided the fate of mortals from an early stage in their lives.

And anyone facing any form of threat, be it from physical danger or disease, or of a psychic or spiritual nature, might be prompted to use a phrase from the *Book of the Dead* invoking her name:

Erta-na-hekau-apen-Ast
("May I be given the Words of Power of Isis.")

Erta-na-hekau-apen-Ast—
"May I be given the Words of Power of Isis."

Just a Little Imagination

Jenine E. Trayer

Magickal people exhibit a wealth of ingenuity in choice of clothing, jewelry and home decorating. Let's face it; you can't go to the local department store and ask for a Yule Wreath decorated with runes to hang on your front door! But Pagan people have been decorating items by stenciling for hundreds of years. The design created can be as magickal and elaborate as the crafter chooses.

A stencil can be made of coated cardboard, tin, or mylar plastic. I prefer the mylar because it has a longer life through repeated use.

To create your own pattern, select a design appropriate for the technique (see examples). Each block of color should be separated by at least 1/8".

Supplies
Utility knife
Tracing Paper
Black Marking Pen
Mylar
Illustration Board
Transparent Tape
Stenciling Brushes: Sizes 2 and 4 for small designs; 6 and 8 for larger patterns
Paint—Ready mixed stencil paint or artists' acrylic. I use ceramic stains. They are of acrylic composition, come in a varied number of colors, and are cheaper and durable.

Wet and dry rags for boo-boos and clean up
Paper Plate

Cutting Your Stencil

Trace design on paper with a pencil. Outline with black marking pen. Stack materials on clipboard—illustration board first, design next, mylar last.

Double check design for color separations and leave at least 1" uncut around entire design for easier stenciling.

Hold utility knife like a pencil and slowly cut design. Use ruler to assist on straight edges, turn clipboard (not knife) for curved lines. Always cut *toward* the body with even pressure on knife—one stroke only for each cut—until entire design is finished. Place your hand under the mylar to check cuts. If cuts have not gone through, place light pressure on cut with knife. Mylar will easily separate. Slightly stronger pressure may be needed for corners or points of the design.

Before removing from clipboard, check that all cuts have been made. The mylar pieces pop out easily (don't force, just lightly re-cut).

Painting the Design

Place the stencil on piece to be decorated. Center, and tape all outside edges securely.

Choose first color and lightly load brush. Paint will crawl up the bristles of brush after repeated use. To assist in controlling loaded bush, place small amount of paint in shallow dish, then dab brush on paper plate until you are comfortable with the technique.

Hold brush perpendicular to surface to be painted. Place the fingers of your free hand as close to the edges of the color area as possible, holding down edges of stencil. The more you can surround the area with your fingers, the better. The trick of stenciling is to keep the paint from bleeding under the edges of the mylar. Always apply pressure to the rim of the stencil around the color areas you are painting.

Bounce the bristles of the brush off the surface. A good looking stencil design has concentrated color in the center that fades (like the technique of an air brush) to the edges.

Bounce out from center of color area. Three coats are required for even color coverage. Let color dry between coats or the bouncing effect will pick up what has already been painted, leaving bare spots.

Clean brush after each color is complete. Wrap and squeeze in dry rag to remove excess water before picking up next color.

When design is finished, carefully remove stencil. Clean under hot, running water. For repeated patterns, wash after every two applications. If you do not, you risk bleeding in your design.

Stencil designs will have a stippled effect. The edges won't be perfectly straight; that is the beauty of the craft.

If your design does bleed, use an artist's liner brush loaded with background color to cover the error.

Colors can be blended on stencil. Choose three shades of the same color. A leaf can look three dimensional by applying two coats of the lightest shade, then touch edges with remaining colors. Do not wash brush between these color uses.

Children enjoy stenciling too. Yule Cards, wrapping paper, tree decorations, talismans, and jewelry are great projects.

After all, necessity, creativity, and fun are the ingredients for any Pagan craft!

The Dragon Bride

Tara Buckland

In the beginning Heaven sent its son, Dragon, to deliver life-giving waters to the Earth. Ordained the most supreme God in nature, Dragon demanded temples, priests and tribute. In adoration, a young Chinese maiden was chosen to be Dragon's bride. The young maiden was set adrift in a wooden boat upon the swift and dangerous currents of the Yangtze River. Humanity hoped this union would ensure proper rainfall and regulate the flood tide.

To this day, the Chinese honor the union of Dragon and his bride with one of the most widely celebrated of Chinese holidays—the Dragon-boat Festival. Each year in early spring, thousands of wooden Dragon-boats are set upon the Yangtze River to pay tribute to the Dragon and his lovely bride. There is still a reluctance, in some of the more rural regions of China, to save a victim drowning in a river for fear of depriving the River Dragon of His tribute.

In many parts of the world the Dragon is a mysterious and often dangerous, if not downright evil, character. To the Chinese, however, Dragon is the bringer of great prosperity, happiness and health. He is life-giving, benevolent and restorative. He is the guardian of treasures and controls all the waters of the earth. He can often be found in rivers, lakes and even (when he magickally shrinks himself) in raindrops. Dragon is also the Giver of Laws and the Supreme Instructor in the ways of Magick. The art of painting is said to have been introduced by Dragon, as was the appreciation of beauty.

Dragon is very fond of glittering jewels and likes to spend His afternoons basking in the warmth of the sun. He also enjoys eating the occasional careless swallow who happens to accidently fly into His mouth while chasing mosquitoes. As beneficent and bountiful as Dragon is, He could become very annoyed if offended or disturbed. At such times His pouting could eclipse the sun. If really angered he would gather up all the fresh water in His baskets and so cause a tremendous drought.

Dragon is a mysterious concoction of many creatures. Although He is generally referred to as a male, it is noted in the ancient literature of China that He is both male and female, although the male (yang) energy is in greater proportion. Dragon is a mixture of animals which makes Him more powerful than any other animal on the earth. The ancient Chinese writer Wang Fu wrote of Dragon in the 1600's: "... Dragon is ... the largest of scaled creatures. Its head is like a camel's, its horns like a stag's, its eyes like a hare's, its ears like a bull's, its neck like a snake's, its belly like a frog's, its scales like a carp's, its claws like an eagle's, and its paws like a tiger's. Its scales number 81, being nine by nine, the extreme odd and lucky number. Its voice is like the beating of a gong... When it breathes the breath forms clouds, sometimes changing into rain, at other times into fire... it is fond of beautiful gems and jade. It is extremely fond of swallow's flesh; it dreads iron, the *Ma Huang* plant (*Ephedra sinica*), the centipede, the leaves of the Pride of India (the azedarac tree) and silk dyed in five different colors. When rain is wanted a swallow should be offered; when floods are to be restrained, then iron; to stir up the Dragon the *Ma Huang* plant should be employed."

The Dragon is described in the old Chinese *Book of Rites* as one of the four benevolent spiritual animals, the unicorn, phoenix and tortoise being the others. Generally He is associated with the East, the direction of the ancestors and the renewal of spring.

The Dragon-boat festival is celebrated at the Chinese New Year, which occurs on the first New Moon after the Sun enters Aquarius. This generally falls sometime between January 21st and February 19th and lasts for four days. In 1992, the Chinese New Year will fall on February 3rd and will usher in the Year Of The Monkey.

To celebrate the awesome, life-giving powers of Dragon, you also may make a Dragon-boat to set adrift on a nearby river. If you don't live near a river, any body of water will do, as Dragon dwells in all water—even bathwater!

Serious thought should be given to the materials used to make your Dragon-boat. It is not recommended that you use any material that could be considered "litter" after the boat floats away and gets struck on a bank. This makes your job harder but I'm sure your creativity will rise to the occasion. Here are some suggestions for making a natural, non-littering Dragon-boat:

Use a piece of driftwood, plaited rushes, the "lid" of a dried gourd, naturally fallen bark or even a dried leaf as the base of the boat. Or, you can tie twigs together, raft-style, using small amounts of sisal twine. It would probably be all right to use very small amounts of Elmer's glue for any fancy construction, but don't glue it too strongly. After all, your gift is *supposed* to be consumed by Dragon—not a permanent structure. Do not use store-bought timber for the boat. Even though it is wood, it just won't look natural cluttered up on the bank of a river.

Do not use any candles, as these would litter too. Instead, use a flower to symbolize the Dragon Bride. Decorate the boat with pretty pebbles or spices. You could make a soft bed for the Dragon Bride with moss. You might even try very small amounts of non-toxic, water-soluble tempera paint for tiny splashes of color.

Celebrate the event with the lighting of incense and music. Chinese music is full of percussion instruments, so take cymbals, drums, rattles or anything else you feel like using. Launch your boat with your prayers and wishes for the New Year and ask Dragon and His Bride to bring you health, wealth and happiness for the coming year.

Robin Hood, Witch
(and More . . .)
Amber K

The legend of Robin Hood: merry men hunting in the green depths of Sherwood Forest. Little John, Friar Tuck, Maid Marian, and the Sheriff of Nottingham. Everyone knows that he is an English folk hero; few understand that he is much more.

Clad in Lincoln green (a very Pagan color), he and his men comprise a group of 13—including, of course, Maid Marian. Robin Hood a Witch? The Merry Men a coven? Maid Marian his High Priestess? The evidence suggests this, and more.

Robin Hood, or Robin Wood, or Robin of the Woods, is a thinly disguised version of The Lord of the Greenwood, the Horned God Himself. Sherwood Forest, claimed by Prince John as a royal hunting preserve, really belongs with all its creatures to Robin. The old phrase *'round Robin Hood's barn*—meaning all over the place—suggests this. "Robin Hood's barn" is Sherwood Forest—or by extension, all outdoors.

He is a male analog to Diana, Goddess of all outdoors, associated with deer and the hunt, with freedom. In his defiance of church and state, He is much like Aradia, Who was sent by the Great Goddess to lead Her people against tyranny and oppression.

If He is The Horned One, then Marian can be none other than the Goddess; and indeed Mari is a very ancient Goddess-name. Though Lady Marian's role in the legend is not so active, the Maiden is always in the background, supporting and encouraging Robin. So much does He love Her, that He will risk all at the great archery tournament to win a golden arrow—and Her kiss.

Many of us have seen the American television version of "Robin Hood," who is not so different from "Davy Crockett," "Zorro," or other adventure heroes of that era. But if you have the opportunity, see the British series—where Robin is the chosen hero of Herne the Hunter, the stag-antlered God Himself. This version suggests the truth, that Robin is the Son of the Horned God or the Horned One in human form.

And every one of the Merry Men ("Merry meet...") has his part in the drama. Little John, Robin's right hand man, a Pagan St. Peter. Will Scarlet, the Summoner perhaps. Alan a'Dale, the bard. And Friar Tuck, outwardly obedient to the Church, but in his actions Pagan to the core.

The legend of Robin Hood was created in a time when the Old Religion still lived, but it was dangerous to openly celebrate the God and Goddess. But who could object to a harmless folk tale? Thus the common people could celebrate the old ways in song and story, in the face of an oppressive Church and state, without reprisal.

Sherwood Forest still stands, its ancient and massive oaks shading paths which lead deep into history. Nearby there is a tiny church and graveyard where Robin and Marian are said to rest in the Earth; but Their spirits live on in the greenwood, and in the hearts of Pagans.

Magical Secrecy

Scott Cunningham

One of the basic principles of magic, as they are often taught, is *secrecy*. Don't speak of your magical workings, we're told. Don't tell your friends of your interest in magic, let alone discuss the candle ritual that you performed last night.

Be still, we're taught. Talk not. Let the power cook. Some say that, by speaking of your magical operations, you'll disperse the energies that you've put into them. Others state that non-magicians, upon hearing of a magical ritual that you've performed, will send out unbelieving, negative energies that will block your spell from manifesting. A few magicians will say that secrecy about one's magical proclivities was once a necessity for saving one's neck. Others give no reason. They simply repeat the old code: "Be silent."

Is this superstition? Perhaps. Many magicians, who work with energies that scientists haven't yet been able to locate or identify, simply don't know everything about these energies. They may have seen the effectiveness of rituals that they've performed. They may even have told close friends about these rituals prior to their manifestations, with no ill effects. But soon, the secrecy issue begins ringing a bell.

"Should I talk about these things?" they'll ask themselves. "After all, that book stated that loose lips sink spells. That woman I know does rituals all the time, but only tells me about them *after* they've taken effect. And I'm sure that there are lots of magicians who'd never breathe a word about that blue candle that they've been burning, their herbal baths, their visualizations or chants or moonlit rites."

Doubt soon clouds the magician's mind. Eventually, the magician buttons up and doesn't speak of rituals. Secrecy has once again been conferred on the process.

This is unfortunate and unnecessary. True magic, the movement of natural energies to create needed change, is limitless. Speaking of a ritual to others doesn't disperse the energies. On the contrary, it gives you a new opportunity to send more power toward your magical goal.

Disbelief also isn't a satisfactory reason for magical secrecy. The disbelief of others has about as much effect on magic as does an unschooled person's doubt that a calculator can add 2 and 2 to equal 4. The calculator will work regardless of this observer's doubt. So, too, will magic.

There are other reasons why the calculator possibly wouldn't perform this simple operation: faulty microchips, low battery power, a lack of batteries, an operator who pushes the wrong buttons, or a switch turned to "off." But an observer's disbelief can't be the cause.

The same is true of magic. Properly performed, magic will be effective. If energy is raised within the body, programmed with intent, and projected toward its goal with the proper force and visualization, it will be effective. Perhaps not overnight. Many repetitions of the magical ritual may be necessary. But it usually is effective, if the operator (the magician) knows how to use this process.

The problem of magical secrecy is the doubt that it instills within the magician. If a magician believes that speaking of her or his rituals to others will somehow diminish their power, it just might—precisely because of this belief. This is similar to going to bed late one night, all the time thinking, "I just know I'll sleep in tomorrow morning and be late for work," and doing just that. This is negative programming, and negative programming is remarkably effective.

The third reason often proffered for magical secrecy, that it's a tradition handed down from earlier times when magicians were rounded up and charged with heresy, is at least historically accurate. But speaking of rituals to close friends today isn't likely to cause you to be hanged.

Secrecy, then, isn't a necessary part of magic. It's no guarantee of magical success. This doesn't mean that you should walk around wearing a green button that states, "I did a money ritual last night!" It also doesn't mean that you *must* discuss your magical affairs with others, especially if you're working on intensely private matters.

You certainly may wish to be silent about your magical rituals among friends who know of your interests, and even among other magicians. If so, be certain of the reasons you're silent.

Magical secrecy concerning rituals is a superstition that should have no place in our lives.

Runes

Norman Frankland

Erce, Erce, Erce,	mother of earth
May the Almighty One,	may the Eternal One,
Grant thee acres	flourishing and fruitful
Acres bountiful,	acres sustaining;
Birth of Bright	millet harvest,
Birth of Broad	barley harvest,
Birth of White	wheat harvest,
And all the harvests of earth.	

The runic alphabet is the oldest form of Germanic writing. It was in use as early as the third century. *Futhark*—24 runes of Gothic alphabet, arranged in three groups of eight letters.

ᚻ	–	cēn	(C)	–	torch
ᛎ	–	ȳr	(Y)	–	bow
✕	–	nyd	(N)	–	need
ᛗ	–	eoh	(E)	–	horse
ᚹ	–	wynn	(W)	–	liss
ᚢ	–	ur	(U)	–	bull
ᚴ	–	lagu	(L)	–	water
ᛄ	–	feoh	(F)	–	wealth

Magical Personalities of Egypt: Tutmose III

Gordon T. G. Hudson

There is a statue of Tutmose in the Cairo Museum on which the neck is short and the chest powerful, suggesting a determined man. He was in fact a formidable man, but his nose was his dominant feature, giving character to his face. He certainly bore no love for his stepmother, Hatshepsut (who was also known as Merkare), and he proved this almost certainly at the outset of his reign. Anyway, he had many other concerns. Early in his predecessor's reign the princes of Djahi and Retjnu had noticed that the Queen had no aptitude for military campaigns, preferring to embellish her noble city of Thebes, and they began concentrating forces at Megiddo. They didn't directly threaten Egypt, but they could be construed as dangerous. Tutmose gathered an army and crossed the frontier near Pelusium where he held a council of war. The Egyptians decided to fight, and engaged the Syrians near Yehem. The engagement was short, as the enemy abandoned their horses and chariots in their headlong rush to shut themselves up in Megiddo. It took seven months for Tutmose to break the siege but break it he did.

It was a hard lesson for the Syrians, but as nothing is ever ended in the Middle East, Tutmose was to fight them again. Until now the Egyptians had hardly gone beyond the second cataract. It was perhaps under Tutmose that they reached the Gebel Barkal, a little way downstream from the fourth cataract. Stele were discovered there which recount Pharaoh's exploits in detail. It was important to advertise the exploits, thank the Gods and edify the populace. In Thebes everywhere one looks one sees the name of the warrior king.

There were occasions for the king to show himself in public. When he decided to reward his most faithful servants, he appeared on the balcony, which was designed for royal appearances. The herald summoned the elect who were presented to the Pharaoh. They had to catch a golden bowl and a golden cup which His Majesty tossed them (the Louvre museum has a cup which Tutmose gave to one of his officials). It was the king's duty to be generous to his servants. Whenever Tutmose was leading one of his victorious campaigns, he never strayed very far from his troops, and as soon as the royal herald signaled some remarkable deed, he would take a valuable gift from a coffer and present it to the brave warrior. He himself was extremely brave in war and readily exposed himself to danger.

At Karnak there are countless proofs of his piety. He paid great reverence chiefly to Amen, but didn't neglect his ancestors. In the Akh-menu building, he caused the names of 61 kings to be engraved, beginning with Snofru the Beneficent, but presented in an order which has caused much trouble to historians.

One of the first acts of his reign was to restore the statues of Amenhotep I and Tutmose II. At Sinai he restored an ancient inscription of Sesostris III, a king with whom he felt he had an affinity.

The king's favorite wife was probably Meryetre, for it was she who gave him the hereditary prince Amenhotep. Mother and son are sometimes shown side by side, and we know that Tutmose watched most attentively over his son's education— his education as a sportsman, that is. He gave him a Prince of This and of the Oasis to teach him archery and under such a master the young man made rapid progress, soon becoming the equal of his father. In the art of breaking horses, the young prince was soon unrivaled. He had his royal sire before him as an example. Tutmose himself was so fond of horses that he had set up a magnificent stable. Pharaoh taught his son to scorn physical softness and to appreciate toughness. Just as he had once prepared himself for his royal duties, so he now prepared his heir.

A story is told that, during the reign of Tutmose, a certain Prince of Joppa rose in rebellion and murdered all the Egyptian soldiers quartered in his town. This news excited people's wrath, and he called together his nobles, generals and scribes to see what could be done. None of then had any suggestions to make, except one a brilliant young infantry officer called Thoutii.

"Give me your magic cane, O my king, and a body of infantry and of charioteers, and I undertake to kill the Prince of Joppa and to take the town."

Pharaoh, who esteemed this officer highly, granted all that he asked—not exactly a modest request, for the cane was a talisman supposed to render invisible anyone into whose possession it fell and also anyone it touched.

Thoutii then marched to Palestine with his men. Arriving there, he had a large skin bag made, big enough to hold a man, and he had irons made for hands and feet; also shackles and yokes of wood, and 400 jars.

He sent to the Prince of Joppa the following message:

"I am Thoutii, the Egyptian infantry general. King Tutmose was jealous of my bravery and has sought to kill me, but I have escaped from him and stolen his magic cane which is hidden in my baggage. If you like I shall give it to you, and I shall join forces with you, I and my men, the pick of the Egyptian army, 400 strong."

This message was very pleasant news to the Prince of Joppa, for he knew Thoutii's reputation and knew that he had no equal in all of Egypt. He sent to Thoutii, accepting his offer and promising him a share of his territory. He then left Joppa to greet the man whom he took to be a new and powerful ally. While he was on his way, Thoutii's men hid in the jars which were then lightly sealed. The Prince welcomed the general and invited him into his camp to dine.

While they were dining the Prince asked about Tutmose's magic cane. Thoutii went out to fetch it and, before the Prince could make a move, Thoutii struck him on the forehead and the Prince became unconscious. Then Thoutii put him into the big leather sack, clapped the handcuffs on his wrists and the irons on his feet. As the face of the unconscious Prince had become invisible from the touch of the magic cane, Thoutii instructed one of his men to say that it was he, Thoutii, who had been made a prisoner. The man was to go to the Princess and announce that Thoutii had been captured and bound and that it was now safe to assume they had no more to fear from the Egyptians. This the man did and the town gates were opened and at the same time Thoutii's men leapt out of the jars, rushed in and took the town almost without resistance.

Though Tutmose was a tough warrior, we find that he had human feelings in that he loved and venerated his mother and his wife. For his companions-in-arms who had more than once saved his life, he felt friendship. In all, he lived a very fruitful life of great accomplishment.

Both Hatshepsut and Tutmose III built on a monumental scale unprecedented until then. They, as well as other pharaohs and nobles, had their dancers and musicians, their jugglers, acrobats and professional storytellers, all of whom maintained a perpetual vaudeville performance for their patrons.

Continuing the saga of his dislike of Hatshepsut, then—he erected a 105-feet-tall obelisk close to hers (anything you can do

I can do better). That is now outside the church of St. John Lateran in Rome, and its companion is in Istanbul.

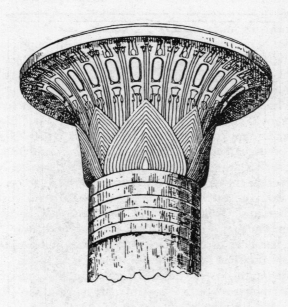

A Ritual for Scrying the 27th Path of Tarot: The Tower

Chic Cicero and Sandra Tabatha Cicero

The cards of the Tarot are perfect vehicles for scrying and astral projection. Sometimes referred to as "pathworking," this experience is uniquely personal to each individual. The practice of astral projection involves altering consciousness through meditation, concentration and ceremony in order to turn inward, traveling through the paths of the mind to unlock the spiritual truths hidden in the psyche.

A true "pathworking" is an astral journey unto one of the paths which connect the different Sephiroth, or spheres, on the Qabalistic Tree of Life. The 27th Path is represented by the 16th key of the Tarot known as *The Tower*. This path connects the Seventh Sephirah, Netzach, to the Eighth Sephirah, Hod. These spheres symbolize the concepts of Emotion and Intellect. A person scrying the 27th Path is undertaking to harmonize these seemingly contrary ideas. A perfect balance between emotional desires and the rational, logical mind has been a goal of Initiates of the Mysteries since ancient times. The Tower card alludes to a fortress of old ideas and old "realities" which are suddenly altered by the powerful energy of Mars. This results in the collapse of an obsolete way of thinking and the rebuilding of a new outlook. It is a new "bridge" built between the right and left sides of the brain, which results in an open channel for communication between the various parts of the "self."

The methods used in this ritual follow the traditional teachings of the Hermetic Order of the Golden Dawn.

The Ritual

(1) Prepare the temple or sacred space in your usual fashion. You will need a consecrated pack of Tarot cards with the traditional Qabalistic symbolism. Remove the 16th Key of Tarot, The Tower, from the deck. Put the remaining cards away. Provide a comfortable place to sit or lie down for the main part of the ritual. You will also need a Lotus Wand or any other personal wand that you normally use for invocation.

(2) Take a Ritual Bath: First shower with soap and water. Then fill up the bathtub with warm water and bath salts or perfumed oil. Soak for a few minutes and release any negativity you may be feeling into the water. Remain in the tub, but pull the plug to drain both the water and your daily problems. Dry off and robe up.

(3) In the temple area perform a ritual of protection such as the Lesser Banishing Ritual of the Pentagram. You should then follow this with the Lesser Banishing Ritual of the Hexagram. (Both of these rituals are described in Israel Regardie's book, *The Golden Dawn.*)

(4) Place the 16th Key of the Tarot upon the Altar.

(5) With wand in hand, say, "I (give Magickal name), in the Divine name IAO, invoke Thee, thou Great Angel HRU (Herru), who art set over the operations of this secret Wisdom. Make this talisman of the ROTA (row-tah) a true and accurate portal through which I may enter and partake of the knowledge of THE TOWER."

(6) With the wand, draw the invoking Hexagram of Mars (the planet which rules The Tower) over the card and intone the following Divine names: While tracing the hexagram, vibrate "ARA-RITA" (Ah-rah-ree-tah); when drawing the sigil of Mars in the center of the hexagram, intone the name "ELOHIM GIBOR"

(El-oh-heem G'boor); and finally vibrate the name of the Hebrew letter "ALEPH" (Ah-Lef) while tracing the letter over the
planetary sigil. Thrust the head of the wand through the center
of the hexagram and visualize a doorway opening into infinite
space.

(7) Again with the wand, draw the Hebrew
letter *peh* in the air above The Tower card.
Visualize the letter in flaming red. Intone the name
of the letter, PEH (Pay), several times.

(8) Place your hands beside the card or hold the trump
with both hands. With all your powers of concentration, look
upon the card and comprehend it, consider all its symbolism
and interpretations.

(9) When your mind is steady upon the image, give the
Sign of the Rending of the Veil (fold hands as if praying, then
step forward and thrust the hands straight out in front of you.
Separate hands and bring the arms straight back so that you re-
semble a T or a cross.) Close your eyes, but keep the image of The
Tower clearly in your mind's eye. At this point you may sit or lie
on the floor in a comfortable position, yet still concentrate on the
card.

(10) Maintain a disassociation from the surrounding room.
The Tarot card of The Tower exists as a huge curtain before you.
The background of the curtain is flaming red with highlights of
green. In your vision, part the curtain with the Sign of the Rending of the Veil. As the curtain is drawn aside, its colors change—
turning to red highlights on a green background. Project your
consciousness beyond your physical body and see *within* the
symbol before you. The following is an example of the experience you are likely to have:

You step through the curtain of the 16th Key to find that
you are in a great eight-sided room. The walls are draped with
orange silk and the floor is covered with fire opals. Eight alter-
nating columns of water and flame encircle the inner sanctuary.
Above you the ceiling is dominated by a large blue sigil of Mercury. Within the circle of the sigil is the image of a cup. You realize that you are in the Water temple of Hod, the 8th Sephirah.
There is a blue altar in the middle of the room upon which is a

chalice of water and the Book of Knowledge—the figure of an octogram graces its cover. In each corner of the room, you see a statue of the God of Knowledge, given various names and images by humanity: Enki, Thoth, Hermes, Mercury, and other forms of the God you do not immediately recognize.

You perform the Qabalistic Cross. This has the effect of lighting you up and announcing your presence in the Sphere of Hod. Almost immediately a form appears before you, a great flaming being who carries a large sword. On instinct, you draw a pentagram before the being, who walks through it and responds by giving the LVX Signs. You suddenly realize that this is the great Archangel, MICHAEL, who has been sent to guide you on the 27th path.

He turns to a door concealed under the cloth to your right and beckons you to follow. Together you start down the path. It is sunrise; the solar disc is beginning its ascent to your left.

You pass low rolling hills and pasture with grazing sheep. Eventually, the landscape begins to change, becoming more rocky and mountainous. The footpath seems treacherous, full of potholes and sharp, loose stones that cause missteps. Michael says not a word as he walks effortlessly in front of you, but his protective presence is reassuring.

Ahead of you, behind a craggy hillside, a wondrous sight appears—a great crown sparkling with many jewels. As you get closer, you see before you a very high stone tower with the shining crown at its summit. The fortress looks impenetrable and there are no windows. The path you are on leads straight to the entrance of the structure. The solid oak door seems to be ajar. Michael gestures for you to enter the tower and continue on without him. From here on you must face what awaits you alone and make your own decisions.

Once inside the damp building you feel a bit closed-in. The tower has been badly neglected. Before you is a stone staircase which leads to the crown. With a renewed confidence you begin the ascent. As you climb the steps, you pass all kinds of armaments, cannon balls and gunpowder, shields, lances, broad swords and more. Yes, the tower is well-fortified.

As you near the top, you hear sounds of movement and

laughter. Who, you wonder, could call such a place as this *home*? Your Will drives you forward. Thrusting open a door at the top of the stairs, you gaze out onto a richly dressed group of nobles in silken robes and jeweled headpieces. They sit atop the shining crown of the tower under the shade of a raised cloth. In front of them are enormous quantities of food and drink, so much food in fact that some of it appears to be spoiling. Yet tethered to a rock away from the food is a small monkey weak from hunger with nothing to eat. The royals have obviously forgotten about the animal. This makes you angry. How dare these people be so neglectful?

Your presence has startled them. It is as if they have never seen anyone besides themselves. They seem to consider you an intruder. Frightened, they sound the alarm. From the door behind you and another beyond the nobles, armored guards come running with raised swords. If only Michael were here now!

Before any hands are able to grasp you, there is another sudden commotion. The aristocrats are now frantic because the sun has abruptly disappeared behind a great black cloud. Without warning there is a huge explosion of light and stone. A great lightning bolt has struck the tower! Within an instant there are no longer bricks beneath your feet and you are sailing through air. For a moment, you think that this must be the end of the journey. As you fall, you yell out, "I am Free from the Bonds of Darkness!"

You are lying on the ground, but you are puzzled. You did not feel the landing. Opening your eyes you see Michael standing above you, smiling. The archangel offers you his hand and you pull yourself to your feet. Remembering what happened, you stare at the tower in amazement.

The mighty crown which surmounted the structure has been utterly destroyed. The entire upper portion of brickwork has been knocked away. Three gaping holes have been blown into the wall and the fire from the blast is still roaring. The nobles are nowhere to be found.

Without speaking, Michael informs you that you have done well on this difficult test. What you rebuild out of the ashes of the Tower struck by Lightning will be far greater than anything you can now imagine. It is now up to you to create a better-kept, more balanced structure. The new tower must be built using knowledge *and* compassion, never the one without the other. But for the moment you must return to the temple of Hod.

The landscape becomes less rugged and the road widens. You feel revitalized by having survived the ordeal of the Tower. Michael walks beside you now, as if he is more confident of your abilities. A noise to your right brings your attention to an apple tree beside the path. The monkey from the tower sits amid the branches, happily munching on a piece of fruit.

Once again you find yourself back at the Water temple. You are reluctant to leave this place of learning, but you know that what you have accomplished today will take time to fully comprehend. You thank Michael and perform the Qabalistic Cross. Michael responds by giving the sign of Osiris, Slain and Risen. Then you step back through the curtain of the 16th Key, giving the sign of the Closing of the Veil (the reverse of the Opening Sign).

Bring your consciousness back into your body and make yourself slowly aware of physical room around you. Take your time and do not move too quickly.

(11) Perform the Lesser Banishing Ritual of the Pentagram.

(12) Perform the Lesser Banishing Ritual of the Hexagram.

(13) Say, "I now release any spirits that may have been imprisoned by this ceremony. Depart in peace to your abodes and habitations. Go with the blessings of YEHESHUAH YEHOVASHAH (Yeh-hay-shoe-ah Yeh-hoh-vah-shah). I now declare this temple duly closed. SO MOTE IT BE!"

Isis and the Warrior Queens of the Ancient Near East

deTraci Regula

The Goddess Isis, worshipped first in Egypt and then throughout the Greco-Roman world, is well-known as a goddess of love, motherhood, and magic. Her role as a maker of kings and as a goddess of war is often forgotten in the crowd of titles which generated for her yet another, that of "Goddess of the Ten-Thousand Names." In fact, Isis was not only a creator and patron goddess of kings but was also a maker of queens, several of whose stories have survived to the present day.

Setting aside the religious and mythological associations, the basic story of Isis and Osiris is that of a benevolent royal couple attempting to further the cause of civilization. While Osiris travels to bring Egyptian culture to adjacent nations, Isis rules alone. However, their success and love for each other incites the jealousy of Set, their brother, who succeeds in murdering Osiris and plans to force the right of kingship from Isis, who confers the power of the throne on whomever she takes as her husband. Isis discovers that she is pregnant by Osiris, and, with the help of her advisor Thoth, escapes to the concealing swamplands to bear and raise her son alone. Using the knowledge she has obtained during her years of rulership, she instructs Horus in the arts of politics and war so that he may avenge his father and reclaim his throne. Through many conflicts complicated by Set's treachery and shrewd political maneuvering, Horus nonetheless triumphs repeatedly with Isis fighting at his side and negotiating on his behalf. Finally, the issue of succession is settled in their favor and Horus becomes Pharaoh.

Many queens and royal princesses must have found this story familiar, particularly the family squabbles and forced marriages to assure politically acceptable unions. Isis Victrix, the Isis of Victory, was a natural choice to become the personal salvatrix of powerful queens.

Cleopatra the Seventh is the best known of the warrior queens who worshipped Isis and the most openly devoted to her faith. Cleopatra styled herself "The New Isis" and often appeared dressed as the goddess. Forcibly married to her younger brother Ptolemy, in an echo of the brother-sister marriage of myth, her brother's advisors plotted to rid themselves of the intelligent, strong-willed queen in favor of her more pliable sister Arsinoe.

But apparently Isis, the goddess called "The One Above Fate," had other plans for her priestess Cleopatra. Although Rome was more likely to support her brother's claim instead of hers, a mighty advocate came forward in the form of Julius Caesar. Although his aid to Cleopatra is generally attributed, understandably enough, to her great beauty and powers of persuasion, it may have been her role as High Priestess of Isis which predisposed Julius Caesar to support her claim.

Although Rome at the time was so violently opposed to the foreign worship then making converts at all levels of Roman society, Julius Caesar exhibited a curious tolerance toward the alien faith. Although he acted to suppress independent guilds, believing that they were a covert threat to the stability of government, he left the Isian fraternities in peace. He apparently met with an individual termed "The High Pontiff of Isis" in Egypt, although the identity of this leader is unclear, and may have been assured of the cooperation of the international and influential Isian priesthood if he supported their claimant to the throne of Egypt. Cleopatra may or may not have gained access to Julius by being hidden in and then unrolled from a rug.

However their first meeting occurred, their first encounter may have been orchestrated by the Isian clergy, who recognized in the devout Cleopatra and the powerful general a chance for a royal union on the scale of the divine Isis and Osiris. On a more pragmatic level, their union would end the tearing down of temples and shrines by the Roman authorities.

Despite the setbacks of later events, this is the scenario that unfolded. Although Julius was murdered by the treachery of those he trusted, in a curious parallel with the death of Osiris, the faith of Isis continued unchecked. And when Cleopatra recreated her divine union with Julius Caesar by allying herself with his friend and "heir" Marcus Antonius, she was again transferring the power of the throne of Egypt to another Roman known to have sympathy for the religion of Isis and who could be counted on not to interfere with the growth of that worship. Although Cleopatra was ultimately defeated after having taken to her embrace two of Rome's finest warriors, the faith she embraced expanded and flourished for centuries after her death.

One of the greatest evangelists for the faith of Isis came in the person of the little-known Cleopatra Selene, one of the set of twins Cleopatra the Seventh bore to Antony. Raised in Rome after her mother's death, she was married to King Juba of Mauretania, who apparently needed the marriage to legitimize his claim to that throne. Very calmly, Cleopatra's daughter proceeded to follow in her mother's footsteps, establishing a major temple to Isis in her capital of Caesarea. Shortly after the founding of this temple in the heart of a Roman city, Rome itself permitted a Temple to Isis to be erected inside the walls of Rome.

Cleopatra Selene ruled alone when her husband was detained in another part of the Empire and she issued coinage as a Ptolemaic Queen, sharing her coins with depictions of Isis and other Egyptian symbols. She continued to dress as Isis for occasions of great significance, as her mother had done. Remembering the brilliant city of her childhood, Cleopatra Selene attempted to recreate the glory of the city of Isis, Alexandria, on the shores of her new homeland. She was also an astute politician and might well have taken armies to battle with her had her skills as a diplomat and negotiator not made this unnecessary. For years she met with troublesome chieftains and artfully prevented open rebellion against the Roman Empire she ironically represented. Within a year after her death, the delicate balance she had maintained was shattered and Mauretania was torn by strife between different factions.

Both Cleopatra and Cleopatra Selene might have seen echoes of themselves several centuries later in the form of Zenobia, Queen of the Nabataeans, who claimed both physical and spiritual descent from Cleopatra the Seventh. The Nabataeans were a mysterious, semi-nomadic people who nonetheless carved cities out of mountains and deep desert canyons. Petra, the hidden city which for many centuries was the Nabataean capital, held a rose-red temple to Isis carved from the walls of the canyon city. It was the need for incense for the temples which first drew the Nabataeans and the worship of Isis together in about the third century b.c.e. Zenobia's possible ancestress Cleopatra once waged war on the Nabataeans to preserve access to the frankincense, the trade of which the Nabataeans almost completely monopolized.

As Roman power grew, the wealthy and independent Nabataeans became a source of irritation to the Emperors, and repeated attacks on their stronghold at Petra led the Nabataeans to relocate their capital to the mountain city of Palmyra. However, the Emperor Severus conquered Palmyra as well, killing the chief of the city, Odenathus, when he was suspected of plotting a rebellion. But Rome erred in believing that the death of Odenathus would be sufficient to break the spirit of the desert-hardened Palmyrenes. His younger son, also called Odenathus, went back into the desert and gathered the support of the Bedouin and other tribesmen, training them to fight against Roman forces. In the daughter of his chief military advisor, a tribesman named Zabba, Odenathus found his future queen. Supposedly descended from Cleopatra through her Greek mother, Bath-Zabbai (or Zenobia) was beautiful and brilliant as well as being a superb military strategist. She took under her own supervision the training of the calvary of Palmyra, whom she taught to triumph over traditional Roman-style tactics by using a harassing, insect-sting style of warfare. Emulating Cleopatra, Zenobia mastered the Egyptian language, perhaps studying with one of the native Egyptian priests at the Temple of Isis-Aphrodite in

Palmyra. She and Odenathus lulled Rome into believing that they were content vassals fighting only to further the interests of Rome against the unconquered nations of Mesopotamia. This unlikely argument, supported by a careful list of enemies of Rome whom they had subjugated, so persuaded the Roman Senate that they named Odenathus the Emperor of the East.

But in 267 tragedy struck. Odenathus was murdered by a nephew and Zenobia was made regent of the East, holding the throne for their eledest son. As a widow, Zenobia found herself in power over an empire reaching from the Caucasus mountains to the Libyan deserts. She led her troops in battle to defend her possessions, wearing a helmet and armor and a robe secured by a buckle made of diamonds. She continued to expand Palmyrene power and finally attacked and conquered a large portion of Egypt. Rome realized that perhaps her interests and ambitions were not the same as that of the Empire and the Emperor Gallienus went against Palmyrene might. He was defeated and killed.

But a different emperor, Aurelian, rose up to challenge the Empress of the East. Aurelian had another challenge to meet as well. The Roman senate, safe in Rome, was questioning why their emperors seemed to be having such trouble subduing an adversary who, after all, was a mere woman. Aurelian detailed his difficulties in a letter to the Senate which answered any questions about the strength and ability of Zenobia as a ruler and as a warrior. He wrote: "My accusers would not know how to praise me enough, if they knew this woman—if they knew her prudence in council, her firmness of purpose, the dignity with which she directs her army, her munificence when need requires it, her severity when it is just to be severe." If any Roman suspected that her so-called victories were actually due to her husband or her father, Aurelian quenched these thoughts by adding: "I must remark that the victory of Odenathus over the Persians, the flight of Sapor, the march to Ctesiphon, were her work. I can assert that such was the dread of this woman among Orientals and Egyptians that she held in check Arabians, Saracens, and Armenians..."

Ultimately Aurelian defeated Zenobia. Unlike her predecessor Cleopatra, Zenobia did not avoid walking in the triumphal parade of her conqueror. Yet Zenobia's history, which along with Aurelian's becomes surprisingly obscure for two such dynamic personages, is not yet finished. She may have been beheaded by him after the triumphal procession at Antioch, as one account gives, or, following Cleopatra to the last, she may have committed suicide. But it is also rumored that Aurelian had a daughter by Zenobia, or that he married a daughter of hers. It is likely that she survived walking in his triumphs at Antioch and Rome and lived out her years in a villa on the Tibur near to the Villa of Hadrian with its extensive Isian statuary and shrines, but on what terms it is not known.

Late Egyptian literature of the post-Imperial era gives another example of a warrior queen relying on Isis to bring her victory. A portion of the Petubastis cycle of stories is called *Egyptians and Amazons* and deals with a warrior queen ruling over a nation of women. In the story fragments translated in Miriam Lichtheim's *Ancient Egyptian Literature*, Queen Serpot, ruler of the land of Khor, is in her fortress which is about to be attacked by Prince Pedikhons, who has been wreaking havoc in the area. Knowing that she is severely outnumbered, Queen Serpot prays: "Give me help, O Isis!" The queen, who is designated in the text by the feminine version of the word "Pharaoh," calls on her younger sister, Ashteshyt, for help. Ashteshyt, whose name may be derived from the Egyptian name of Isis, Aset, agrees to disguise herself as a man and go to reconnoiter the enemy camp. Based on Ashteshyt's information, the pharaohess decides to attack. She again invokes Isis to help her and orders her people to make preparations for the attack.

The battle goes in Serpot's favor. She is described as fighting like a hawk falling on prey, like the serpent Apophis attacking Ra. Prince Pedikhons retreats and decides that his only chance at victory lies in defeating Serpot in single combat the following morning. Serpot accepts the challenge despite her sister's offer to fight in her stead. "By Isis, the Great Goddess, the Mistress of the Land of the Women, it is I who shall don armor and go to the battlefield against the evil serpent of an Egyptian today!"

She and Pedikhons meet alone at the battleground. Savagely, they engage in combat. The text says that "They took death to themselves as neighbor," fighting with all the bravery, guile, and skill they gained in years of battle. Neither submits to the other. Finally, after fighting from dawn until dusk, they agree to a truce for the night to commence anew in the morning. For the first time they see each other outside the heat of battle. Although the end of the text has many missing portions, Queen Serpot is now laughing and Prince Pedikhons is calling her "My sister," the traditional Egyptian endearment between lovers.

As with the rest of these warrior queens, mere military victory is not sufficient. Invariably the good of the entire nation is their goal, and war is pursued as a means to an end rather than an endeavor complete in and of itself. The Isian concept of true victory entails a dynamic, harmonious uniting of opposites for the benefit of both attacker and attacked, not unlikely for a goddess who proclaimed: "I am she who made men and women to love one another."

The Ritual of Soul Caking

Raymond Buckland

Soul, Soul, for a Soul Cake.
I pray you, good mistress a Soul Cake.
An apple, a pear, a plum or a cherry;
Or any good thing to make us all merry!
One for Peter, two for Paul,
Three for Them as made us all.
Up with the kettle and down with the pan,
Give us good alms and we'll be gone.

These were the words of the Soul Cake song that used to be sung all over the British Isles at the start of November, and still may be heard in some outlying districts. Soul Caking tied in with the old Pagan festival of Samhain. This was the start of the old Keltic year, the time when the "veil between the worlds" was thin and those who had crossed over could come back briefly to see their loved ones. It was the time when "ghosts" were about the land, when old souls came a-visiting.

It was felt that the returning souls would be in need of sustenance, and so special cakes were made to offer to them at this time. They were generally filled with fruit—"An apple, a pear, a plum or a cherry"—the fullness of life.

As with so many similar traditions, people—especially children—would go from house to house, singing the song and receiving gifts of cake, fruit and money—charity from those better off than they were.

The ingredients of the Soul Cake varied in different areas. In Yorkshire it was a small fruitcake but in Northamptonshire it had to contain caraway seeds. In other areas it was more a small loaf, or bun, than a cake, being made of wheat or barley flour.

Christina Hole, in *A Dictionary of British Folk Customs* (London, 1978), states that in Staffordshire there was a version or a verse of the song which dealt more with the origins of the custom:

> *Soul Day! Soul Day!*
> *We've been praying for the souls departed;*
> *So pray, good people, give us a cake,*
> *For we are all poor people, well known to you before,*
> *So give us a cake for charity's sake,*
> *And our blessing we'll leave at your door.*

The version I give at the start of this article includes the line: "Three for Them as made us all." The "Them" would seem to indicate the old Pagan belief in gods, or a god and a goddess, rather than the Christian concept of a single, male deity.

Together with the making of the cakes, a lighted candle was usually placed in the window, to guide back the soul. Sometimes, too, the fire would be banked up in the fireplace and whole meals would be spread out on the table, occasionally even with offerings of tobacco left out overnight.

Throwing the Bones—
Zulu Style

Brian Crowley

The art of throwing the runes as a form of divination is as old as Africa itself and the Zulu witchdoctors, or more correctly, *sangomas*, wield an immense influence over their fellows in the kraals, or traditional country villages, and in the modern townships and cities. The sangoma, male or female, is accepted at once as counselor, psychologist and prophet to the tribe or community. Some are also doctors or *nyangas*, healers and herbalists, and each tribe will also have its *iznyanga zezulu*, the "herder of the sky," who controls lightning, thunderstorms and life-giving rain. The proper name of the tribe, amaZulu, means in fact "People of the Sky," and there is even one Zulu legend which claims original ancestry from another world, the Earth being the seventh home so far of this proud people.

Traditionally, Zulu spiritual life revolves around the practice of reverence to the *amaDlozi*, the ancestral spirits who are considered to be as alive as anyone else and highly capable of influencing events in our own world. (The Zulus and other tribes of Southern and Central Africa also, incidentally, pay due homage to the *Nkosi Yezulu*, "The Chief of the Sky," also known as *Nkulunkulu*—"the old, old, one," and hold sacred the African version of the Tree of Life—the *Shivhakava* Tree.) Contact is generally made with the ancestral spirits by the sangoma when in a trance state, or alternatively when "throwing the bones" or using some other form of divination.

Other than bone-throwing, methods of divination employed include beating the ground with sticks (done by the inquirer and interpreted by the sangoma) or using a set of falling sticks, somewhat like the Chinese *I Ching* yarrow stalks. The bone-diviner usually carries a bag of various bones at his waist, ready for use. Traditionally, these magical dice were made of the bones of wild animals, but today all sorts of objects are used— shells, fruit seeds, pieces of colored glass, carved wooden fetishes, seashells, pieces of tortoise shells, claws, beaks, hooftips and peculiarly shaped stones. Only the sangoma has any idea of the true meaning attached to each individual piece and to the patterns they form. There are no ground rules. Each diviner selects or manufactures his/her own set and uses the bone-kit as a point of focus in making contact with the inhabitants of other dimensions.

Typical bones of animal origin used for bone-throwing divination are generally related in some way to the meanings attached to them. They include:

antbear (lord of the underworld)—loss, death
baboon (a gregarious creature)—family and domestic affairs, home, huts, kraals
crocodile—sorcery, defilement, doom, death
hyena—intrigue, bewitchment, untrustworthiness
duiker (a type of deer)—travel, change
kudu—vigilance
leopard (the clever hunter)—dignity, prosperity, longevity
lion (king of the beasts)—authority
monkey (agile and cunning)—all actions etc. requiring quick thinking
springbok—speed
steenbok—gentleness, humility

Tortoise shells might be used for indicating future events; fruit seeds in connection with agricultural matters; hooftips in relation to cattle (the wealth of the African); seashells with regards to battle, power and emtional concerns; the claws and beaks of birds as direction pointers.

My own set of throwing bones is made up entirely of sea-washed stones. The symbols I have painted on them link up the ancient African art of bone-throwing with Zulu numerology, as recorded by the current Zulu hereditary High Sangoma, Credo Vuzamazulu Mutwa. (For full details see book written under the pseudonym "Ulufudu," *The Zulu Bone Oracle*, Wingbow Press, 1989.)

Some African tribal diviners inlude four "special" carved pieces in their bone kit, made of horn, ivory or wood, depicting the men, women or children for whom the bones are being thrown. In my own kit I have replaced all of these with a single stone bearing the traditional mark of the "warrior" in a picture script that is universally used by nyangas and sangomas throughout Southern Africa.

Each "bone" possesses its own "praise name" or *isibongo*, and prior to use praise songs may be sung to activate the selected pieces.

Before commencement of a "reading" for a client, some bone-diviners will first chew *muti* or special herbal medicine. All will invariably first blow upon the bones in their cupped hands. My own method in "getting my bones ready to speak" is to blow life into them four times—once for the originators of the oracle, once for myself, once for my higher self working through me, and once for the One and Only Creator who guides and protects us in all we do. I also sometimes ask the sitter to blow on the bones.

The bones are well shaken before being thrown, and when they fall, those that lie face down (the lazy ones) may indicate unseen forces at work. Those that fall upright are ready for immediate interpretation. Any seen lying on their sides are considered asleep and of no immediate importance. How the bones fall in relation to each other is of significance, as well as the positioning of the pointer bones.

From the disposition of the bones, the sangoma can tell what has occurred in a person's life, what may now be happening, and what can be expected in the future, much as is the case with other time-honored divinatory tools such as the I Ching, Tarot and rune stones.

Tarot and Stone Correspondences

Amber K

For years I have been drawn to both the Tarot and stones for divination, and recently I decided that it is possible to use both at once by casting stones which would each symbolize one of the Tarot major arcana.

Such lists have been published before, but I would like to offer some new and occasionally more exotic suggestions.

THE FOOL, who is Everyman and Everywoman, could be either a common stream pebble, borrowed from its journey to the sea, or an unfaceted diamond ("a diamond in the rough"), or a large rock salt crystal ("salt of the earth").

THE MAGICIAN's colors are red for courage and white for purity—nicely combined in the striped sardonyx. Or, consider Icelandic spar, a clear crystal which doubles images—that is, changes perceptions.

THE HIGH PRIESTESS might be represented by a moonstone for the Goddess, or by a holy stone, or by two stones combined: amber and jet, the traditional stones of a Wiccan High Priestess's necklace.

THE EMPRESS, related to growing things and abundance, might be green calcite, or moss agate, or "rain forest" jasper.

THE EMPEROR's position and strength are suggested by royal sugalite or imperial jasper.

THE HIEROPHANT is easy: the staurolite, sometimes called a "fairy cross." Some of these unusual brown crystals grow like a

Christian cross, others are equal-armed. Another option is marble, which suggests the halls of authority.

THE LOVERS might be rose quartz, a stone of blessing and affection, or rhodochrosite, a more jazzy pink stone.

THE CHARIOT with its black and white steeds suggests zebra agate, though the rich dark blue of sodalite is also reflected in the garments of the charioteer.

JUSTICE seems to call for the black robes of judges, so perhaps black onyx would be appropriate—or obsidian, though it has fiery origins.

THE HERMIT carries a lantern in the darkness, and the mysterious interior dragon-scale light of a fire agate seems perfect; or an opal in matrix; or a small geode, which has a crystalline interior which suggests a hermit's cave.

THE WHEEL OF FORTUNE connotes the rise and fall of fortune and chance. There is a hexagonal Chinese stone which looks like an ancient coin or gambling piece, though its name eludes me; or how about a polished white angel agate, marked with black dots to suggest a die?

STRENGTH might be "tiger iron," Australian compound of iron and tiger's eye; or a similar stone which has red jasper as well; or hematite, which is mostly iron; or a smooth or spiked bojo stone. Nor would granite be amiss.

THE HANGED MAN could only be a piece of stalactite from a cave. Needless to say, cave formations should not be broken—but cave onyx does break naturally sometimes, or is accidentally broken when a cave is opened, so it is obtainable.

DEATH could also be a zebra agate—the black of death and white of rebirth. Or perhaps a fossil, which is a dead replica of a once-living creature; even a gastrolith, found in the gullet of a (very dead) dinosaur.

TEMPERANCE must be amethyst (from the Latin, "no alcohol"), which has long represented that quality and moderation in general.

THE DEVIL might well be iron pyrite ("fool's gold"), or magnetite ("lodestone"), which is "attractive" in a different way but equally valueless.

THE TOWER should be lightning-fused sand, which I think is called fulgarite; or brecciated red jasper also looks suitably disastrous.

THE STAR might be a star sapphire, which need not cost a fortune; or a nice clear quartz crystal, or perhaps a natural octagonal fluorite crystal.

THE MOON, you would think, would be moonstone; but some scientists think that the mysterious tektites were ejected by lunar volcanoes, and what could be more perfect? I suppose the enhydro, a stone encapsulating a few drops of ancient water, would make the traditional connection between Moon and tides.

THE SUN must surely have a golden stone, such as amber, cltrine, sunstone or tiger's eye.

JUDGMENT suggests wisdom, and jade traditionally encourages that quality; or lapis lazuli carries that connotation in a psychic or spiritual sense.

THE WORLD could be symbolized by the lovely sky-blue color of bluestone, actually a glass byproduct of medieval Swedish forges. Or the rich colors of chalcopyrite, or peacock stone, might do well for the richness and diversity for which the card stands.

Will such amazing and unusual stones be easy to find? Many of them—no. But the search will be half the fun! As you discover each one, or whatever stones you may choose to substitute, I suggest that you meditate on the stone and the corresponding card simultaneously (perhaps putting the stone on the card) so as to make the connection in your deep mind. Enjoy!

The Fool	Stream pebble, salt crystal, rough diamond
The Magician	Sardonyx, Icelandic spar
The High Priestess	Moonstone, holy stone, amber and jet
The Empress	Rain forest jasper, green calcite
The Emperor	Royal jasper, royal sugalite

The Hierophant	Staurolite, marble
The Lovers	Rose quartz, rhodochrosite
The Chariot	Zebra agate, sodalite
Justice	Black onyx, obsidian
The Hermit	Fire agate, opal in matrix, geode
The Wheel of Fortune	Six-sided Chinese stone
Strength	Hematite, tiger iron, boji stone; granite
The Hanged Man	Cave onyx
Death	Zebra agate, gastrolith or other fossil
Temperance	Amethyst
The Devil	Iron pyrite, magnetite (lodestone)
The Tower	Brecciated red jasper, lightning-fused sand
The Star	Crystal, fluorite crystal, star sapphire
The Moon	Moonstone, tektite, enhydro
The Sun	Sunstone, amber, tiger's eye, citrine
Judgment	Jade, lapis lazuli
The World	Bluestone, peacock stone

Shamanic Dog Magic

Tara Buckland

This ceremony is designed to bring dog and dog-friend (owner) closer together. It has been inspired by ancient Shamanic techniques used to transform a Shaman into an animal—usually an animal to which the Shaman is closely allied.

Native people of the Americas believe that every human is under the protection of at least one Animal Spirit whether they are aware of this animal's presence or not. It is also generally believed that this animal cannot be domestic. This animal is called the Power Animal.

The belief in Power Animals was, at one time, widespread among all the cultures of the world. Native peoples of Europe more commonly used the term "Familiar" to refer to a Power Animal. In European mythology, however, we find that no distinction was made as to whether the animal was domestic or wild, and so we find that cats, dogs, horses, chickens and cows were used as well as swans, bears, wolves, snakes and other wild animals

Dog, along with other scavengers like Magpie, Crow and Raven, was originally identified with funerary functions and death. Dog was the companion of the Crone—the Goddess of death and what comes after. Dog was the guardian of the gate to the spirit world. The fact that dogs often howl at the moon was seen as a sign that they could see into the world of spirit and warn of impending death.

The Personality of Dog is one of personal sacrifice and loyalty. Dog willingly sacrifices personal needs for the good of the family. Dog feels a fierce sense of loyalty to this family and will defend it to the death. The ceremony to become closer to your "pet" dog is basically one of bonding. You are formally cementing the relationship and acknowledging that the two of you are members of the same pack or family. Dog respects and needs the strength of a leader, and you will also recognize and accept the responsibilty of this position of power.

If the dog lives with more than one person and the other members of your family are willing to participate, then you must decide among yourselves which of you is to be the dog's leader. It is this person who should lead the ceremony.

For this ceremony you will need candles (to imitate a campfire) or firewood (if you are lucky enough to be able to perform this ceremony outside), a plate of cooked meat, a rattle or hand drum, and a nice big meat bone that your dog has chewed clean.

Clean the bone that your dog has "worked over." Soak it in a Clorox water solution for 30 minutes and then boil it for a couple hours to soften any remaining food bits. When the bone is clean, dry it in a low-heat oven until it is gleaming white (about two hours). This bone is to become a symbol of your link to your dog. Decorate the bone. Wrap bits of fur on it or tie colorful beads, crystals and feathers to it. Make a pouch or find a special cloth or leather to bundle it in. (A sacred object should always be kept out of sight when not in use, to preserve its power.)

If you are to have the ceremony outside, then you will want to build a fire that will be the center of your circle. If you are inside then use several candles clustered together to imitate a fire in the center of your circle. The symbolism is that in the very early days the dog was the guardian of the campfire. Humans depended on Dog to be their eyes and ears to the possible dangers of the night. You will be inviting your dog into your campfire, into your circle of family.

The cooked meat is for you to share with your dog. This is an important point to be made. The dog shares from your bounty and you share from the dog's bounty. Dog was a companion to the hunt and was often responsible for hunting successes that might otherwise have been unfruitful.

Vegetarians should also be willing to share the cooked meat. It won't kill you to do it once for this ceremony. Dog is not a vegetarian and by providing for Dog (even if you only feed canned or dried food) you are responsible for taking the life of an animal. If you are to keep a dog this responsibility must be acknowledged and accepted. Please do not try to make your dog a vegetarian.

The rattle or drum is for you to use while you dance. It is a Shamanic tool to induce trance. The dance is a gift of energy to the spirit of Dog. During the dance you will imitate the motions of Dog and imagine yourself becoming Dog. Trot around the circle, howl, bark, sing and allow yourself to become one with Dog—the drum or rattle will keep time. You may find at some time during the ritual you may not be able to continue using the rattle or drum because the trance has become too deep. Resist going to this final level as it will inhibit your being able to function for the rest of the ceremony. It is not necessary to go that deep at this time (although at another, earlier time you may wish to do that sort of journey in preparation so that you may get further instruction as to how to personalize your ceremony).

As Dog has been associated with the Full Moon it seems natural that the best time to perform this ceremony would be at the Full Moon. Prepare your circle. Have ready the plate of meat, the decorated bone, the fire or candles and the rattle or drum. Have your dog in the same room or area. He doesn't have to be in the circle at this time.

While holding your bone amulet, begin your ceremony by rattling or drumming to each of the seven directions—west, south, east, north, above, below, within. If you are lunar oriented, begin in the west and move counterclockwise (to many cultures life begins in the darkness of the womb and a new day begins at sunset). If you are solar oriented, begin in the east and move clockwise. You may say whatever words you feel are appropriate. Begin your dance and keep it up for at least 10 or 15 minutes, at which time you should feel a link with Dog and be in a light trance (a sort of sleepy feeling). Bring your dog into the circle. If you have a special collar which links him to your family you may present him/her with it at this time. The decorated bone is also a link between you. Show it to the dog. You will use it as an amulet to link you to your dog. Share the meat with your dog. Eat it in dog fashion by taking it off the plate without the aid of your hands. Now simply sit quietly with your dog and listen to each other. When you feel within yourself that the ceremony has ended, thank the spirit of Dog and shake your rattle or beat your drum four times to signify the conclusion.

The feeling that you evoked during the dance is a spiritual link to the energy of Dog. From now on all you need do to link into the energy of Dog is dance to Dog with your bone amulet. The more often you dance the more quickly you will be able to tap into this energy. Eventually you may only need to unwrap the bone to flash into communion with Dog.

When to Use the Calendar

It had long been considered the very worst of luck to hang a calendar for the new year on the wall before the old year has ended. Calendars received at Christmas time should be put away safely until January 1st.

Similarly, it is bad luck to change the date on a daily calendar before the old day is finished. To change a calendar ahead of time is tantamount to wishing your life away.

RB

The Magic of Shells

Scott Cunningham

A wave washes up, spilling foam onto the glistening sand.

Within the surging water tumble treasures from the deep. As the wave recedes, these jeweled wonders sit patiently on the sand, waiting the next wave or an interested collector.

Many children gather shells. Many adults, too, have traveled widely to garner vast collections of these fascinating objects, and are willing to pay $800 and more for an extremely rare shell, such as the exquisitely beautiful golden cowrie.

Few children, and even fewer adults, however, know of the hidden powers contained within seashells. Long used in magic and religious rituals, shells continue to hum with oceanic power, and can be utilized to bring love, money and protection, good fortune and many other energies into their finders' lives.

For years I've wandered up and down Pacific, Atlantic and Gulf of Mexico beaches, searching for treasures that have washed up from the ocean's depths. Walking beside the water, breathing in the crisp, saline air, is an invigorating and healing experience. This wonderful exercise holds yet another possible benefit: finding a magical object or two.

Though different types of shells are found in various parts of the country, certain forms are widely distributed, or can be purchased in specialty stores or craft shops.

Because destroying life is against all magical principles, use only those shells that you find without living creatures inside. Many times I've had to leave a shell on the beach when I discovered that its original occupant was still in residence.

To use shells in magic:

Charge the shell by holding it between the palms of your hands. See in your mind's eye the effect that you wish the shell to make: protection, love, purification, banishment of negative thoughts or illness, peace. Push and pour out this mind—and body—generated energy into the shell.

Once the shell has been magically charged, you have many options. You can toss the shell into the sea to release its powers; carry it with you or wear around your neck (if the shell is small enough); place on an altar near candles; fill or surround it with herbs and stones. You're limited only by your imagination. (For recommended candle colors, stones and herbs, see the table at the end of this article.)

Here's a small sampling of these gifts from the sea.

Cowries are found throughout the world in warmer waters: off the coasts of California ard Mexico; in Polynesia, Micronesia and Melanesia, India, China and elsewhere. A certain form of cowrie was used as money in China as early as 600 B.C.E. They were soon heavily traded around the globe as a valuable commodity. Some contemporary religions use a cowrie shell to represent the Goddess in sacred rituals, and among certain sects of Yoruban religion, cowries are a highly prized divinitory tool. They've also been used as symbols of royalty and of warriors. Magically, cowrie shells are charged and used to attract money energies.

Oysters, long eaten to promote sexual arousal, have another use: a piece of the shell is carried to promote good fortune. Alternately, charge an oyster shell to find someone with whom to share a loving relationship.

White "clam" shells (bivalves) are common on beaches throughout the world. Some species grow to be the largest shells (the famous "giant clam"). Magically, they're charged and used in rites of purification.

Cone shells, of which there are many varieties, can be found on beaches off California, Mexico, the Gulf States, the Atlantic side of Florida, and elsewhere. Though the creature that inhabits them can be quite dangerous when alive, the shell itself is useful for protective rituals.

Abalone shells are uncommon but can occasionally be found on the beaches of California, Mexico and Hawaii. The Navaho used water-filled abalone shells in rain-producing rituals. During many summers at Laguna Beach, California, I collected dozens of tiny abalone shells that had washed up on secret beaches. The irridescent, prismatic colors of the inner shell make them perfect for all magical purposes. Fill them with herbs or stones; anoint them with oils; carry or wear a small shell after charging it with power.

Left-handed whelks, found in Gulf of Mexico waters, are fine instruments of making dramatic changes in your life, such as halting negative habits. Charge with power as you visualize yourself making this change. (Use the herbs, stones and candle colors listed under "purification" below.)

Conches, which are so popular in Florida, are fine, large, orange shells with a flaring pink lip. Charge a conch with love-attracting energies and put it in a place of importance in your bedroom.

Olive shells, found in Gulf of Mexico waters, are soothing shells that can assist in healing. Charge and place the shell near a blue candle.

There are many more shells, but these few words should provide a start. For more information regarding the magical and ritual uses of shells, see the two books below:

Katlyn, *Ocean Amulets*. Long Beach: Mermade Magickal Arts, 1988.

Safer, Jane Fearer, and Frances McLaughlin Gill, *Spirals From the Sea: An Anthropological Look at Shells*. New York: Clarkson N. Potter, 1982.

LOVE: Pink Candles. Stones: Rose Quartz, Green Tourmaline, Amethyst. Herbs: Lavender, Rose petals, Basil.
PROTECTION: Red Candles. Stones: Obsidian, Carnelian, Garnet. Herbs: Black Pepper, Hyssop, Juniper.
PURIFICATION: White Candles. Stones: Aquamarine, Calcite. Herbs: Chamomile, Cedar, Fennel.

HEALING: Blue Candles. Stones: Bloodstone, Jade, Lapis Lazuli. Herbs: Sage, Eucalyptus, Fennel.
MONEY: Green Candles. Stones: Aventurine, Olivine, Bloodstone. Herbs: Ginger, Cinnamon, Clove.

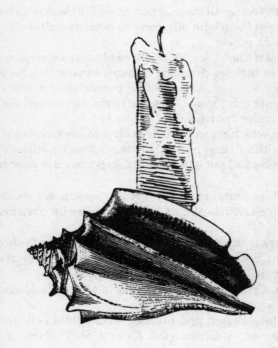

Cats Can See in the Dark

Sandra Tabatha Cicero

Astarte's Moon
A Pagan Rune
In Eyes Cryptic and Stark;
A Templar's Tale
Seen Through a Veil
Cats can See in the Dark.

> Elementals follow
> Mary Magdalo
> To Ishtar's Celestial Ark;
> Scene in a Crystal
> Fur-bearing Missile
> Cats can See in the Dark.

Seeds need Sowing
Clockface glowing
Though the Once-born set their Mark;
Sauniere Knew
Poussin did too
Cats can See in the Dark.

> Sacred Chalice
> Devoid of Malice
> Carved from Arcadian Bark;
> Hide and Seek
> But Gnostics Peek
> Cats can See in the Dark.

The karamat or mosque/tomb of a famous Cape Muslim saint, Prince Sayed Abduraamen Motura, who died in 1754, is perched high on Signal Hill. The sacred karamats form a holy circle of protection around the city.

Lighting the Candle

Brian Crowley

There have been claims that there are in total 3,000 names of Allah. Sufis and other Muslim mystics place great store on the power generated during *majalis adh-dikhr*, sessions at which litanies invoking the Divine names of Allah are chanted. The writer has been a witness at several similar gatherings involving so-called *khalifa* groups from among the large community of Muslims of Malay origin living in Cape Town, South Africa. The Cape Malays' forebearers were either slaves of the Dutch East India Company during the late 1600s or political exiles under British rule at the Cape. They have mixed little with other races and have for the most part remained devout Muslims noted for their law-abiding character and high morals.

The actual ceremony is known as *Ratiep*. The leader of the group, usually a Sheikh who has been to Mecca, is known as the *Khalifa* (caliph or vice-regent). At these sessions, during incessant chanting of the names of Allah and beating of *ghomma* drums and tambourines, participants slash themselves with razor-sharp swords and pierce their faces, tongues and other parts of their bodies with red-hot skewers. This is done to prove the strength of Allah over the material flesh. Amazingly, no blood is drawn, nor is there any scar or mark left once the swords and/or skewers are withdrawn! The performance can last for many hours and is closed when the chanting and beating of drums and tambourines ceases on a single note at the signal of the Khalifa. The sudden silence can be an eery experience.

The city of Cape Town is almost encircled by a string of

karamats, Muslim holy burial places, most placed high on mountain paths on the massive Table Mountain and its accompanying
Signal Hill, overlooking the city. These tombs of especially holy
persons have been buried beneath colossal stone slabs. Miniature mosques, some quite grand, have been built over the rest-
ing places. It is believed that the positioning of these buildings
will forever ensure the safety of the city from any great catastro-
phe.

The almost magical karamats of the Cape peninsula are favorite places for prayer and meditation. More than 20 years ago,
during a particular early evening session of simple chanting of
the Holy Names inside one of these mosque-like buildings, just
as the setting sun became lost behind Table Mountain, some
who were present (including the teller of this tale) were stunned
when, during a high-point in the chanting, an unlit candle set in
the *mihrab*, a wall niche common to all mosques, suddenly burst
into flame as if lit by an unseen hand. No one was sitting within
three or four feet of the candle, and there was simply no way in
which the event could have been rigged. Regular participants in
these rituals took it all as a matter of course. Although the sun
was setting fast when they had arrived, and there was no elec-
tricity for lighting, none of them had even bothered to bring
along a box of matches!

A Child's First Wand

Jenine E. Trayer

The New Generation of Witches is upon us, and we, as magickal parents, are bearing the inheritors of the future in greater numbers than ever before. It is time to unlock those closets, break out the candles, and invite our children to join us in the world of magick.

Yes, that Magickal Baby Boom is definitely upon us.

As parents, it is important for us to involve our children in our religious beliefs and practices. Our purpose should be two-fold: To provide our children a leading edge as they advance to adulthood and to ensure the continuance of the Old Religion itself—or at least the proper education therein.

Even if a child eventually chooses a different religous path than that of its parents, we can make an effort to assure that h/she has been properly educated to the extent of not joining the ranks of our untrained persecutors.

Regardless of their eventual personal choice, training in practical magick will allow our children to emerge from the family unit with a greater sense of self-sufficiency and maturity.

An easy way to begin tool training is to provide a child with his or her own simplistic version of the *wand*. Now, you could cut a branch from magickal wood and continue to fashion a standard wand, but I have found that my children relate better to the tool if it carries a brightly colored, handcrafted appearance.

Many cartoon characters today, such as He-Man, Shera, and Luke Skywalker, indicate to children that the ability to

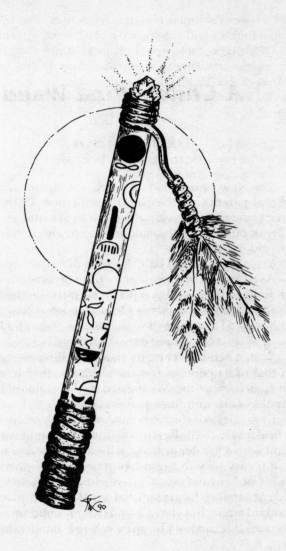

A Child's First Wand

wield a magickal tool is real. It teaches them that by the use of this tool the Self will experience a positive transformation.

Often, these tools are colorful and bright; therefore, a plain wand carries less appeal to a child of four or five. Imagination can always stand a little handcrafted fun.

To make a child's first wand you will need the following materials:

1 dowel rod—1/2" diameter
White rawhide strip(s)—36" in length
1 small piece of rose quartz
3 white feathers
7 silver beads
Glitter (silver or gold)
Varied colors of acrylic paint
Glue
A wood-burning tool

Before you begin, go through your library and search for symbols you feel would be appropriate for the wand. You could choose runes, astrological signs, a magickal alphabet, suns, moons, stars, etc. On our wand, we used the symbols from Scott Cunningham's *Wicca: A Guide For The Solitary Pratitioner.*

Now you are ready for the actual crafting of the wand. If you can, have the child present while you fashion it for him or her. Draw the symbols on the rod with a pencil. Leave one inch at the top and five inches at the bottom clear of any drawings.

Next, go over them with the wood-burning tool. Some you may merely wish to outline; others, such as the symbol for the New Moon, you may darken completely with the tool. Paint in some of the symbols with bright colors, such as vivid green, gold, silver, white, pink, baby blue, etc.

Wrap the bottom five inches of the wand with the white rawhide strips—about four to five inches,where the child's grip will be.

Finally, glue the piece of rose quartz to the top of the wand and secure with rawhide wrapped around the top of the wand.

Leave about two inches hanging. Thread the beads and knot. Place a little glue on the shaft of each feather and thread them between the beads and the rawhide.

Cleanse and consecrate the wand as you would in your personal workings.

In our home, Mommie keeps the wand locked in her magickal cabinet. The children use it in their "circle time," to begin a family holiday, or in a general working under the supervison of an adult. It is also used as a "speaking stick" when in the children's circle environment. The child holding the wand is permitted to speak on whatever subject chosen. Since we have four children, it gives each one a sense of authority to express themselves without being interrupted by the others.

Not only does giving a child a wand teach tool handling and respect, it also gives them "hands-on" training at an early age. I can tell you from experience that it will keep you from having heart failure when you have forgotten to lock up a tool or two of your own. That was my reaction when, on one too-quiet afternoon, I found my four-year-old son jumping up and down on my bed, wielding my wand over his head, valiantly whispering, "He-Man! Power of the Universe!"

Well, at least he wasn't pretending to be Darth Vadar, but I made him his own wand anyway.

A Look at
Magical Symbolism

Gerald and Betty Schueler

Magical symbols play an important part in the practice of magic. They serve as visual reminders of various universal truths. They also act as inspirational, mediational, and focal devices.

Magical symbols have been used since the beginning of humankind to represent ideas that were too complex to be articulated by the average person. For instance, the ankh (shown below) was used in the ancient Egyptian religions to represent life.

In the same religion, the symbols of the snake and the frog (shown on the following page) were both used to represent re-embodiment. Just as a snake periodically sheds its skin, so man periodically sheds one identity for another. And just as the frog disappears in the fall and reappears in the spring, so man reappears after death.

The early Israelites used the hexagram to represent the two main forces of the universe, materiality and spirituality (see below). The hexagram is made up of two interconnected triangles, one pointing upward, representing the upward force of spirituality, and one pointed downward, representing the downward force of materiality. The interconnection of the two symbols represents the duality of the universe and their inseparable relationship.

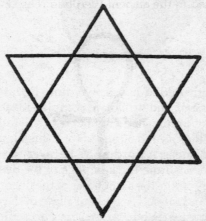

The Chinese developed a symbol that also represents the duality of the universe, called the Yin and Yang (see next page). The outer circle represents the universe divided into two parts, the material and the spiritual. One half of the symbol is white, representing the spiritual part of the universe, while the other half is black, representing materiality. The small circles, used in some versions of the symbol, represent the seed of conscious-ness of its dualistic opposite; that is, the white half has a black seed while the black half has a white seed. Again, this interac-tion represents the inseparable relationship between spiritual-ity and materiality. The dramatic nature of this relationship is suggested in the symbol by the two sides appearing to be in rota-tion.

While humankind has grown more literate and is better able to understand and articulate complex ideas, the need for symbols has not diminished. Symbols are still important for in-spiration, meditation, and as an aid for focusing the mind on an idea or group of ideas. According to the Swiss psychologist Carl Jung, symbols constitute the language of the deepest layers of our mind—they clothe the archetypes of the unconscious. As we better understand ourselves and our place in the universe, new symbols are constantly being developed to represent our new consciousness.

Most symbols are developed by using already existing, universally understood symbology and expanding on it. For in-stance, everyone knows that a circle with a line drawn diago-nally through it means "no." By combining this symbol with the picture of a cigarette, a new symbol is developed which warns people that smoking is not permitted (see below).

In the same way, traditional religious or magical symbols can be combined to form new, complex concepts. We did this when designing a warning symbol for the back of the cards used in our Enochian Tarot deck (shown below). We wanted a symbol that would represent universal truth free of materialistic influence. To represent this idea, we combined the Christian cross (a symbol for self-sacrifice), with the Jewish hexagram (a symbol of the universe) and the Eye of Horus (the Egyptian symbol for initiated consciousness or the developed intuition). Thus, the symbol becomes a reminder to the Tarot reader that he or she must sacrifice his or her personal selfhood and invoke the intuitive Eye of Horus so that the true, universal meaning of the card spread will be revealed and understood.

Symbols have played an important part in religion and magic since the beginning of humankind. New symbols continue to be developed, as needed, to serve as simple, universally understood representations of complex ideas.

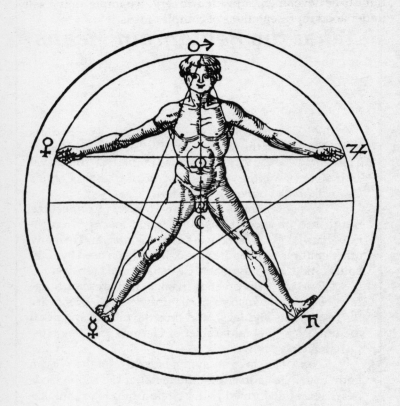

What the Pentagram Means

Amber K

It has had many names: Pentalpha, The Endless Knot, The Seal of the Microcosm, The Star of Knowledge, The Pentacle of the Virgin or of the Templars. To medieval churchmen it was the Witch's Foot, Wizard's Star, Cobin's Cross, Druid's Foot or Devil's Sign.

The pentagram is an ancient symbol of protection, health and balance. It has been found inscribed on ceramic jars for grain storage in ancient Sumer, and in many other cultures all over the world. It has been used by Kabbalists and Celts, Egyptians, Christians and Gypsies.

To many who practice magick, it represents a human being as microcosm of the universe (the points are the head, arms and legs), and thus the famous magickal dictum of the Emerald Tablet of Hermes Tristmegistus, "As above, so below."

Today it is a favorite symbol for those of the Wiccan faith, usually cast in silver (the metal of the Moon Goddess). It is often formed with a circle around it, symbolizing the cycle of life, death and rebirth; the wheel of the year; and the magick circle cast to create sacred space before each ritual.

When inscribed on a disc of wood, stone, metal or ceramic, it is the Pentacle, the ritual tool and symbol of Earth. Often it will have talismanic sigils engraved about it, or sometimes the Names of God or the archangels.

To those of the Craft, each point has a meaning. Starting at the right and moving deosil (clockwise or sunwise), we have first the Element of Water, which is also emotion and intuition. Next is Fire, which is the will and the energy of life. The next point is Earth: the body, the material world, and foundations of things. At upper left is Air, or mind, intellect, and imagination. And at the top we find Spirit: Goddess, the Source. Taken together they represent wholeness, all elements in balance. The single point of Spirit is placed at the top, ruling the other elements.

When the single point is down, it shows one of two things. In some branches of the Craft, it can depict the Horned God's head, and represent the second degree of initiation in the Craft. But unfortunately, this form is also used by some Satanic groups—just as they might use a broken or inverted cross—to represent Spirit in subjection to the material world.

To many uninformed people raised on cheap movie thrillers, any pentagram connotes negative occultism and worse. But to many who are aware of its history, it is a sign of power and blessing to be worn with pride and honor.

Treasured Sources

Scott Cunningham

The scent of herbal tea rises and mixes with the resinous aroma of incense. Candles and firelight create a bright glow in the room. A figure bends over a book, running a finger down a page, searching for an age-old ritual.

Suddenly, the magician's cat springs onto her lap. One errant paw flips over several pages of the book. The magician stares down at the page and smiles as she realizes that she's finally found the ritual for which she's been searching. The cat kneads. The magician pets her. The book seems to shine with energy.

Most practitioners of magic spend hours poring over old books. Classics of the hidden art line their bookshelves, waiting for use when needed. Years of searching have garnered a collection of time-honored works. The magician's reference library is, indeed, a valuable magical tool.

Most magicians have their own treasured sources of information, the books that have sparked their imaginations when searching for or devising new rituals, or altering others. Though each magician has her or his own favorites, I thought that I'd present some of mine to you.

Many of these books aren't magical texts, yet they contain much material of this nature. It was years before I realized that some of the best "magical" information is to be found in books of superstition and folklore, for both of these topics are solely concerned with the magic of past ages.

Some of these books are out-of-print and rather difficult to find, but most were printed within the last 30 or so years and may be available in new editions. Ask for them at used book stores, or write to book search services for assistance in locating them.

And most of all, treasure these books for the knowledge that they contain.

Budge, E. A. Wallis, *Amulets and Talismans*. New Hyde Park: University Books 1968. (A monumental collection of magical objects and their uses, from all parts of the world throughout history.)

Cirlot, J. E., *A Dictionary of Symbols*. New York: Philosophical Library, 1962. (A fascinating, world-wide look at the meaning of symbols, including plants, animals, birds, natural features and much more.)

Elworthy, Fredrick Thomas, *The Evil Eye: The Origins and Practices of Superstition*. New York: Julian Press, 1958. (First published in 1895, this is a wonderous collection of folk magical rituals: everything from magic nails to ritual gestures to amulets and other protective devices.)

Fielding, William J., *Strange Superstitions and Magical Practices*. New York: Paperback Library, 1966. (Despite the sensationalized title, this is an excellent guide to natural magic. Topics include rings; stones; fertility; healing; love and weddings; protection and much more.)

Frazer, James, *The Golden Bough*. New York: Macmillan, 1958. (Much magic is hidden among the dense pages of this book, which was culled from the original 13-volume work. Patience in reading it will be rewarded with an amazing array of magical techniques.)

Kitteridge, George Lyman, *Witchcraft in Old and New England*. New York: Russell and Russell, 1956. (Love spells, image magic, herb rituals, divination and treasure-finding methods, culled from actual trial records.)

Leland, Charles Godfrey, *Etruscan Magic and Occult Remedies*. New Hyde Park: University Books, 1963. (A collection of Etruscan and Roman spells, incantations, divinations, amulets and other wonders. Originally published in the late 1890s.)

Leland, Charles Godfrey, *Gypsy Sorcery and Fortune Telling.* New Hyde Park: University Books, 1963. (Orginally published in 1891, this is a goldmine of Gypsy charms and spells.)

Opie, Iona, and Moira Tatem, *A Dictionary of Superstitions.* New York: Oxford University Press, 1989. (An instant classic, this scholarly work records many magical practices, including those related to the moon; eggs; cats; mirrors and much, much more.)

Radford, Edwin, and Mona A. Radford, *Encyclopedia of Superstitions.* New York: Philosophical Library, 1949. (A collection of British and Continental superstitions and magical practices.)

Randolph, Vance, *Ozark Superstitions.* New York: Columbia University Press, 1947. (Love charms, ghosts, divinations, healing rituals and more, culled from living informants in Missouri and Arkansas.)

Thompson, C. J. S., *The Mysteries and Secrets of Magic.* New York: Causeway, 1973. (A remarkable collection of magical history and practice. Chapters discuss magical rings; ritual perfumes; quartz crystal; numbers; ointments and so on.)

Superstitions Concerning the Moon

Raymond Buckland

If the first time you see the New Moon it is straight ahead of you or to your right, it is said that you will be very lucky for the next month. If it is to your left, it will be an unlucky month. If it should be behind you, it will be the worst possible luck.

If you should first see the New Moon through a window pane, it is unlucky. In some parts of England it is said that the bad luck will take the form of breaking glass, since you saw the Moon through glass. Gypsies consider it unlucky to see the New Moon through the boughs of a tree but, in this case, the bad luck can be broken by immediately taking a coin from your pocket, spitting on each side of it, and holding it up to the light of the Moon.

An old English superstition had it that the first person in a group who saw the New Moon should kiss one of the opposite sex and say what he/she most desired. The object would shortly be received, it was said. Another superstition has it that if you are alone you should kiss the first person that you meet, of the opposite sex, to obtain what you desire.

An 11th century English manuscript says that if you approach the king when the Moon is only one day old, the monarch will grant whatever you request. Later books modify this to say that whatever you wish for, on first seeing the New Moon, you will receive before the end of the month (or the end of the year, in some areas). Gifts are frequently associated with the New Moon, in many countries.

In Scotland men and women would bow and curtsey to the

New Moon when first seeing it. In other parts of Britain people would kiss their hand to it. In Ireland the people would kneel and say, "May you leave us well and safe as you found us."

The New Moon was frequently taken as a good time to do divination, especially for finding out who you would marry. A 17th century manuscript says: "the first time you see (the New Moon), hold your hands across, saying this three times, 'New Moon, New Moon, I pray thee tell me this night who my true love will be.' Then go to bed without speaking any more that night and you will certainly dream of the person you are to marry." Another contemporary manuscript says you should say, "All hail to thee, Moon, all hail to thee! I prithee good Moon, declare to me, this night, who my husband must be." Two examples from the 19th century are from Scotland and from Berkshire, England: Chambers' *Popular Rhymes of Scotland* states, "The young women of the Lowlands, on first observing the New Moon, exclaim as follows, 'New mune, true mune, Tell unto me, if _____, my true love, he will marry me. If he marry me in haste, let me see his bonny face; if he marry me betide, let me see his bonnie side; gin he marry na me ever (if he never marries me), turn his back and gae awa'." While in Berkshire the maidens go into the fields, look up at the Moon, and say, "New Moon, New Moon, I hail thee! By all the virtue in thy body, Grant this night that I may see he who my true love is to be." They will then see their "true love" in their dreams that night.

Another form of divining one's "true love" is to hold up a black silk handkerchief between you and the Moon while you pray to see your lover. Also, by looking through such a cloth, it often appears that you are "seeing" more than one Moon. The number you see is an indication of the number of months or years that will pass before you marry. One ancient book instructs that the querant go to a stream and "hold a silk square over the water with the moon behind you. The silk diffuses the light and several little moon reflections appear in the water. The number of moons denotes the number of months you must wait before becoming a bride."

Perhaps most superstitions connected with the New Moon

are to do with money. As far back as 1507 c.e., in *Gospelles of Dystaues*, we are told, "He that hath no moneye in his purse ought to absteyne hym from lokynge on the newe mone, or elles he shall haue but lytell all alonge that mone." Many books, before and since that time, have instructed that to be without money at the time of the New Moon is to be in for a very hard time, if you look at the New Moon. Some writings are specific about the money being silver. In other words, if you have no silver in your pocket, you will be unfortunate—no matter how much copper or even gold you might have.

Turning the money you have—especially silver—is very important at this time. On the first day of the New Moon, when you first see the Moon, you must put your hand in your pocket and, with eyes closed, turn over the coins. Some say, specifically, that you must turn only the silver; some say it should be the smallest coin in your pocket. In Devonshire, England, you are expected to shake your pocket to turn the money in it. In some areas you are instructed to actually take out the money and hold it up (and turn it) in the light of the Moon. The turning of your money is to encourage it to increase during the coming month. In the north of England they really take no chances— there you are expected to take out your money, turn it over, turn yourself around three times, and make a wish!

Full Moon

Although most neo-Pagans and -Wiccans associate the Moon with the Goddess, in fact in many countries (*e.g.*, Germany) the Moon is regarded as masculine, from which we probably get the idea of "the Man in the Moon." The Harley Manuscript of 1340 c.e. refers to him: "Man in the Moone stand and strit; On his bot-forke his burthen he bereth." Similarly, Shakespeare (in *A Midsummer Night's Dream*) has Flute speak: "The Lanthorne is the Moone; I, the man in the Moone." In *Household Tales*, a popular book at the turn of this century, we find: "The 'Man in the Moon' is said to have a bundle of sticks on his back, and it is said that he was put there because he gathered sticks on a Sunday."

Regardless of the sex of the Moon, it has always been considered unlucky to point at it. In Lancashire, England, it is recorded as "a sin to point at the moon." While the above-mentioned *Household Tales* states, "If you point nine times at the moon you will not go to heaven."

Much magick is done at the Full Moon, or when the Moon is increasing (waxing) to the full. A manuscript of the mid-1600s states: "The most easie deliverie a woman can have, is alwaies in the increas, toward and in the full of the Moon, and the hardest labors in the new and silent Moon." Aubrey, in 1688, said: "According to the Rules of Astrologie, it is not good to under-take any Business of importance in an Eclipse (of the Moon)."

In Somerset the belief is that a child born in the waning Moon will need far more care and attention to survive than will a child born in the waxing Moon. Shaw's *History of Moray* (1775 c.e.) states that "the Druids avoided, if possible, to fight till after the Full Moon."

In Scotland it is unlucky to marry during the waning cycle of the Moon. It is also unlucky to move house, unless: ". . . the moon be waxing, the tide be flowing and the wind blow on the back of the person who removes."

Trees cut down during the Full Moon produce harder wood than those cut in the waning cycle, according to Welsh beliefs. Also, fruit and vegetables gathered at that time will last longer than those gathered in the waning cycle. A similar belief holds throughout much of Europe regarding the planting of crops; they need to be planted in the waxing cycle, unless they are root crops, in which case they may be planted when the Moon wanes.

It can be dangerous to sleep in the light of the Full Moon, according to many old beliefs. A 17th century work warns: "When thou goest to thy bed, draw close the curtains to shut out the Moone-light." Another book, written 200 years later, states, "Human beings are said to be injured by sleeping in the moon's rays," while a 20th century work mentions, "As children we were cautioned against going to sleep with the moonlight shining on our faces. We were told that if we did, we should go blind."

However, moonlight can be very beneficial as, for instance, in the removing of warts. There are several traditional wart-removing cures that involve holding the hand or other afflicted part in the light of the Moon. A 17th century book states: "For warts we rub our hands before the Moon." Another, contemporary work says: "One should offer to wash his hands in a well-polished silver basin wherein there is not a drop of water, yet this may be done by the reflection of Moonbeams only."

Similarly, it is traditional to "charge" a crystal ball or other scrying tool by exposing it to the light of the Full Moon.

The Olde Old very Olde Man or Thomas Par. the
Sonne of Iohn Par of winnington in the Perish of Alberbury
In the County of Shropshire who Was Borne in 1483 in
The Raigne of King Edward the 4th and is now living in
The Strand being aged 152 yeares and odd Monethes 1635

The Secret of Longevity and Everlasting Beauty

Raymond Buckland

Thomas Parr lived to the ripe old age of 152 or so they say. Born in 1483, he survived ten Kings and queens of England, finally dying in November 1635. He claimed that the secret of his long life was his diet. He existed on coarse bread, milk, rancid cheese and whey. Whey, of course, is the water part of milk that remains when the rest has become curd. (Remember "Little Miss Muffet," on her tuffet, eating her curds and whey?) Certainly for hundreds of years, in Europe, young ladies have drunk whey believing it to cause their skins to remain soft and beautiful. It is said that whey is especially delicious in May and June, when the grass eaten by the cows is so full of flowers and young sweet herbs.

Thomas Parr lived a rigorous life, working his farm daily until he was nearly 150. His home was in the village of Wollaston, but such was his fame that he was finally buried in Westminster Abbey. It is said that he would still be alive today had he not been invited to London by Charles I and eaten heartily of the "junk food" available in the capital!

Sex in Enochian Magick

Gerald and Betty Schueler

The famous magician Aleister Crowley said that Magick is the science and art of causing change to occur in conformity with the will. In other words, any conscious or deliberate act is a magical act. Through common usage, this definition has now been accepted as the New Age definition of Magick and is in accord with the teachings of Enochian Magick. According to this definition, you can do Magick by exalting your will to a point where it is in control of any given situation. You can focus and exalt your will by ordering every thought, word, and act in such a way that your attention is completely absorbed in the desired object. Sex is a tool that can be used to assist in this process.

Enochian Magick makes use of sex and sexual forces. Sexual techniques are not necessary, and are, in fact, dangerous (in a karmic sense). However, they are sometimes incorporated into Enochian Magick in order to produce various degrees of bliss, or to control ecstatic states, when they occur in the course of magical practices. At least four degrees of bliss, or ecstasy, are known: bliss, supreme bliss, special bliss, and innate or natural bliss.

Why do we encounter the extremely pleasurable sensation of bliss in a high spiritual state of consciousness? Because of man's nature. According to Enochian Magick, man has a subtle body, complete with subtle senses for each cosmic plane. For example, we have an astral body, with astral senses, that is located in the Watchtower of Water on the astral plane. We have a mental body with psychic senses that is located in the Watchtower of

Air on the mental plane, and so on. The highest such subtle body, the spiritual body, is sometimes called the Body of Bliss because its vibrations are so high that, whenever we become conscious of it, our physical body is filled with a blissful sensation similar to that obtained in orgasm but much more acute. In the East, this bliss is called *ananda*, and the Body of Bliss is known as the *ananda-maya-kosha*. This body is the *Sambhoga-Kaya* of Mahayana Buddhism.

A large gap exists between spiritual consciousness, which is formless, and normal human consciousness, which has forms. In rituals we sometimes put our body into special positions or postures, say certain words, and visualize in certain ways in order to lessen this gap. The idea is that, by lessening the gap as much as possible, the easier it will be to shift consciousness from its normal human state (with forms) to an exalted spiritual state (formless). In the same way, sex can be used to lessen the gap between orgasmic bliss and the ecstasy of spiritual consciousness.

One of the goals of Enochian Magick is to unite duality into a divine blissful oneness. You must combine knowledge with action, theory with practice, formless consciousness with bliss. The goal is to unite all dualistic opposites, including masculinity and femininity. This is not as easy as it may sound.

In order to understand sex in Enochian Magick, it is essential to first understand the doctrine of dualities. A duality implies any twofold force or two-sided expression. The concept of dualities is an important concept to grasp. A duality often seems to be two separate things or forces. Big and little for example, are two sides of a duality. We usually think that big is not the same thing as little. But actually they only exist in relation to each other. Big is only meaningful if something small is compared to it. For example, a mouse is small when compared to an elephant, but is big when compared to a grain of sand. Man is small when compared to the universe of planets and stars, but is big when compared to the atomic world of atoms and molecules. The concept of "up" is meaningless when used by itself. When you think of "up" you usually think of what is over your head or above you. But to someone on the other side of the world, your "up" is their "down" and vice versa. You can see from this that relativity is an important part of duality. The modern doctrine of relativity, described mathematically by Einstein, says that everything exists relative to something else—nothing has absolute existence. This doctrine is very similar to the ancient Buddhist doctrine of dependent arising, which states that the existence of every object in the universe depends on something else—nothing has independent existence.

The term *duality* denotes any force or expression that has two sides to it such that either side is meaningless without the other. When you see another person and think in terms of ugly or beautiful, you are mutually comparing that person with other persons. If only one man existed, he would be neither ugly nor beautiful. The dualistic idea of beauty and ugliness would disappear. Similarly, a baby has no concept of good or bad. The child must learn about that duality as it grows up. It is impossible to become aware of one side of a duality without the other side. The very nature of dualities is that we become aware of both sides simultaneously and that we can only eliminate one side at the expense of the other. We can only hold onto one side by clinging (in some cases unconsciously) to the other. This concept is extremely important to understand. It is the foundation of the Enochian magician's code of ethics and morality. A magician's morality is not society's morality. They look at life differently.

The following three laws of duality are from our book, *Enochian Physics*:

Duality Law 1. When one side of a duality is created, the other side comes into existence simultaneously.

Duality Law 2. When one side of a duality is eliminated, the other side ceases to exist simultaneously.

Duality Law 3. Everything that exists is one side of a duality, even existence itself.

The concept of dualities, and the philosophical implications of dualities, have been known for many centuries. Gotoma Buddha taught that existence and nonexistence were two sides of a duality. The psychological thrust of Buddhism is to tread a "middle path." This implies that one should live in-between the extreme points of dualities by combining/uniting them. Duality leaves its stamp on all things in the universe. From subatomic structures to the cosmos itself, all things express a dual nature, including man. As a magical tool, sex is used to eliminate the duality of masculinity and femininity.

In Tibetan Tantricism, sex with a physical partner is known as *karmamudra*. Sex with an imaginary partner is called *jnanamudra*. Much has been written about karmamudra, which has two main schools: those who reach climax while concentrating on the goal and those who focus on the goal while deliberately avoiding climax (*karezza*). But little has been written about jnanamudra, wherein sex takes place with a deity.

Enochian Magick uses a system of sex magick similar to jnanamudra, except the deity is usually a ruler of one of the four Watchtowers or 30 Aethyrs. This is sexual union with an imaginary (magical) partner. In psychological terms, it is union with the inner man or woman—the anima or animus of Carl Jung. Because of this, such a union has psychological benefits as well as achievement of the physical goal of the ritual. A ritual for this type of sex magick can be found in our book, *An Advanced Guide to Enochian Magick*.

The Aethyrs and Watchtowers of Enochian Magick are said to contain sexual currents where either masculinity or femininity is especially strong. The sexual currents of the cosmic planes of manifestation are a result of the three laws of duality. As soon as manifestation descends below LIL, the first Aethyr, it becomes dualistic. Subjectivity separates from objectivity to form the basic polarity of existence. The split into masculinity and femininity, which begins in PAZ, the fourth Aethyr, leads to sexuality and the sexual currents.

The masculine current is characterized by consciousness. The feminine current is characterized by love. As manifestation proceeds deeper into time and space (the *spacetime* of Einstein's theory of relativity), the masculine current precipitates the mind and the feminine consciousness precipitates the emotions. The masculine current tends to be hot and dry. It is stern, unyielding, continuous. The feminine current tends to be warm and wet. It is soft, yielding, and periodically changing. The highest manifestation of the masculine current in our solar system is the Sun. The highest manifestation of the feminine current in our solar system is the Moon.

Parallels exist between the sexual currents and electromagnetism. In electromagnetism, every magnet is comprised of two poles, called north and south. Isolated magnetic poles do not exist. If you cut a bar magnet in half you will not get two separate poles. Rather you will get two smaller bipolar magnets. There is no way to produce an isolated north or south pole. In the same way, a single pole of a duality cannot exist without a feminine current. Every Aethyr and Watchtower Square contains both. However, in most regions, one current is emphasized over the other. One current may be experienced in a region while the other is so weak as to appear nonexistent. Despite appearances, both currents must always be present.

The following five laws that govern the sexual currents are from *Enochian Physics:*

Law 1. Opposite currents will attract while like currents will repulse.

Comment. In general, male magicians will find the feminine current to be sexually stimulating, attractive, and alluring. The masculine current will not seem sexually charged at all. Female magicians will be sexually aroused by the masculine current but not by the feminine current.

Law 2. A sexual current will be induced by a magician whenever he/she moves through a field/plane.

Comment. A magician who enters a region, such as an Aethyr or Watchtower Square, will not automatically encounter a sexual current. Sexual currents can only be encountered while "moving about" in such regions. Here "moving" is not motion through spacetime but rather an acceleration of consciousness. It can be viewed as an increase or decrease in the vibratory rate of the magician's aura (Body of Light).

Law 3. The type of sexual current induced is such as to oppose the sexuality of the magician.

Comment. A male magician will induce the feminine current. A female magician will induce the masculine current.

Law 4. As a sexual current can influence a magician, so a magician can influence a sexual current.

Comment. In the same way that a sexual current can influence a magician who encounters it, so a magician can influence the current. Any sexual current can be bent to the will of the trained magician. Sexual currents are used in many magical operations as energy sources much like a battery is used as a source of electrical energy.

Law 5. A magician who induces a sexual current over a given region can influence any other being within that region.

Comment. Two people within the same sexual current can easily influence each other, whether conscious or unconscious of that current. A strong thought in the mind of one can cause that thought to be shared by the other. In other words, the power of telepathy increases in a sexual current.

The theory of sexual currents is important for the Enochian magician to understand. For one thing, sexual currents can be used to transmute your physical body. You can induce a sexual current throughout your physical body for longer and longer periods. The general effect is the conversion of mechanical energy into electromagnetic energy, or matter into spirit/energy. The result is that your body will become a psycho-spiritual dynamo. This process is identical to the awakening of Kundalini as taught in Kundalini Yoga and tantricism.

Whether you use sex as a magical tool with a physical or

magical partner or not is a personal decision. However, sooner or later in your practice of Enochian Magick, you will encounter sexual currents, and you should strive to understand these currents beforehand.

Solution to Mystical Cryptic Crossword on page 41.

C	U	P	▨	A	A	▨	A	A	▨	M	A	B
H	▨	S	E	P	T	E	M	B	E	R	▨	R
A	H	▨	L	I	E	▨	S	H	E	▨	S	E
R	E	E	V	E	▨	M	▨	O	R	S	E	A
M	A	G	I	C	K	C	I	R	C	L	E	S
S	D	M	▨	E	A	▨	D	S	▨	E	S	T
▨	D	▨	▨	▨	▨	▨	▨	▨	▨	G	▨	▨
S	R	O	▨	M	O	▨	R	S	▨	O	H	S
T	E	T	R	A	G	R	A	M	A	T	O	N
U	S	H	A	S	▨	A	▨	U	L	O	S	E
P	S	▨	S	T	E	▨	E	D	B	▨	T	A
I	▨	T	H	E	V	I	R	G	I	N	▨	K
D	U	O	▨	R	E	▨	G	E	▨	B	U	Y

Magical Personalities of Egypt: Ramses II (The Great)

Gordon T. G. Hudson

Ramses II earned the accolade "Great" by doing things on a grand scale and with enormous gusto. In an opulent 67-year reign he waged an extravagant war against a coalition of Asian states led by the Hittites, sired more than 100 children and erected Egypt's biggest and showiest buildings.

Having succeeded his father, Ramses II turned his attention to the Nubian gold mines in 1301 B. C., the third year of his reign. He was in Memphis when he devised plans for digging wells on the road to Akita (Wadi el Alaki) because there was much gold there and, water lacking on the way, half the caravaners and their pack animals were dying of thirst during the journey. Ramses caused reboring of his father's wells and succeeded in finding water at a depth of 132 cubits (224 feet), 12 cubits below the depth abandoned by his predecessor. A cubit measures roughly 1.7 feet.

As in Egypt, so in Nubia; the building activities of Ramses II were on an immense scale, and in addition to the masterpiece at Abu Simbel, he built temples as far down and even further than the Second Cataract.

The Temple of Abu Simbel, one of the largest rock-cut structures in the world, is indeed a masterpiece of ancient architectural design and engineering. Carved in a great head of rock on the west bank of the Nile opposite the modern village of Farek, its setting is magnificent. But this was not the only reason for the selection of the site, for there is evidence to show that these hills were considered important and sacred, even before the construction of the temples. Near the temples there are the small towns of Maha and Absheck, so we may conclude that in the days of Ramses these great structures were situated in a well-populated district. Even so, it's difficult to understand why such magnificent monuments should be located in such a distant part of the country. Only two explanations seem plausible. Either because the hill at Abu Simbel was for some reason considered sacred or, at a point near the head of the Second Cataract (which, by that time, was considered the frontier of Egypt proper), the pharaoh wished to impress his unruly neighbors further south with his power and wealth.

One Temple was built on a suitably heroic scale and celebrated the Sun-God Ra-Harakhti and Ramses II as a living God, the four colossi of the facade representing the seated pharaoh and towering 67 feet from the ground. The other Temple, a few hundred feet away to the north, portrays Ramses paying homage to Hathor, goddess of love, music and the dance, and to his favorite consort, Queen Nefertari. This, the smaller of the two Temples, shows six colossal figures standing.

Ramses made it quite clear that he was boss in the family, for Nefertari was granted only two statues on the facade a mere 33 feet high, even though standing, each flanked by two statues of Ramses. He ordered at least 18 other colossi of himself for the Luxor Temple alone. Despite his martial boasts, he was an inept general, although a smart treaty-maker. He was also a notorious usurper of his ancestors' monuments.

There is evidence suggesting that the original conception of a temple at Abu Simbel was made by Seti I, and certainly a large part of the interior excavation must have been complete before Ramses ascended the throne in 1304 B.C. But to what extent Seti was responsible for the final design, particularly of the facade, is not known. However, as it was usual in the construction of such rock-cut monuments to complete the facade before excavating the interior, we must consider it possible that the four colossal statues which are the principal feature of its design are portraits of Ramses' predecessor. However, Ramses takes the sole credit for the creation of the magnificent edifice, as in the building inscription he is shown instructing an official called Ramses-eshabat to build the temple.

The monument was completed before the year 1280 B.C. and, like many other temples in Nubia, it was dedicated to the worship of Ra-Harmathis, identified with the Sun and usually represented as a man with a falcon's head wearing the solar disc. The whole purpose and position of the temple was devoted to the adoration of the Sun at dawn, and it was only at sunrise at certain times of the year that the vast interior was illuminated, when the light penetrated the sanctuary. This, I feel, is what Akhenaten was seeking, a vehicle proper to the adoration of his beloved Aten, one which eluded him and which became the death knell of the dynasty. Ramses, in all his exuberance for life, had the intelligence to build what he may have conceived as being a temple for Sun worship, but didn't go as far as Akhenaten had.

As it must have been for the ancients, so it is for the modern visitor an unforgettable experience to stand in the main hall at dawn and watch the life-giving light of the Sun gradually reveal the splendor of this architectural masterpiece, finally penetrating into the Holy of Holies of an ancient faith. But impressive as the spectacle is today, it can only be a shadow of what it must have been when the sculptured scenes on the walls were painted in brilliant colors in the selection of which the Egyptian artist was a master.

The Egyptian style of building is sometimes confusing for the modern person because sacred buildings and profane ones superficially look alike. There is, however, a difference: the walls of the temple and shrine are covered with holy inscriptions while the commemorative monument may have in it some inscriptions which are more mundane. For instance, in a building at Deir are contained reliefs depicting scenes from Ramses' Nubian campaign. The reliefs show him charging panic-stricken Cushites, who flee to their camp in the hills and leap into trees. Yes, he actually treed some! All is confusion and panic, while the Egyptians round up their prisoners.

When Ramses died in 1237 B.C., he was succeeded by his

13th son Merenptah, under whose rule the biblical exodus was supposed to have taken place. It was within 50 years or so of this event that the siege of Troy took place, but that is another story.

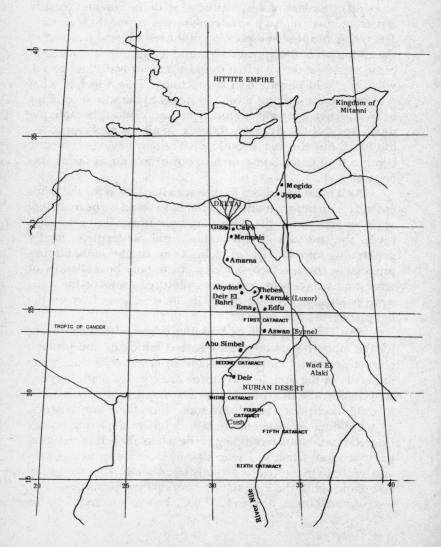

How to Get Low-Cost/High-Quality Egyptian Art

Gerald and Betty Schueler

Ancient Egyptian art has recently become very popular, but obtaining it is difficult and often costly. There are, however, inexpensive ways to obtain your own high-quality, low-cost, Egyptian art.

There are many New Age specialty shops that offer papyrus greeting cards made by the Papyrus Paper Co. of Houston, Texas. Some shops also carry a line of unframed artwork from the same company. The cards and artwork are of high quality and very reasonably priced, starting at $3. Commercial framing of the pictures can run anywhere from about $15 for the cards to several hundred dollars for the larger pieces of artwork available. But, compared to the pre-framed artwork that we have seen offered, the savings can be substantial—especially if you do your own matting and framing.

If you do not have a local source for the papyrus cards or artwork, you can order them from: Harford Writers Group, 680 W. Bel Air Ave., Aberdeen, MD 21001. A catalog and price list is available for $1. Please write clearly when requesting your catalog, and include a home phone number in case there are any questions.

Another good source of artwork is found in the back of E. A. Wallis Budge's book, *The Gods of the Egyptians*, Vol 2. There is a full-color pullout in the back of the book that can be cut out of the book with a razor blade. On the front of the pullout are five pictures of various Egyptian deities. On the back is the famous scene of Ani's heart being weighed in the balance. Both sides are suitable for framing. They are especially stunning when matted in a dark forest green and framed with a burnished gold frame. The smaller pictures cost about $25 each to professionally mat and frame. The scene of Ani's judgment costs about $100 to professionally mat and frame. The book sells for $10.95 and can be purchased locally at almost any Walden's, Dalton's, or specialty bookstore. The book is distributed by Dover Publications, Mineola, N.Y.

Our book on Egyptian Magick, *Coming Into The Light*, illustrated by Bill Fugate, can be a source of artwork for those who have a more modern decor. The book costs $14.95 (plus shipping) and is available from Llewellyn Publications, 84 S. Wabasha, St. Paul, MN 55107. The book contains a number of modern interpretations of the ancient Egyptian gods. Matting and framing will run about $20 per picture, but again, you can also mat and frame it yourself for a lot less money.

One of the very best sources of high-quality Egyptian artwork can be found in the two-volume set, *Monuments of Egypt*. This set of books is not cheap, but it offers a wealth of suitable art work. The book is published by Princeton Architectural Press, 37 East 7th Street, N.Y., 10003. The books contain both black and white and color art work on high-quality paper. The pictures vary in size from 3 x 5 to 9 x 12-inch artwork. The pictures are from the Napoleonic expedition of 1798 and are exquisitely rendered.

There are many other books available on ancient Egypt which contain pictures in black and white and/or color. Quite often, you can find these books on the sale tables at local booksellers. The majority of picture books are printed on quality paper, and once properly framed and matted, can offer a very inexpensive source of quality artwork.

Using pictures from books is a fairly easy process. First, you must select the pictures you want to display. Next, you must carefully remove each picture from its book with a new razor blade (never use an old blade as it may tear your picture). Once you have your pictures, you will have to group them to see which way to best present them.

If you are going to hang a group of pictures together, you will want complementing mats and frames which will go well with both the pictures and their surroundings. If the artwork is to be hung individually, you will only have to consider the colors in the picture and the picture's surroundings. If you want the pictures to blend in with their surroundings, you should mat them in colors similar to their surroundings. If you want the pictures to be a focal point in the room, you will want to use contrasting colors. If you have problems figuring out what colors to use, ask an artistic friend to advise you.

Once you have the colors of your mats and frames picked out, take your pictures to the local framing shop. Select the exact mats and frames you want for each picture. You will also have to decide whether you want nonglare glass or regular glass. You may want to have your pictures dry mounted. Discuss this with the framer.

Framing usually takes several days, so be prepared to wait for your pictures. Once they are back, however, you should be delighted with the finished product.

Collecting and exhibiting ancient Egyptian artwork can be a very rewarding hobby. With only a little imagination and money, you can amass a collection worth many times the money you spent on it. In the process, you will gain new appreciation for a culture that contributed much to our modern civilization.

The Enchanting Goddess Calendar

The 1992 Goddess Calendar will enchant you
with its brilliance and splendor.

Let *The 1992 Goddess Calendar* grace its radiant beauty to you. This year artist Hrana Janto's original full-color paintings decorate the pages of this beautiful calendar. The radiant Goddesses come from a variety of eras and cultures. Featured Goddesses include Rhiannon (Wales), Morgan Le Fay (Celt), Nut (Egypt), Skadi (Scandinavia), Yemaya (Africa), Sophia (Judeo-Christian), Artemis (Greece), Inanna (Sumer), Tara (Tibet), Estsanatlehi (Navaho Indian), Pachamama (Bolivia) and Amaterasu (Japan).

The Goddesses and the symbolism of the paintings are described in the accompanying text. Plus, the date pages include the four quarters of the Moon and important holiday information. *The 1992 Goddess Calendar* makes a beautiful gift for any occasion. Order yours today!

**O-87542-469-4, Full-color, 12" by 13", $9.95
Please use order form on last page.**

Bring Some Light Into Your Life!

Let *Llewellyn's 1992 Sun Sign Book* help you see the light in the coming year.

This popular yearly guide gives the whole year's horoscopes for all twelve signs so you can check out the trends for you and all your friends. With this easy-to-read guide you'll receive special activity tables giving you the best dates for each month's activities; from finances and career to romance and relationships.

All forecasts are written by Gloria Star, best-selling author, professional astrologer, lecturer, counselor and radio and television personality. Her knowledge and insights are truly amazing!

Llewellyn's 1992 Sun Sign Book also includes exciting articles by leading astrological authorities including: Roxana Muise, Bruce Scofield, Philip Sedgwick, Ninah Kessler, Anthony Louis, Vince Ploscik and many others. Order your copy today and bring some light into your life!

0-87542-468-6, 416 pp., mass market, $4.95
Please use order form on last page.

Not Just Another Appointment Book!

Llewellyn's 1992 Daily Planetary Guide is the most complete datebook for astrologers.

Llewellyn's 1992 Daily Planetary Guide is, without a doubt, the most popular datebook among astrologers. It includes all of the astrological information necessary to plan your day as well as, essential, accurate information for anyone who makes a hobby or business of astrology.

Just open to a page in the Guide and you will find all of the lunar data, the aspects for the day with their exact times, voids, retrogrades, planetary motion, holidays and more. Data is given in both Eastern and Pacific times so everyone can use it with ease.

Other features include an introduction to astrology for the novice, a planetary hour guide with sunrise and sunset tables, a new graphic retrograde ephemeris, a chart blank and more. See why *Llewellyn's 1992 Planetary Guide* is not just another appointment book. Order one today!

0-87542-466-X, 176 pp., spiral bound, $6.95
Please use order form on last page.

Don't Be Left Out In The Dark!

Let *Llewellyn's 1992 Moon Sign Book* help you with the shadows of the coming year.

This world-popular lunar almanac is a must-have for gardeners and anglers alike. Based on the timing of the Moon's phases and signs, it determines everyday activities from buying a car to moving. No smart person will be without this guide. There are over 100 different activities included.

With this handy guide you'll be able to determine what are the best days for any activity. You'll also find the tables easy to read and understand.

Llewellyn's 1992 Moon Sign Book and Lunar Planting Guide also includes feature articles by Louise Riotte on planting and monthly horoscopes by astrologer Anne Lyddane. There are even weather reports, stock market forecasts, earthquake predictions and lots of entertaining almanac material. It's the only natural guide around!

0-87542-467-8, 432 pp., mass market, $4.95
Please use order form on last page.

Navigate By The Stars

Llewellyn's 1992 Astrological Calendar will guide you through the year with ease.

Forecasting during the year is easy with **Llewellyn's 1992 Astrological Calendar**. This famous full-color calendar is a remarkable reference for astrologers and non-astrologers alike. Each month features personal horoscopes. There are also major daily aspects, important lunar data, a handy ephemeris and the best fishing and planting dates. With all this, there's even room for personal entries.

Llewellyn's 1992 Astrological Calendar also features articles on vacation and financial planning, lunar gardening, lunar activity, political trends, celestial phenomena for the year and a comprehensive introduction to astrology for the beginner. It even includes interesting articles by leading astrologers. This full-color wall calendar is your complete daily guide to the heavens. Order one today!

**0-87542-465-1, Full-color, 10" by 13", $9.95
Please use order form on last page.**

The Magic in Food
Legends, Lore and Spellwork

Everyone knows that food is the storehouse of natural energy. Choosing specific foods, properly preparing them, eating them with a magical goal in mind: these are the secrets of *The Magic in Food*, an age-old method of taking control of your life through your diet. Author Scott Cunningham explains the mystic qualities of everyday dishes, their preparation and the method of calling upon their powers. He also includes numerous magical diets, each designed to create a specific change within its user: increased health and happiness. This is Cunningham's 10th Llewellyn title. Don't miss out on this one!

The Magic in Food, 380 pp., $14.95, L130

Year of Moons, Season of Trees
Mysteries and Rites of Celtic Tree Magic

Many of you are drawn to Wicca, or the Craft, but do not have teachers or like-minded people around to show you how the religion is practiced. *Year of Moons, Season of Trees* serves as that teacher and as a sourcebook. Most of Witchcraft in America comes from or has been influenced by that of the British Isles. The Druidic sacred trees native to that culture are the focus of this book. The essence, imagery and mythology behind the trees and Seasons is vividly portrayed by author Pattalee Glass-Koentop. Her explanations give subtle meanings that will be remembered long after the rite is complete.

Year of Moons Season of Trees, 240 pp., $14.95, L269

Cosmic Keys
Fortunetelling for Fun and Self-Discovery

This book invites those of you just starting out in psychic mysteries to jump in and take a revealing and positive look inside yourself and the people around you. Through the hands-on application of the Cosmic Keys, you'll come away with insights into your individual personality and life situation. You'll also uncover hidden opportunities from new-found knowledge of future events along with personal challenges. Author M. Blackerby gives explanations for the difficulties experienced in life and shows you how you can feel good about yourself, and how to keep things that way. Send for your copy today!

Cosmic Keys, 200 pp., $12.95, L027

To order, use form on last page.

Kundalini and the Chakras
A Practical Manual

Today there is an explosion of interest in using Kundalini energy as a personal evolutionary tool. This interest has motivated people to gain understanding of these mysterious forces. *Kundalini and the Chakras* shows you how to release Kundalini gradually and safely. It is a must for those who have experienced a spontaneous rise of Kundalini and for those who wish to release more of this powerful energy. As the planetary energies intensify, everyone's evolution will make a quantum leap. Knowing and understanding Kundalini will make this process much easier on your body, mind and spirit.

Kundalini and the Chakras, 240 pp., $12.95, L592

Growing the Tree Within
Patterns of the Unconscious Revealed by the Qabalah

The Qabalah, or Tree of Life, has been the basic genetic pattern of western esotericism, and shows us how to make our climb steadily back to Heaven. When we study the Qabalah, we open ourselves to it and work with it as an Inner Activity. *Growing the Tree Within* presents an exhaustive and systematic analysis of the 22 Paths of the Tree of Life. It includes a detailed and comprehensive study of the symbolism of the Tarot cards in which author William Gray presents a viable yet unorthodox method of allocating the Major Arcana to the Paths. Send for your copy today!

Growing the Tree Within, 464 pp., $19.95, L268

The Sacred Cauldron
Secrets of the Druids

The Sacred Cauldron examines the actual practices of the Druids in their most ancient and timeless forms. Author Tadhg MacCrossan has reconstructed the early pre-Christian Celtic tradition using such scholarly methods as structuralism, comparative mythology, Indo-European comparative linguistics, archaeological findings and etymology. He also presents a comprehensive course in the history and development of Celtic religious lore, the secrets taught by the Druids and the modern performance of the veritable rites and ceremonies. Find guidance with *The Sacred Cauldron* today!

The Sacred Cauldron, 304 pp., $10.95, L103

To order, use form on last page.

The New Golden Dawn Ritual Tarot
Keys to the Rituals, Symbolism, Magic and Divination

This is an indispensable companion to Llewellyn's "New Golden Dawn Ritual Tarot Deck." It provides a card-by-card analysis of the deck's intricate symbolism, an introduction to the Qabalah, and a section on the use of the deck for practical rituals, mediations and divination procedures. The Tarot newcomer as well as the advanced magician will benefit from this groundbreaking work. The highlight of this book is the section on rituals. Instructions are included for everything from ritual baths to dream work with the Tarot. This book and companion deck is just what everyone has been waiting for!

Golden Dawn Ritual Tarot (book), 256 pp., $12.95, L139

The Wheel of Destiny
The Tarot Reveals Your Master Plan

Announcing an irresistible new tool for self-knowledge found nowhere else. *The Wheel of Destiny* delves into the "Master Plan reading" of the Tarot's Major Arcana and provides detailed information about the individual, much like a reading of an astrological birth chart. Author Patricia McLaine explains how to lay out the 22 cards and delineates the meaning of each card in whatever position it falls. All you need is this book and a Tarot deck. No previous knowledge of the Tarot is required. The Master Plan Reading has been field tested by the author on clients the world over. Order a copy today!

The Wheel of Destiny, 480 pp., $17.95, L490

Archetypes On the Tree of Life
The Tarot as Pathwork

The Tree is the Kabbalistic Tree of Life, the ageless mystical map to the secrets of the Universe. By working with its 10 circular paths and 22 linear ones, you can find answers to life's most profound questions. *Archetypes on the Tree of Life* symbolically examines the meanings and uses of the 22 paths based upon their correspondences with the Tarot trumps and Hebrew letters. Throughout the book author Madonna Compton also investigates the mystical and allegorical interpretations of the Old and New Testaments, and compares these and other worldwide mythologies to the Tarot Archetypes.

Archetypes On the Tree of Life, 336 pp., $12.95, L104

To order, use form on last page.

The Complete Book
of Amulets & Talismans

Let *The Complete Book of Amulets and Talismans* avert evil and
bring good fortune into your life. With this complete reference guide
you'll learn how to make use of these religious and magical symbols
for protective purposes, inner strength and self-assurance. Through
detailed illustrations you'll be able to travel around the world to
examine the variety of these charms and fetishes found in every
civilization, from the distant past to the present. Author Migene
González-Wippler presents the history of these good-luck pieces,
their geography and how to make and use them in a simple format.

The Complete Book of Amulets & Talismans, 268 pp., $12.95, L287

Dream Alchemy
Shaping Our Dreams to Transform Our Lives

People are rediscovering that what we dream can become real.
Learning to shift the dream to reality and the reality to dream—to walk
the thread of life between the worlds—to become a shapeshifter, a
dreamwalker, is available to everyone. Dream Alchemy is one of the
safest and easiest ways to bridge your consciousness to higher realms.
No tools are necessary, and cost is minimal—only limited waking time
and persistence. These two, when used with the techniques of Ted
Andrews' book, will stimulate greater dream activity, lucid dreaming,
higher inspiration and even controlled out-of body experiences.

Dream Alchemy, 264 pp., $12.95, L017

Ancient Ways
Reclaiming the Pagan Tradition

Ancient Ways is filled with magick and rituals that you can perform
every day to capture the spirit of the seasons. It focuses on the
celebration of the Sabbats of the Old Religion by giving you practical things to do while anticipating the sabbat rites and helping you
harness magical energy. The wealth of seasonal rituals and charms
are drawn from ancient sources, but are easily performed with
materials readily available. Most Pagans and Wiccans feel that the
Sabbat rituals are all too brief and wish for the magick to linger on.
Ancient Ways can help to heighten this feeling of magick.

Ancient Ways, 336 pp., $12.95, L090

To order, use form on last page.

Words of Power
Sacred Sounds of East and West

Within our human heritage is a vast storehouse of magical words, mantras, invocations and chants handed down from ages past. These sounds are a gift to us and are revealed, at last, in this fascinating and instantly usable manual. *Words of Power* is the first such work of a universal nature. It is presented in an easy-to-read format and contains simple keys to correct pronunciation, suggested meditations and detailed explanations of esoteric meanings and functions. This book also explains the tone patterns designed to initiate communication with other dimensions, and how to use the power of sound.

Words of Power, 326 pp., $10.95, L135

How to See and Read the Aura

Anyone can learn to see and experience the aura more effectively. There is nothing magical about the process. It simply involves a little understanding, time, practice and perseverance. *How to See and Read the Aura* shows you how to do a variety of exercises to practice alone and with partners to build your skill in aura reading and interpretation. Author Ted Andrews also explains how you can balance your aura each day to keep it vibrant and strong so others cannot drain your vital force. Learning to see the aura not only breaks down old barriers, but also increases sensitivity. As you develop the ability to see and feel the aura, your intuition will unfold and increase.

How to See & Read the Aura, 160 pp., $3.95, L013

How to Make an Easy Charm to Attract Love Into Your Life

Enter the fascinating world of Egyptian magick and learn how to make a charm that is extremely effective in attracting love. With the step-by-step instructions in this book, you'll become highly regarded and much sought after. You'll also learn the valuable secret of drawing love from others. All charms are easy and inexpensive to make, and have no adverse affect on you or anyone else . . . and they work! The knowledge in this book works equally well for both males and females. Take some tips from the ancient ones and order today!

How to Make an Easy Charm to Attract Love Into Your Life
112 pp., $3.95, L087

To order, use form on last page.

Secrets of Gypsy Dream Reading

Let *Secrets of Gypsy Dream Reading* show you how to interpret your nocturnal visions. Written by Gypsy Raymond Buckland, this guide features explanations of hidden meanings and a complete dream dictionary. Learn how to engage in lucid dreaming and to recognize and use the prophetic nature of your dreams. Also learn how to dream the future, dream for profit, direct your dreams, remember your dreams and accurately interpret dreams. If you are mystified by your nighttime movies, let the popular *Secrets of Gypsy Dream Reading* guide you to greater understanding. Order your copy today and experience the magic of your midnight visions.

Secrets of Gypsy Dream Reading, 224 pp., $3.95, L086

Secrets of Gypsy Fortunetelling

Secrets of Gypsy Fortunetelling, written by Gypsy Raymond Buckland, discusses the history, language and divination of the Gypsies. It explores such subjects as palm reading, tea leaf reading, tarot reading and reading regular playing cards. It interprets the actions of animals and the weather, and covers reading the future with knives, dice, needles and sticks. Most of these items are easily attainable and with them the secrets of magical life will be revealed. By using these simple objects and following the traditional Gypsy ways shown, you will become a seer and improve the quality of your own life and the lives around you. Send for your copy today!

Secrets of Gypsy Fortunetelling, 220 pp., $3.95, L051

Secrets of Gypsy Love Magick

For centuries the Gypsies have traveled all over the world collecting and dispensing magickal knowledge. In *Secrets of Gypsy Love Magick* you will find a collection of love spells and magick formulas that are time-tested and reliable, taken from a long tradition of successful Gypsy practice. Author Raymond Buckland explains how you can discover your future spouse, attract a lover, keep a spouse faithful, retain youthful beauty and virility plus much more! Gypsy magick is both positive and practical—it can be followed using ordinary, easily obtained materials. Don't wait any longer! Bring some Gypsy love magick into your life today!

Secrets of Gypsy Love Magick, 159 pp., $3.95, L053

To order, use form on last page.

Earth Power
Techniques of Natural Magic

Author Scott Cunningham shows you how to work with the forces and energies of Nature to bring about desired changes. He gives a full range of charms, spells and rituals for nearly every practical purpose. Included are spells for breaking bad habits, healing, divination, protection, attracting love and more. There are also spells involving the sea, rivers and springs; the Sun and Moon; storms and rain; trees and knots and mirrors. Here is magic that anyone can perform with surprising results because it works! Once you have opened your eyes to Nature, you will discover true peace. Order today!

Earth Power, 153 pp., $8.95, L121

Magical Aromatherapy
The Power of Scent

Magical Aromatherapy is the gentle art of using the power of fragrance to enhance your life. It is the most natural form of magic, because its only tools are the scents of flowers, spices, herbs and essential oils. Author Scott Cunningham explains how these natural perfumes are storehouses of energies for everything from love to psychic awareness to protection. The age-old lore has been brought up-to-date in this practical guide to scent magic. When you learn to experience the magic of these powerful scents you will achieve harmony and inner peace. There is no other book like this one!

Magical Aromatherapy, 206 pp., $3.95, L129

Magical Herbalism
The Secret Craft of the Wise

Certain plants are prized by ritualists for the range of magical energies they possess. In *Magical Herbalism* author Scott Cunningham unites the powers of plants and man to produce, and direct, changes in accord with human will and desire. He presents the magic of amulets, charms, sachets, incenses, oils, simples, infusions and anointments. He also includes full instructions, recipes plus many important rituals and spells. With the knowledge in this book you will be able to lead a better life. Send for your copy of *Magical Herbalism* today, and see how your life can be more fulfilling!

Magical Herbalism, 240 pp., $7.95, L120

To order, use form on last page.

Tarot Spells

Tarot Spells is a beautiful and simple book of creative and enjoyable rites which can enhance your daily life. With no more than a pack of Tarot cards, you can use the meditations, visualizations and affirmations included in this volume to gain greater control and understanding of personal relationships, career and money concerns, major life events and your own emotional frame of mind. No expertise, study or technical skill is involved—merely an open mind, a willingness to learn and a desire to improve your surroundings, your circumstances and your fortunes. Author Janina Renee includes every category of spells, from self-improvement to emotions.

Tarot Spells, 228 pp., $12.95, L670

Coming Into The Light
Rituals of Egyptian Magick

Coming Into Light is the name that the ancient Egyptians gave to a series of magickal texts known to us today as *The Book of the Dead*. In this updated rendition of the texts of *Coming Into Light*, authors Gerald and Betty Schueler provide extensive evidence that these rituals were a vital tradition of Magick which has formed the basis of Western occultism as it is known today. With this book you'll meet all the major deities of the Egyptian pantheon in these ancient rituals and see them in beautiful full-color pictures. You'll also read about Egyptian Magick in a way that has never been presented before!

Coming Into The Light, 359 pp., $14.95, L713

Enochian Yoga
Uniting Humanity and Divinity

Enochian Yoga is the only book currently available that combines magick and yoga into a single, easy-to-use system that is suitable for everyone, from beginners to advanced magicians and yogis. Authors Gerald and Betty Schueler describe eight graduated paths of development, and include a complete description of the subtle Centers and Channels of Enochian Yoga, which are equivalent to the chakras and nadis of Kundalini Yoga. With this book you will be rewarded with a deeper understanding of both yoga and magick, as well as an improved ability to access the spiritual dimension of existence.

Enochian Yoga, 408 pp., $12.95, L718

To order, use form on last page.

The Complete Book of
Spells, Ceremonies and Magic

This is a study of all aspects of magic through the ages. With this book you'll learn how to follow detailed instructions to concoct love potions and gambling charms. Practice spells from various magical systems for love, wealth and success. If you aren't interested in performing magic but just want to explore the history, this book will explain everything from the Astral Levels to Zen Buddhism. This book will excite you, educate you, but most of all serve as a valuable reference for years to come. Don't miss out on this one!
The Complete Book of Spells Ceremonies and Magic
376 pp., $12.95, L286

A Kabbalah for the Modern World
Revealing the Oneness of All Things

This is the first book which presents the Kabbalah from a scientific orientation and shows how it clearly relates to such modern scientific models as the theories of Quantum, Relativity and the Big Bang. It also includes new revelations of the practical Kabbalah and how to gain material and spiritual prosperity. With the aid of the diagrams, tables and easy-to-read style, author Migene González-Wippler reveals the inner structure of the psyche and the secrets of God. Journey into new dimensions of being and discover a new spiritual harmony. Send for your copy today!
A Kabbalah for the Modern World, 227 pp., $8.95, L294

Dreams and What They Mean to You

Everyone dreams, but not everyone remembers their dreams. Now you can learn how to recall your dreams so that you can solve problems and gain better understanding of your deepest feelings. This book explores the nature of sleep, dreams, the human mind and consciousness and analyzes the different types of dreams that people often have. Included is an extensive dream dictionary, giving the meanings for hundreds of dream images. With this book you'll be able to learn to recall your dreams, practice creative dreaming, explore dream travel, plus much more. This book guides you every step of the way and helps you to expand your life. Order soon!
Dreams and What They Mean to You, 217 pp., $3.95, L288

To order, use form on last page.

SOME THINGS ARE FOR NOTHING.

With your **FREE** subscription to the *New Times*, you'll be among the first to hear about exciting new books, kits, audiotapes and videos in the fields of astrology, metaphysics and human potential. Every other month the *New Times* comes to you full of products, services, columns, interviews and events. It even includes regular articles by leading New Age authors. To get your name on the mailing list, just check the box on the order form on the last page or write to the address below. Send for a copy today!

**The Llewellyn New Times
P.O. Box 64383, St. Paul, MN 55164-0383**

WE EXPLORE THE UNEXPLAINABLE.

Each month *FATE* gives you what no other magazine does: we explore and explain the latest-breaking events and discoveries in the world of the paranormal. *FATE* won't give you rehashes of the same old reports you've heard for years. Instead, we focus on the most bold and exciting accounts of the strange and mysterious! To receive your one-year subscription, send $15.95 (a savings of up to 32% off the cover price) with this coupon. Don't miss another spellbinding month! Order now and explore the unexplainable!

Name _____

Address_____

City_____

State _____ Zip_____

**Mail to:
Fate Magazine
170 Future Way
P.O. Box 1940
Marion, OH 43305**

- Start my one-year subscription at the low price of $15.95!
- I save $7.45 off the cover price!
- Allow 6-8 weeks for delivery of 1st issue.

D464

True Magick: A Beginners Guide

In this book Amber K, a High Priestess of the Wiccan religion and experienced practitioner of magick, explains not only the history and lore of magick, but also its major varieties in the world today. She also explains how to prepare yourself, how to find or create your ritual tools, how to establish a temple in your home, how to plan a ritual and cast a spell—and how to do it ethically and safely. Whether you are just curious, or an aspiring magick-worker, order this magickal guide today!

True Magick, 252 pp., $4.95, L003

Please use order form.

MIRACLES

begin to happen when you commit your life to unfoldment and purification.

ARE YOU READY?

Health reading by powerful healing psychic, $25. For reading I need only name, address, & age. Please include your phone number! Send with money order to: **ZEMLACH**, P.O. Box 3332, West Palm Beach, FL 33402. I will send you an individual report, suggestions, & special prayers.

Universal Love to All & Peace On Earth PRAISE TO GOD!! IT WORKS!!

Ghosts, Hauntings and Possessions: The Best of Hans Holzer, Book I

FATE magazine presents a collection of the best stories from best-selling author and psychic investigator Hans Holzer. Dr. Holzer takes you on a remarkable journey into the vast, often frightening, realm of the unknown. You'll read about accounts of restless ghosts, authentic haunted houses, and famous people like the Kennedys, Abraham Lincoln, Elvis plus many more. This is for readers of all ages!

Ghosts, Hauntings & Possessions, 288 pp., $4.95, L367

Please use order form.

ESP, Witches and UFOs: The Best of Hans Holzer, Book II

In this book Dr. Hans Holzer, best-selling author, examines many fascinating and ever-changing subjects. Read about true accounts of the powers of extrasensory perception, prophetic dreams, UFOs and visitors from other worlds and survival after death. Dr. Holzer also dispels preconceived misconceptions by presenting new ideas and new evidence to endorse and correct old falsehoods.

ESP, Witches & UFOs, 288 pp., $4.95, L368

Please use order form.

SUPER DISCOUNTS ON
LLEWELLYN DATEBOOKS AND CALENDARS!

Llewellyn offers several ways to save money on our great line of almanacs and calendars. With a four-year subscription you receive your books as soon as they are published. The price remains the same for four years even if there is a price increase! Llewellyn pays postage and handling as well. *Buy any 2 subscriptions and take $2.00 off! Buy 3 and take $3.00 off! Buy 4 and take an additional $5.00 off the cost!*

Subscriptions (4 years, 1993-1996)

☐	Astrological Calendar	$39.80
☐	Sun Sign Book	$19.80
☐	Moon Sign Book	$19.80
☐	Daily Planetary Guide	$27.80

Order *by the dozen* and save 40%! Sell them to your friends or give them as gifts. Llewellyn pays all postage and handling on quantity orders.

Quantity Orders: 40% OFF

1992	1993		
☐	☐	Astrological Calendar	$71.64
☐	☐	Sun Sign Book	$35.64
☐	☐	Moon Sign Book	$35.64
☐	☐	Daily Planetary Guide	$50.04
☐	☐	Magickal Almanac	$71.64

Include $1.50 for orders under $10.00 and $3.00 for orders over $10.00. Llewellyn pays postage for all orders over $50.00.

Single copies of all Llewellyn's Almanacs and Calendars

1992	1993		
☐	☐	Astrological Calendar	$9.95
☐	☐	Sun Sign Book	$4.95
☐	☐	Moon Sign Book	$4.95
☐	☐	Daily Planetary Guide	$6.95
☐	☐	Magickal Almanac	$9.95
☐		Goddess Book of Days	$12.95
☐		The Goddess Calendar	$9.95

Please use order form on last page.

LLEWELLYN ORDER FORM
LLEWELLYN PUBLICATIONS
P.O. Box 64383-471, St. Paul, MN 55164-0383

You may use this form to order any of the Llewellyn books or services listed in this publication.

Give Title, Author, Order Number and Price.

_____

_____

_____

_____

_____

_____

_____

Shipping & Handling: We ship U.P.S. when possible. Include $1.50 for orders under $10.00 and $3.00 for orders over $10.00. Llewellyn pays postage for all orders over $50.00. Please give street address.

Credit Card Orders: (minimum $15.00) call 1-800-THE-MOON (U.S.A. & Canada), during regular business hours, Monday through Friday. Other questions please call (612) 291-1970. You may mail in your charge order:

    ❒ Visa   ❒ MasterCard   ❒ American Express

Account No. _____

Exp. Date_____ Phone _____

Signature_____

Name _____

Address_____

City_____ State _____ Zip _____

    ❒ Please send me your **FREE** *New Times* catalog!